How to Find God

Also by Harold Klemp

Animals Are Soul Too!
The Art of Spiritual Dreaming
Ask the Master, Books 1 and 2
Autobiography of a Modern Prophet
The Call of Soul
Child in the Wilderness
A Cosmic Sea of Words: The ECKANKAR Lexicon
ECKANKAR's Spiritual Experiences Guidebook
ECK Essentials
ECK Masters and You: An Illustrated Guide
ECK Wisdom Temples, Spiritual Cities, & Guides: A Brief History
Is Life a Random Walk?
The Living Word, Books 1, 2, 3, and 4
A Modern Prophet Answers Your Key Questions about Life, Books 1 and 2
Past Lives, Dreams, and Soul Travel
Soul Travelers of the Far Country
The Sound of Soul
Spiritual Exercises for the Shariyat, Book One
Spiritual Exercises for the Shariyat, Book Two
The Spiritual Exercises of ECK
The Spiritual Laws of Life
The Temple of ECK
Those Wonderful ECK Masters
Welcome to the Wonderful World of ECK! Your Membership Guidebook
The Wind of Change
Wisdom of the Heart, Books 1, 2, and 3
Your Road Map to the ECK Teachings: ECKANKAR Study Guide, Volumes 1 and 2
Youth Ask a Modern Prophet about Life, Love, and God

The Mahanta Transcripts Series

Journey of Soul, Book 1
How to Find God, Book 2
The Secret Teachings, Book 3
The Golden Heart, Book 4
Cloak of Consciousness, Book 5
Unlocking Your Sacred Puzzle Box, Book 6
The Eternal Dreamer, Book 7
The Dream Master, Book 8
We Come as Eagles, Book 9
The Drumbeat of Time, Book 10
What Is Spiritual Freedom? Book 11
How the Inner Master Works, Book 12
The Slow Burning Love of God, Book 13
The Secret of Love, Book 14
Our Spiritual Wake-Up Calls, Book 15
How to Survive Spiritually in Our Times, Book 16
The Road to Spiritual Freedom, Book 17

The Immortality of Soul Series

The Awakened Heart
The Awakening Soul
HU, the Most Beautiful Prayer
The Language of Soul
Love—The Keystone of Life
The Loving Heart
The Spiritual Life
Touching the Face of God
Truth Has No Secrets

ECK Wisdom Series

ECK Wisdom on Conquering Fear
ECK Wisdom on Dreams
ECK Wisdom on Health and Healing
ECK Wisdom on Inner Guidance
ECK Wisdom on Karma and Reincarnation
ECK Wisdom on Life after Death
ECK Wisdom on Solving Problems
ECK Wisdom on Soul Travel
ECK Wisdom on Spiritual Freedom

Spiritual Wisdom Series

Spiritual Wisdom on Prayer, Meditation, and Contemplation
Spiritual Wisdom on Relationships

Stories to Help You See God in Your Life

The Book of ECK Parables, Volumes 1, 2, and 3
Stories to Help You See God in Your Life, ECK Parables, Book 4

MAHANTA

This book has been authored by and published under the supervision of the Mahanta, the Living ECK Master, Sri Harold Klemp. It is the Word of ECK.

How to Find God

HAROLD KLEMP

Mahanta Transcripts
Book 2

ECKANKAR
Minneapolis
www.Eckankar.org

How to Find God
Mahanta Transcripts, Book 2

170203

Printed in USA

Library of Congress Control Number: 2020902545

Compiled by Joan Klemp and Anne Pezdirc

Edited by Mary Carroll Moore and Anthony Moore

Cover design by Doug Munson
Cover painting by Edith Freimanis
Text illustrations by Fraser MacDonald
Spine photo and text photo (page xii) by Art Galbraith

Second edition—2020

∞ This paper meets the requirements of ANSI/NISO Z39.48-1992 (Permanence of Paper).

Contents

Foreword

The teachings of ECK define the nature of Soul. You are Soul, a particle of God sent into the worlds (including earth) to gain spiritual experience.

The goal in ECK is spiritual freedom in this lifetime, after which you become a Co-worker with God, both here and in the next world. Karma and reincarnation are primary beliefs.

Key to the ECK teachings is the Mahanta, the Living ECK Master. He has the special ability to act as both the Inner and Outer Master for ECK students. The prophet of Eckankar, he is given respect but is not worshipped. He teaches the sacred name of God, HU. When sung just a few minutes each day, HU will lift you spiritually into the Light and Sound of God—the ECK (Holy Spirit). This easy spiritual exercise and others will purify you. You are then able to accept the full love of God in this lifetime.

Sri Harold Klemp is the Mahanta, the Living ECK Master today. Author of many books, discourses, and articles, he teaches the ins and outs of the spiritual life. Many of his talks are available to you on audio and video recordings. His teachings lift people and help them recognize and understand their own experiences in the Light and Sound of God.

How to Find God, Mahanta Transcripts, Book 2,

is a collection of his talks from 1982 to 1983. May they serve to uplift you on your journey home to God.

To find out more about Harold Klemp and Eckankar, please turn to page 353 in the back of this book.

Sri Harold Klemp, the Mahanta, the Living ECK Master shows each Soul Its own path to spiritual freedom in this lifetime.

1
The Two Plum Trees

An ECK chela once told a story about being out jogging one day. He came to a track at a high school and saw a man a few years older than he running around the track, just taking his good-natured time. The ECKist, being younger, thought, Well, I'll just start running around the track and use him to set my pace.

An ECK chela out jogging one day saw a man older than he running around the track, just taking his good-natured time.

After about half a mile, while the other fellow kept right on going, the ECKist had to stop for a rest. He waited until the man had come around a second time and then ran behind him so he wouldn't be embarrassed by having this older fellow pass him.

The man continued to run with a very smooth, flowing motion, but pretty soon the ECKist had to stop again. And this time he just admitted it: The other man was in better shape than he was.

He drew the parallel that this is how the individual who is first getting on the path to God has to build up his endurance. It may take a while before he can run around the track and keep pace with the individual who has done it longer, who seems to move very steadily and keeps right on going.

Experience on the Path of Life

There is one difference between Eckankar and any other religious teaching, and it is simply this: that whosoever does the Spiritual Exercises of ECK faithfully can reach the kingdom of heaven while still in this physical body.

This is the unique feature of Eckankar. I know this to be so, but I'm not able to prove it to you. It is something you have to find out for yourself. I can talk to you about experiences of all kinds, and yet this does little more for the God seeker than a sermon from the pulpit. It is our own experience on the path of life that is important in our spiritual unfoldment.

In ECK we don't retreat from life; we use our common sense, and we go out and enjoy life.

In ECK we don't retreat from life; we use our common sense, and we go out and enjoy life. We do the best we can every day. If we have interests such as school, hobbies, or sports, we keep up with them. Just because we are on the path of ECK does not mean we give up our friends who are not on the path of ECK. There is no need to make abrupt changes in your life. Changes can be made gradually. Friendships that stand between us and our goal of God-Realization will dry up quite naturally, just like the river of karma.

The Heart of the ECK Teachings

At the heart of the ECK teachings is the Sound of God. In ECK, we have both the Sound and the Light. Those of you who have studied the ECK discourses for several years or have read the ECK books have become aware of this Sound of Spirit. It is an actual sound. It has a reality that is unknown to most religions. A few have a diluted form, a faint memory of the Sound and Light.

We can hear the Sound of God clearly when we do the Spiritual Exercises of ECK. These are found in books such as *ECKANKAR—The Key to Secret*

Worlds. There are four or five given there.

In the book *In My Soul I Am Free,* by Brad Steiger, which is a biography of Paul Twitchell, there is a technique called "The Easy Way."* This is the technique that I used when I began studying Eckankar, and I was actually quite surprised to find myself in a higher state of consciousness. I wrote to Paul Twitchell about it, and my experience—the one about the young serviceman overseas—was included in the book.

When *In My Soul I Am Free* came out in 1968, I was in the service in Fort Meade, Maryland. I walked into the bookstore one day, and there it was. When I took it off the bookshelf and saw the name Paul Twitchell, I was very happy for Paul that these pure teachings could now come out to the public. Until then, I had thought Eckankar was some kind of private little study group.

Although I was an ECK student at the time, I had absolutely no contact with any other ECKists. There were very few when I joined in 1967, and even a year later, in 1968, I still hadn't met any. So when I opened the book and started to read, naturally I got very excited to see the experience of that young military person in Japan.

There are four states of consciousness that I can speak of here. There's the sleep state, the waking state, the self-knowledge state, and then the objective realization. The self-knowledge state is what we know as Self-Realization, and the objective realization is what we know as God-Realization.

Very often I work with individuals in the dream state.

Very often I work with individuals in the dream state. The Living ECK Master is empowered to work both in the dream state and outwardly, where I can direct you to one of the ECK books.

* *In My Soul I Am Free* is now out of print, but "The Easy Way" can be found in *The Spiritual Exercises of ECK* (exercise 104). —Ed.

I don't expect to prove to anyone that this is the only way to God. It won't be the way for all of you. If all of us found ECK compatible with our needs on the spiritual path at this time, I would say that would be a very happy coincidence.

Aspects of Eckankar

There are different aspects to Eckankar such as the ECK-Vidya, the ancient science of prophecy. Someone said to me this afternoon, "You are the Living ECK Master and the Inner Master, the Mahanta; you're supposedly in the know about all things. Why didn't you know about a particular situation?" Maybe I did and maybe I didn't. I had practiced the ECK-Vidya a long time ago. It takes discipline just as it does to learn to work with the dream state.

The ECK Masters led me to that discipline, or showed it to me, and I took the disciplines upon myself. I'm not speaking of something highly esoteric like doing breathing exercises, but simply keeping a notepad by my bed and having the self-discipline to crawl out at night when it's ice-cold in the room and start writing from the state of total sleep. It's hard. It takes a lot of discipline.

I could look at the ECK-Vidya to foresee some of the situations that come up at the ECK Office. But it would take an entire staff of people that is ten times larger than we have just to carry out the troubleshooting. I'd have to tell them that we had something going on in some area even before anybody wrote in or recognized the situation.

I give you the opportunity to learn by your own experiences.

Do you see how it would put me in the position of telling somebody what to do every time? I do this as little as possible. I give you the opportunity to learn by your own experiences.

DREAM TEACHINGS

The ancient Egyptians taught through the dream state; they had temples established for this purpose. The Greeks picked it up from them and had over three hundred temples devoted to learning by dreams. But the priests and the oracles put themselves between God and man.

As the Living ECK Master, I don't do this. I put out help only if you want it. I don't ever say that the way is through me. I don't say that either I or those appointed under me are the only ones who can interpret a dream correctly for you. It's not true. You have to learn how to interpret your own dreams; your dreams can give you the secret knowledge of the other worlds.

Your dreams can give you the secret knowledge of the other worlds.

We can be disciplined about studying our dreams or we can just not bother, but our success depends somewhat upon how much of ourselves we put into it. This is true whether we are going for a bachelor of arts degree or for an eighth-grade diploma. It's all the same thing. Success doesn't happen overnight.

Although I'm out in public, there is a whole line of ECK Masters who stand in the background, who give support, and who work in all the different worlds of God. One individual wanted to see Rebazar Tarzs, the great ECK Master who usually is portrayed as walking around in a short, knee-length maroon robe.

This individual had an inner experience but saw only lights moving around. Someone else who had been there and was able to see those lights explained that they were actually the ECK Masters—Wah Z, which is the spiritual name for myself on the inner planes, and Rebazar Tarzs. Rebazar Tarzs took this individual to the House of Imperishable Knowledge on the fifth plane, the Soul Plane. He had earned the right to be raised in consciousness to this particular level of heaven which is beyond that known to orthodox religions.

Rebazar Tarzs may come to you in the dream state and work with you. Another individual didn't recognize him because he came in a tan shirt and trousers, rather than the short, knee-length maroon robe.

When Rebazar Tarzs came, though he seemed to be a good person and there was a kind of dynamism about him, it never occurred to this individual that he might be an ECK Master. This man had let an image put a box around him, and he couldn't step beyond it. Eventually he learned that the ECK Masters can walk around in any attire they choose.

The ECK Masters work with us in all ways, at all times, to give protection, to give healing.

The ECK Masters work with us in all ways, at all times, to give protection, to give healing, but often we do not understand the method of healing that comes.

Spiritual Growth

I met with several individuals today who are still learning their spiritual lessons. We all are. I'm still unfolding, and so are all the ECK Masters. They, too, are looking to take another step.

One of the individuals I met with was trying to put a measure to the state or the quality of his spiritual life. He asked what he could use as a yardstick or a measure of success. Anytime something happened and he got some money, this individual took it as a sign that the ultimate reality, or God—what we know as Sugmad—had given it to him. Without knowing it, he equated spiritual growth with material success.

There's nothing wrong with this. As we walk the spiritual path, we may have all kinds of success in the spiritual, material, and emotional areas. But if we're not careful it's possible to be misled by the negative power. I don't often speak about the negative power, or Satan, but it does exist. In Mark Twain's day, it was sometimes called Old Scratch, and he wrote about it in *The Mysterious Stranger*.

The negative power, or Satan, is merely an instructor who is in charge of God's earthly schoolroom, the place where Soul gains purification so that It may one day reenter the heavenly states of consciousness and become a Co-worker with God.

You and I—Soul—were created in the heart of God and put in the lower worlds because we simply would not serve others. We were self-serving, enjoying our life on the Soul Plane and other worlds, and we would not give anything in any way. And so we came into the lower worlds.

Many of you write and ask, "What is my mission in life?"

Many of you write and ask, "What is my mission in life?" Very specifically, it is to become a Co-worker with God. How this breaks down for your particular talents is actually between God and you. It's not for me to say.

CARRYING THE MESSAGE OF ECK

Someone wrote to me from his cabin in the northern United States. He described the wind blowing outside, the cabin creaking, and a fire burning in his stove. He was surrounded by these pleasant sounds: the crackling wood and the howling wind. He was safe and secure and warm inside, listening to the Sound of Spirit, hearing the Music of God.

There was such a tranquil sense of harmony in this letter that I wished I could have been up there in his little cabin enjoying it too. He wrote to ask: "For what reason would I join the outer organization of Eckankar when I have the Sound of God with me right now?"

We carry the ECK message forward, out into life, and why do we bother? Because Soul is uplifted and purified in the presence of others. The ECK Satsang—which is the real organization here on earth, not the ECK Office—is an instrument for this Divine Spirit to flow into the community.

We do nothing whatsoever to direct this power, because to direct the ECK becomes black magic. One form of directing Spirit is prayer. I won't include all prayer—just prayer which is done without a person's permission, asking for someone else's healing or asking for someone else to change his religion. This is an attempt to direct Spirit, and it's nothing more than black magic.

Most of the people who pray so earnestly for others don't realize we each have chosen our state of consciousness.

Choosing Our Own State of Consciousness

It takes a while for many individuals, even many ECK initiates, to recognize that we each choose our own state of consciousness. We make our own worlds. What we are today is the sum total of everything we have thought or been throughout the ages.

Often when we look in the mirror we wonder: Is this really the highest of all? Is this what I have reached? I've asked myself that question a lot of times too. I'd look at myself and think consciousness must be something that doesn't show in the mirror.

The ECK Masters stand in the high states of consciousness, ready to help anyone who is willing.

But we don't worry about it. We take our steps on the spiritual path; we climb the ladder to God. The grace of God does not descend upon us. This is something religions often do not understand. They feel the grace of God comes to us merely because we ask. It does in a way, but first we must earn it. We must make at least some effort before the grace of God comes to us; but when it does, we are lifted up into it.

The ECK Masters stand in the high states of consciousness. They stand in the high heavens ready to help anyone who is willing to reach into a knowledge of himself, which we know as Self-Realization, and ultimately the knowledge of God Consciousness. But we have to go through the disciplines, and we know these disciplines as the Spiritual Exercises of ECK. These are done at home, privately, and no one else knows you are doing them. No one else knows whether you are being successful, whether you are making advances on the path or whether you're not. No one except the Inner Master and you.

Another point is to live the karmaless life. To act without creating further karma is to do everything in the name of God or in the name of that Inner Master within you. This is a simple way to go through life.

The path of ECK is an adventurous one.

The path of ECK is an adventurous one. Everything that is given to you is given because you are able to handle it. No matter what comes up in your life, you have enough inner strength or the Master wouldn't have given you that next step in your spiritual unfoldment.

Spiritual Lessons

Too often we think of the healings of Christ as being permanent. We have no record beyond the time of the healings. Did they last or didn't they? Or how long did they last? It never occurs to us that even though a person was healed of a very great illness, can a healing wear out? How about those who were raised from the dead? Are those people still here today? We've never thought about it.

We look for help from Spirit, and we get it. Whether it's a physical healing or whether it's to give us the strength to bear what we must until such time that we've learned the lesson and it can be removed.

We work off the karma that is needed for us to learn the spiritual lesson which got us into a predicament in the first place. Our health problems come from some attitude of the mind in the past where we created what we have today. And it's only for our spiritual unfoldment. The reason is never punishment.

As ECKists, we have the opportunity to reach into those other worlds. We can go into the heavens and have actual experiences in regions beyond the third heaven which Saint Paul speaks of in the New Testament. We can go beyond that, and we do.

Building a Spiritual Foundation

When you get this experience of God in your life, what do you do with it? Often I'll take someone along very slowly. I'll say, "Take your time. Don't hurry with the study of ECK. Please do not read book after book or gorge yourself on as many ECK discourses as possible." You can get spiritual indigestion, and eventually you just run out of steam.

Someone mentioned that an acquaintance of his had gotten success in his daily life by the power of positive thinking, and it worked very well for a long time. He was able to gain money and to go from working for someone else to establishing his own business. One success led to another. Then one day the bottom fell out. Everything caved in, and he wondered why.

We want to go into the pure spiritual worlds that begin at the Soul Plane and go beyond, onward to God.

It was simply because this power of positive thinking is from the lower worlds of matter, energy, space, and time. We want to go into the pure spiritual worlds that begin at the Soul Plane and go beyond, onward to God. This power of the lower worlds has to fail because it is unstable. It will work for a while, and just when you think you've got it all working for you, it'll collapse right out from underneath you and leave you on the floor in a pile of dust and ashes. Then somehow you have to recreate the whole scene and put yourself back together.

I would rather have you build your spiritual foundation carefully so when the psychic waves come, bringing doubt and fear, problems, and health situations, you will be strong enough to see and know why you are going through this, and that it will pass. We know in ECK that whatever is here today must one day pass. It's the nature of life. Spring gives us the example: Nature renews itself each year; it renews all life.

THE TWO PLUM TREES

A woman wrote to me from Europe with a story about two plum trees. The story is an example, in a sense, of reincarnation and spiritual renewal. It's the nature of life to renew itself. When the night looks darkest, stick around; morning's coming. The Master is always with you.

One pretty summer morning this woman was in her kitchen, looking out the window. A friend of hers was working outside in the garden, enjoying the freshness of the day, when a car drove up with two men in it. They stopped right by the driveway and jumped out to look at the garden.

The men stood there, examining two dead plum trees in the woman's garden. They decided to take it upon themselves to do this lady a favor and cut them down for her, since it costs money to cut down trees. They had a chain saw, so they thought they would just cut down the trees, stack up the wood for the lady to use in the winter, and everything would be fine.

The men had a chain saw. They said, "The trees aren't bearing fruit, and what's the point of having two plum trees that have faded?"

They walked up to the friend who was working in the garden and said, "We've come to cut down the two dead plum trees." The friend said, "But why?" They said, "Because the trees aren't bearing fruit, and what's the point of having two plum trees that have faded?"

One of the men then went to the car, got out his

chain saw, and came back to the garden. By this time the owner of the home had left the kitchen and came running outside. "Wait a minute," she said. "I forbid you to cut down my two plum trees." But the man was insistent. Maybe he thought she was too polite to expect anyone to do her this favor for nothing.

Again she said, "Stop," but they kept walking toward the trees. What the men didn't know is that she had plans to graft different branches onto the stumps, and in this way she hoped to renew them without having to dig up the stumps and roots. She knew she had to save those trees.

She came storming up to them and said, "Don't cut down these trees. Come with me. I want to show you something." She led them to the stump of a cherry tree and pointed to the young branches that were growing from it. They had blossomed and borne all kinds of sweet cherries. "Have some," she said. After they had eaten the fruit, she asked, "Now weren't those the sweetest cherries you've ever tasted?" The two men agreed.

The renewal of life. Sometimes we know it as reincarnation. Sometimes we know it as spiritual unfoldment. Other times we know it as Soul making Its way back to God.

She said, "Those plum trees are going to bear fruit again in the very same way." The men just shook their heads. They didn't really believe it, but they finally left.

In explaining this to the two men, the woman was trying to demonstrate something about the renewal of life. Sometimes we know it as reincarnation. Sometimes we know it as spiritual unfoldment. Other times we know it as Soul making Its way back to God.

I would like to thank you for coming tonight. Watch your dreams. Work with them.

May the blessings be.

World Wide of ECK, San Francisco, California, Friday, October 22, 1982.

Although people cursed it, they continued to follow the crooked path the calf had made in centuries past.

2
Calf Paths of the Mind

I would like to welcome you tonight to Eckankar, a universal teaching of the Light and Sound of God. It's a teaching that is unique in that the individual is shown how to get experience for himself with the Voice of God.

Eckankar is unique in that the individual is shown how to get experience for himself with the Voice of God.

We know the Voice of God as Spirit, or the Word. In the New Testament, Saint John says, "In the beginning was the Word. . . . and the Word was made flesh." We know It also as the Audible Life Stream that comes out of the high worlds of God and can be heard as Sound and seen as Light. These sounds and the different colors of light are described in ECK books such as *The Spiritual Notebook*.

Levels of Heaven

There are different levels of consciousness or, if you will, different heavens. Jesus said, "In my Father's house are many mansions." Saint Paul said he knew a man fourteen years earlier who had been lifted up even unto the third heaven. In my preministerial studies, my professors never told me anything about heaven number three, let alone two or one. It was supposed to be enough to know that if I died, I was going either to heaven or hell.

On a radio program the other day, a man was saying that the power of the church lay in the fact that it said it had the answer to a man's life after death. Whoever controls what happens to you after death controls you in this life.

I would like to give you a little understanding about what happens in the other heavens, about the reality of the Light and Sound of God. This Sound can be heard in numerous ways.

There are many sounds of Spirit, many sounds of ECK. One of them is the buzzing of bees. This can be heard on a certain level which we call the Etheric Plane. Another sound is a humming, which can be heard at a different level. Or you can hear the flute of God. The importance of these sounds in our spiritual unfoldment is that when we hear the Sound of God—which usually is heard as music or similar to a sound of nature—Spirit is uplifting and purifying us in our state of consciousness.

Questions from the Youth

The young lady was really asking, What is the role of the Living ECK Master? and What is the relationship of Soul to God?

This afternoon I visited the teen room. The teenagers are the future of Eckankar. One young lady asked me, "What's the difference between God and you?" She was really asking two things: What is the role of the Living ECK Master? What is the relationship of Soul to God?

Soul is the essence of God. Soul is not God—It could never be God. We can never be one with God, although we can be one with Spirit.

Another teenager asked, "What should we do when they make us pray in school?" It's interesting when we come to the point where we have the freedom in our country to pray—or else. I asked, "How many of you who are in public schools are forced to pray, regardless of your beliefs?" Out of maybe seventy or eighty teenagers in the room, about ten hands went up. I said, "What do you do when the time comes?" One young lady answered, "Mostly I just put my head down and look at the Blue Star of ECK."

The ECK Masters don't always like to walk out in public and remind our legislators what the Constitution is all about and its importance to the strength of the United States today. There are many adults who forget that even though a child is not forced to pray and can step outside the classroom, by doing so he becomes an outcast. Have the elders forgotten their own childhood?

Some of the questions from the youth were quite interesting. They ranged from what to do about health to spiritual unfoldment. They are learning about their bodies. All of a sudden at around thirteen, fourteen, and fifteen, they shoot up the same way we did. And however big you used to be inside, now you don't reach to the end of your fingers. You drop things. Others call you clumsy. You trip and do all kinds of awkward things. You're in this body that is a little too big, and you haven't quite gotten used to it. But the dexterity comes.

When we unfold more, what used to work no longer does.

It's the same in our spiritual unfoldment. When we unfold a little bit more, we come to a new level of consciousness where the laws of Spirit that we have learned up to that moment may change and reverse. What used to work no longer does. We may wonder, Why has God forsaken me? This is often called the dark night of Soul, as spoken of by Saint John of the Cross.

A Penny and the Law of Karma

One of the things we as parents can do is to teach our children respect for another person's space and property. When I was young, I would go to the phone booth to see if somebody had left a dime or a quarter in it. That's the kind of thing you do when you're young.

Once in a while I'd find some coins, and I always got away with it. But as you make a little bit of progress in the spiritual life, as you unfold, you're not able to get away with the same things as before. The greater you become in your state of consciousness, the quicker your acts come back to you. In the Bible, Saint Paul speaks of this Law of Karma when he says, "Whatsoever a man soweth, that shall he also reap."

Too often this is not accepted in the orthodox beliefs. The reason is that the karma may not come up for payment for twenty years, or it may not come until the next lifetime. When I went up to a telephone booth and took a dime, I'd say, "Oh, good! It's nobody's dime"—and I'd go buy something with it. But eventually it got to the point where the next time I'd go to a newspaper box, I'd lose a quarter.

Recently I went to the school yard with my daughter, who's in grade school. This little fellow came along—he said he was nine years old, but he looked about seven—and he said he had been playing soccer for four years. I didn't know anything about soccer, and I was twice as tall as he was, but I said, "How do you play it?"

On the path to God we step out boldly and courageously. We learn things.

This is the attitude we take in life on the path to God. We don't say, "I'm afraid to step out in life because I'll be shown up as ignorant." We step out boldly and courageously. We learn things. We're willing to make a fool of ourselves just for the sake of experience or learning.

This little guy was really good. He'd kick the ball, run around, and make a goal. I blocked one of his goals once, and it really bothered him. I had the advantage because my arms were twice as long as his.

When we finished playing, we sat on the swings for a while. I was really swinging high when I started to feel a little swing-sick, so I told my daughter I was going to climb the bars. She kept swinging for a few more minutes and then got off to climb the bars too. As she walked past the place where I had been swinging, she said, "Hey, Daddy, I found a penny." I said, "Leave it there." She's heard the phone-booth story of karma from me so often that, rather than get a lecture, she left it there. A penny's not worth a lecture on karma.

But soon she said, "I found a nickel." I said, "A nickel! We're starting to get up there now."

"And here's a quarter."

"A quarter?" I ran over there, feeling my now empty pockets. As we dug through the sawdust, I said, "I lost a lot of money down here."

She couldn't resist it: "But are you sure it's yours, Daddy?"

"I know it's mine—except I'm not sure about the penny!"

And this is how we go through life.

Levels of Spiritual Consciousness

We are told on the spiritual path to seek first the Kingdom of God. In ECK we know that as we reach the higher states of realization, we are going to get wisdom, power, and freedom.

We gain the wisdom to know how to take another step on the ladder to God. We gain power, but not over others; not to tell them how to live their lives, and not even to pray for what we think is right for them. We don't have that right. And we gain freedom; not to step into another's state of consciousness, because that is sacred, but the freedom to open ourselves to be a vehicle for Spirit. This is the mission of Soul: to become a Co-worker with God.

As we open ourselves for Spirit, there is a lot of baggage we have to throw overboard.

As we open ourselves for Spirit, there is a lot of baggage we have to throw overboard. Someone mentioned a meeting with Paul Twitchell, the ECK Master who brought out Eckankar in 1965. At the completion of a talk he gave one day, Paul looked out over the audience and said, "There are some people here who have to drop a lot of baggage." He was talking about karma.

My role as the Living ECK Master is to link up Soul with this divine essence of God which is known as the Audible Life Current.

In ECK we have levels of spiritual consciousness which we identify by the initiation. This is an initiation into the Sound and Light of Spirit. My role as the Living ECK Master is to link up Soul with this divine essence of God which is known as the Audible Life Current, or the cosmic current. In the Bible It is known as the Holy Spirit, the Holy Ghost, or the Comforter. This initiation comes after two years of study in ECK.

We do not pull people off the street and say, "Become a member of Eckankar!" I did that when I first started in ECK, but I didn't know any better. It's not worth the trouble. Each person ought to have the freedom to choose his own path to God. God has provided many different paths so that Soul can find Its way back again.

Reality of the ECK Masters

Some of the ECK Masters of the Order of the Vairagi work with the initiates of ECK. These ECK Masters come to us sometimes years before we step on the path of ECK, because the way must be prepared.

At one time we were looking into a public-relations firm to see if they had any ideas about how we could get the message of ECK out to the mainstream of the twentieth century, yet keep it pure and simple without getting into the more sensational aspects. For example, Rebazar Tarzs is one of the ECK Masters who has gained the ability of longevity. There also are reports of yogis who have lived a hundred years and more, and some of these ECK Masters have the same longevity.

When the public-relations people learned how old Rebazar Tarzs was—this is mentioned in some of the ECK books—they said, "How about if we take him on a road tour?" It was hard to explain to them that Rebazar Tarzs generally works only in the Soul body, although he does have a Physical body here. They didn't understand, so I guess that project was dropped somewhere along the way.

Many have given reports about meeting Rebazar Tarzs. One of the ECK initiates wrote in and recounted such an experience. As she did the Spiritual Exercises of ECK, she suddenly found herself on a grassy knoll, talking with Rebazar Tarzs. This time he was dressed in his knee-length maroon robe, carrying the large staff that he uses when he walks in the mountains.

As she did the Spiritual Exercises of ECK, one initiate suddenly found herself on a grassy knoll, talking with Rebazar Tarzs.

He talked with her for a while about several things, and then all of a sudden he got up and took this large, strong oak staff and broke it over his knee as easily as if it were a piece of kindling. At first she was uneasy. What had she done to upset this ECK Master? What spiritual lesson had she overlooked?

Then she realized that he had taken on some of the karma that she had to work out. She had learned all the lessons from that particular amount of karma, and he had taken it, in the form of his staff, and broken it over his knee. Through this experience, she came to recognize the love and the help that the ECK Masters are able to give—not just on the physical, which is only a small part of the spiritual unfoldment that is given to any Soul, but on the inner planes.

The ECK Masters have the ability to work with you in the dream state. Many times this is done years before you hear of Eckankar. It would be easy for a psychologist to think the followers of ECK have been programmed to see the image of their teacher in their minds. It would be very easy for him to say they're robots. But how would he explain about the person who had experiences with the ECK Masters years before he ever heard of Eckankar, even years before 1965 when Paul Twitchell brought it out into the open? One explanation is that there is a reality to the ECK Masters of the Order of the Vairagi.

Detached means simply that you can have compassion, you can enjoy life, but if sorrow comes into your life, it does not burden you until the end of your days. You are able to see the hand of God in it.

Vairag is the detached state of consciousness. This goes along with God-Realization. Detached does not mean without compassion, uncaring, without love. It means simply that you can have compassion, you can enjoy life, but if sorrow comes into your life, it does not burden you until the end of your days. You are able to see the hand of God in it.

The Key to the Spiritual Works

There was a poem I learned as a child called "The Two Weavers." It went something like this:

> As at their work two Weavers sat,
> Beguiling time with friendly chat,
> They touched upon the price of meat,
> So high a Weaver scarce could eat.
>
> What with my brats and sickly wife,
> Quoth Dick, I'm almost tired of life;
> So hard my work, so poor my fare,
> 'Tis more than mortal man can bear.

The other weaver looked at him as they worked on a rug, and answered:

> And when we view these shreds and ends,
> We know not what the whole intends;
> So when on earth things look but odd,
> They're working still some scheme of God.

As Soul we are looking only for experience, whether it's in this world or in the other worlds. We have no concept of sin in ECK. That doesn't mean we are hedonistic. We recognize something more powerful, and it's called self-responsibility with instant payment. This is better than the threat of death sometime later for sins committed.

The key to the entire works of ECK is in the spiritual exercises. There are a number of exercises, or creative techniques. These are given in the ECK books, such as *The Spiritual Exercises of ECK*. The spiritual techniques are important.

If you are interested in the path of ECK, the first step is to read a book. Try the spiritual exercises and see if they work for you. Take your time—two or three or even four years.

There are also three good spiritual exercises in *The Spiritual Notebook*, by Paul Twitchell. They are to help you see the Light of God, to hear the Sound of God, and to recognize them both as they come together in the form of the Inner Master. You can then know the reality of the works of ECK for yourself. You do not have to take my word for it or anyone else's.

Choosing Your Path

When Spirit comes into your life, It will uplift you and give you an understanding into the problems and the joys of your daily life.

When Spirit comes into your life, It will uplift you and give you an understanding into the problems and the joys of your daily life. It gives direction, and for many people this is the first time they have found it.

It gives meaning and reason to life and answers to questions such as why a baby dies when it's only five days old or why an individual is required to suffer for years and years before he finally dies. It gives answers, because understanding reincarnation and the Law of Karma gives us a view that goes beyond the borders where scientists dare not tread. Science can't go beyond the laws of the physical world, and the spiritual worlds all lie beyond these borders. They may catch glimpses, but they will never catch the essence of this Light and Sound of God.

So if you are interested in ECK, check it out for yourself; don't let anyone else tell you this is the path for you. I wouldn't want anyone to tell me to do this or that, because I was always very stubborn. I might have felt it was the right way, but I wanted to choose it myself. I wanted the right to make the decision myself.

Someone sent me a poem. The title was "The Calf Path," and one of the lines in it was "the calf-paths of the mind." It tells an interesting story.

Three hundred years ago there was a little calf on its way home. It meandered as it made its way along a path through the forest, and it disappeared into history.

Three hundred years ago there was a little calf on its way home. It meandered as it made its way along a path that led through the forest, and as the calf wandered and made its trail, it disappeared into history. The next day, along came a dog. He was just out for a walk when he smelled these tracks, and he decided to follow the path of the calf. A few days later there came a bellwether, the sheep that leads the flock, and by some coincidence this sheep followed the trail made by the calf and the dog.

After a couple of years, men started to track along this same path, and though they bitterly cursed its crookedness, still they followed it. Time went on, many years passed, and this animal trail became a country road. A few more decades saw it evolve into a city thoroughfare, and finally, after more years, it became the main street of a metropolis. But it was still so crooked that you had to travel three miles to advance one mile.

The people drove down this crooked street by the thousands, by the hundreds of thousands, day after day, year after year. Because they had to travel three times farther than the actual distance, they cursed it, and yet they continued to follow this crooked path of the calf from centuries past.

Eckankar is not the only path to God, but it is the most direct. It is the direct path home. There are other paths, but they are trodden and driven through the centuries by those who can't get off them, who will curse the crookedness, who will curse the darkness but not turn on a light.

In ECK we understand that the mind runs in a rut. We pick up habits as children, which carry into the teen years and become hardened and solidified as we grow older. Anger and other attitudes of the mind stem from these habits. The only thing that is greater than mind is Soul. It is above the power of the mind, and It is the only thing able to nudge the mind out of its rut.

I invite those of you who have any interest in ECK to look at the introductory books; look them over with an open mind, then put them away for a while. Don't do too much reading in the works of ECK any more than you would in any other spiritual path. This leads to spiritual gluttony and spiritual indigestion. Things will go wrong because you will be getting too much Light and Sound within you before you are able to give It back out in deeds of service and love to your fellow man.

Greater than walking any particular path is to be able to exercise the freedom to choose the path to God that is right for you, and to allow the same freedom for others.

I invite you, then, to look at the path of ECK with an open mind. Whether it's for you or not, recognize that something greater than walking any particular path is to be able to exercise the freedom to choose for yourself the path to God that is right for you, and furthermore, to allow the same freedom for others.

Thank you kindly. May the blessings be.

World Wide of ECK, San Francisco, California, Saturday, October 23, 1982

Children imitate their parents, using them as an example.

3
Stories of ECK in Life

As we live the life of ECK, we want to know how It works in our daily life.

A professional musician recently came to me and said he had developed a case of jittery nerves. So much of this creative flow was coming through him that he was not able to take the time to balance it with some kind of physical activity. He used to walk a lot; he was able to spend time out in the fresh air. But nowadays he's so involved with his music that he has not been able to work any physical activity into his daily schedule.

Another musician told about joining a basketball team. The musician was able to get his exercise in this way. It is important to keep a balance in our physical life. When we get the ECK flowing in, all too often we want to put all of our attention on the books of ECK or the contemplative exercises, and we forget that we also have to live day to day.

In the children's room yesterday, I asked some of the children, "Do you ever see the Inner Master?"

The Consciousness of a Child

I was in the children's room yesterday. I asked some of the children, "Do you ever see the Inner Master?" Very straightforward, they said, "Oh, yes." No questions, no explanations. They have experiences but are often unable to put them into words.

As parents, we have to bring forth discipline so that the children can grow up and take their rightful place in society as leaders in ECK. At my daughter's school, there is an old-fashioned teacher. She likes the reading-writing-and-arithmetic approach. She teaches the children to respect the space of other people, not to interfere in their state of consciousness. Her rule is something like this: Keep your hands, your feet, and your mouth to yourself. I teased my daughter about this. But as they get these rules, they learn.

One day my daughter came home beaming and announced, "I'm president of my class!" She was very proud. Then she said, "For today."

My daughter was recently chosen to serve in the food line at school, which is considered a great honor. They also have a program where the students get to be the class president for a day. One day she came home beaming and announced, "I'm president of my class!" She was very proud. Then she said, "For today."

This is the fresh consciousness we see in a child. In the spiritual works it says something to the effect that unless you become as little children, you cannot enter into the kingdom of heaven. It means this fresh consciousness that looks at life through eyes that have never seen before. Everything is new to a child. They have no preconceived notions of how something should be.

It is known that before the age of six a child learns very rapidly. They learn by imitation. Some of us may have forgotten that a child imitates the parent. If you're a father with a small son, you might take a step, look around, and there's your little shadow. They use you as an example.

In Eckankar, too, we look to someone higher on the path and notice how they live the life of ECK. This is why we, as the initiates of ECK, must be examples to reflect that spiritual understanding which is coming into our lives. We don't make a goal of higher ethics, but higher ethics are a natural result of increased spiritual unfoldment. This ought to show in our lives, in our business dealings, and in our interactions with others.

Looking at Past Lives

Some of you have come to love music. I've had a very difficult time with music in this lifetime. In grade school we had music classes where the instructor would sit us up in the bleachers in our music room and we'd have to suffer through music theory and the history of the musicians from the Middle Ages. I never really had an interest, and it has taken years to develop it. I used to like country music, and before that I liked popular music. As we develop, we take a liking to certain kinds of music for a while, and as we go on, we drop them and move forward to something else.

An ECK initiate had gone for years without the kind of inner experience where he could look back into his past lives.

There was an ECK initiate who had gone for years without the kind of inner experience where he could look back into his past lives. He wanted to have the ECK-Vidya opened so that he could look back and see what had caused some of his problems in this life. This is the only point of knowing the past. We can use the ECK-Vidya to gain an understanding of how the past can help us today.

When he did get this experience, he found that in the nineteenth century he was an American musician who traveled widely. He enjoyed his music, had a following of fans, a woman in every port, and broke a lot of hearts. It wasn't because he was of a callous nature; he simply didn't recognize that other people really cared for him.

So in this present life two things happened. He found difficulty in sustaining romantic relationships, and he didn't like music. He had gotten his fill of it in that past lifetime.

In ECK, we have the freedom to like music, to learn to grow to like it if we choose, or not to like it. An individual mentioned to me how he'd had an aversion to music years ago when Paul Twitchell was here. This individual had an opportunity to ask Paul why he had this aversion to music. Paul researched the ECK-Vidya for him and found out that in several past lives, on another plane, he had been a music teacher. If any of you have been music teachers who tried to get a few notes across to a student who didn't want to learn, you might agree it could affect your feelings about music in the coming lifetimes.

The ECK-Vidya can give us an understanding about ourselves so we may unlock the barriers in our present life that have come from the past.

The ECK-Vidya can give us an understanding about ourselves so that we may unlock the barriers in our present life that have come from the past and see that portion of the future that will help us become a clear channel, or vehicle, for Spirit. The whole point of our existence is to open up to the ECK.

The Creators of Our World

I have always found it a great privilege to attend the ECK seminars. There was a time that I loved to sit in the audience and just soak up everything. Paul and the Higher Initiates would speak about one topic or another, and each talk gave me a little greater understanding. Eventually there was too much to hold inside. I'd get restless and would have to get up and start walking around in the halls; I just couldn't sit still in the audience. I found this happened because I could only take in so much, and then I had to give it back out.

So I began to look around for ways to give out this love from Spirit. I'd go out in the hallway and enter into a conversation with someone. Sometimes we would talk about ECK, and other times we wouldn't, but that didn't matter. As I went further, I was able to give service, to help in some way. I'd carry messages or do anything to be helpful, and it made life more fun. It's that way in our personal life too.

Life is a mystery until we come to the path of ECK.

Life is a mystery until we come to the path of ECK. We begin to understand that we can be the creators of our own world and that, in truth, what we are today is a creation of that which we have made from the past. There is a way to change the future, and we can do it. But you don't do it by wishing.

When an individual looks for God-Realization, it has to be more than a passing fancy. It's not like a fashion that you only wear for a season; you don't just forget your high aspirations for God. It must be something that is within your heart in a gentle way. You know that no matter what happens on the path, it is always to lead you closer to the source of Soul's creation in the heart of God. Soul wants to return home.

Inner Surrender to Spirit

Life goes up and down. We have times when everything is going our way, but there are also times when we're at the bottom. If we keep ourselves open to Spirit, there will be an equal balance.

This is what is meant by the detached state: When our fortunes hit bottom, we surrender to Spirit. Then we can go back up more naturally, and we'll maintain this rhythm of life. As life goes on around us, the detached state is that which runs right through the center; we are the balanced individual working in the Soul consciousness.

To reach God-Realization, we must learn surrender to Spirit, where we give up everything on the inner—not outwardly.

An elderly woman had so many physical ailments that she felt she wasn't long for the world. She decided she had better get to a doctor quickly.

Mark Twain told the story of an elderly woman who had so many physical ailments that she felt as though she wasn't long for the world. She decided she had better get to a doctor quickly. After examining her, the doctor said, "Yes, you do have a number of ailments, and we have to see if we can do something to make your life better so that you can get your health back. For one thing," he said, "you are going to have to give up smoking."

"But Doctor," she said, "I don't smoke."

"Well, then you're going to have to give up your drinking."

"I don't drink either," she said proudly.

"Then you'll have to give up your cussing," he shot back.

She sat straight up in her chair. "Doctor, I never swear!"

He threw up his hands in frustration. "Madam, there's nothing I can do to help you. You have neglected your habits!"

These habits Mark Twain was speaking about are what we know as the five passions of the mind. They lead to gossip and gluttony and all of the perversions. There are counterbalances to the five passions, such as humility, contentment, and others. We find this balance by looking to detachment. Detachment doesn't mean a lack of emotional interest in life. It means that we are willing to take life as we find it, with the highs and the lows. Then yesterday becomes no more than yesterday, and we can look through the eyes of the child and say, What is here for me today?

Freedom of Consciousness: Abortion and Prayer

I'd like to read a letter that one of the initiates sent to several government officials and newspapers.

It concerned the issue of prayer in schools. Some of the ECK teenagers were concerned about this and wondered what they could do. The reason I mention this is that we are interested in consciousness.

Some ECK teenagers were concerned about the issue of prayer in schools and wondered what they could do.

All I can do is direct you to the ECK books and show you where to find some understanding as a beginning point to take you into the inner worlds. This is where you can check out whatever you are told here on the physical plane and find out for yourself if there is any validity. This is where you can become the source of knowledge, in that it flows through to you.

In reading this letter about prayer in schools, I'm speaking about the freedom of our state of consciousness, which has been guaranteed by the United States Constitution. It's the reason Eckankar was able to come out in a country such as America, to be used as a fountainhead for reaching out to all the world. We have to be willing to protect the individuality of each person. This is my only concern. When it comes to speaking out and standing up for our freedom of religious belief, we have to make the effort.

The letter reads:

> Dear Editor:
>
> Let me preface this letter by saying that I am not a biblical scholar. When I read the Bible, like many others, I just use common sense to understand its meaning. I would like to address two issues that are very much in the forefront of public opinion. As I read the Bible, it clearly states certain principles that have direct bearing on these issues.

And here he addresses the abortion issue.

> Most of the conflict over the abortion issue has to do with whether or not the human fetus is a living being, because if it is, then abortion is wrong, and if it is not, then abortion makes no difference.

> President Reagan has said that it is impossible to know the answer to this question. I wonder if he has checked his Bible lately. Genesis 2:7 states: "And the Lord God formed man of the dust of the ground, and breathed into his nostrils the breath of life; and man became a living soul."

First man is formed, and when the breath of life is breathed into him, then man becomes a living being. And not until the breath of life comes into the fetus does it become a living being. These bodies are vehicles for Spirit. To become a vehicle for Spirit means we use what we have. Though the body needs to be taken care of, it's the consciousness, the Soul consciousness, which we are concerned about.

In the Soul form, we use whatever we have in order to carry forth the message of the Sound and Light of God. This is to let others know of the reality of these twin aspects which come from the Ocean of Love and Mercy; that they can be used for Soul to ride on the Sound wave, on this Sound and Light, back into the heart of God—back home.

Soul can ride on the Sound wave, on this Sound and Light, back into the heart of God—back home.

The letter goes on:

> According to this, man becomes a living being when he takes his first breath. As far as I know, a baby begins to breathe after it is born, and not before. If what the Bible says about this is true, then the abortion of the fetus would not be taking the life of a living being.

Then he goes into the prayer issue:

> Communication with God is a very sacred part of many men's lives. One form this communication takes is prayer. A personal prayer to God can be an uplifting spiritual experience. There are those who would prefer prayer to be a more public activity. To those who advocate public prayer in the schools, I would only ask that they

> read Matthew 6:5 and 6:6, which states: "And when you pray, you must not be like the hypocrites: for they love to stand and pray in the synagogues and at the street corners that they may be seen by men. . . . But when you pray, go into your room and shut the door and pray to your Father who is in secret; and your Father who sees in secret will reward you."

We go to where we can meet God directly. We have the source; we know the way: through the Spiritual Exercises of ECK.

We speak of this as going within. We go to where we can meet God directly. There is no reason to parade our communication with God outwardly or to make it a law. The children who do not wish to address their God in a particular way, at a particular given time as dictated by someone else, should have this freedom without being expected to leave the room and become an outcast among their classmates.

As you go home, you will take this love of ECK which has entered your heart and carry it with you. Some of you will find that others back home and at work will notice there is a glow about you. Though they may not see it, they can feel it. And they will notice this tranquil peace and contentment which comes from having learned where to find this love of God, this love of Divine Spirit. We have the source; we know the way: through the Spiritual Exercises of ECK.

I'd like to thank you for coming. As you travel homeward, know that spiritually you have my love and protection.

May the blessings be.

World Wide of ECK, San Francisco, California, Sunday, October 24, 1982

To develop the creative imagination, you can work with the Spiritual Exercises of ECK as illustrated in the ECK books. What you're looking for is to have experience with the Sound and the Light, where you will have adventures in other worlds.

4
The Spiritual Exercises: A Key to Heaven

For those of you who are new to the teachings of ECK, which are the teachings of Spirit, I would like to explain the HU chant. HU is an ancient name for God which you can use quietly in your personal life if you run into a situation where you would like to have a little insight or a little spiritual upliftment and protection.

You can use HU quietly in your personal life if you run into a situation where you would like to have a little insight or a little spiritual upliftment and protection.

I don't always like to do the HU chant when there are those of you here who have never heard about Eckankar before, because if I were to go to another group and they said, "OK, we're going to do this chant," I wouldn't want to feel I had to participate. The HU chant is something that we invite you to do only if you want to, but it does help to spiritualize and uplift.

The Many Paths to God

We have talked quite a bit this weekend about Soul's purpose and why we are on earth. I went to a local bookstore and found it quite interesting. The volume of words written about the spiritual path is awesome. You look at all those words, and you figure that somewhere among them there must be truth. Of course, there is, but each one of us requires a different level of truth.

As an example, the people of most Christian denominations say that they follow the same Christian Bible. Yet there are hundreds of different denominations. What could be the explanation? Simply that there are many different levels of consciousness.

You and I are Soul. Soul—each of us—is a unique creation; a spark of God. There are no two of us alike. Those of us who have similar ideas about life, gained from our personal experiences, may get together in a group and call it a church or a fellowship. We are on the path to God in our own way, at our own time, and each of us ought to have this freedom to find God as we will.

We are on the path to God in our own way, at our own time, and each of us ought to have this freedom to find God as we will.

In the early days of Christianity, there was a group of people known as the Gnostics who were said to have a dualistic belief. They worked from the premise that any knowledge of God had to come from personal experience.

As time passed, the religious leaders lost the ability to go to the other worlds and bring the divine wisdom back to their followers. The next best thing they could do in order to keep control was to outlaw any practice that taught or encouraged the individual to explore those inner realms for himself. Gnosticism was one such path, and it was outlawed.

One of the early schools of Eckankar was established in Egypt around 3000 BC. Astrology had a large following in those days, and though its adherents were able to manipulate charts, very few were able to work with what we know as the ECK-Vidya, the ancient science of prophecy. Then persecutions were set in motion, and the ECK teachings were taken underground by the ECK Masters.

From that time until the present, we have worked

quietly in the background. There are many different brotherhoods at work, each one valid in its own right. There is a brotherhood that stands behind the workings of the political scene, and behind that one is another brotherhood, and behind that one is another.

We do what we can to bring the Light of Spirit to those in our community in a way that allows them the freedom to say, "No, I have my own way." We recognize the validity of another individual to choose his own path to God without recrimination or prejudice.

My preministerial background was in the Lutheran Church, and it was a very stringent, very orthodox branch of Christianity. I learned many things about literature; I learned many things about biology. But when I had questions such as, Does a man really go to hell if he hasn't ever heard of Christ? the only answer I got was, Yes, he does. When I would say it didn't seem fair, I was only told to have faith and believe.

The Gnostics rejected faith as the only criterion for experience with God or for accepting God, because it wasn't enough. In ECK we know we must begin with faith, but once we have faith, there has to be something more. Therefore, we speak in ECK of the two aspects of Spirit—the Sound and the Light.

What Sets ECK Apart

We have been seeking for centuries, and some of you may find an answer in the ECK books.

What sets Eckankar apart from most religious teachings—not all, but most—is the Sound and Light of Spirit. Spirit is the Voice of God which comes out of the God realm, the home of Soul, into all the lower worlds of creation. This Voice is also referred to in the Bible as the Word. For example, Saint John speaks of it as, "In the beginning was the Word. . . . and the Word was made flesh."

We have been seeking for centuries, and some

of you may find an answer in the ECK books. Instead of saying, Take my word for anything you hear today, I'll suggest only that you read an ECK book and take your time.

The key to making contact with this Light and Sound of Spirit is the Spiritual Exercises of ECK. Several of them are listed in *ECKANKAR—The Key to Secret Worlds*. It's a very inexpensive way to get an introduction to Eckankar and to try out these spiritual techniques for yourself. Take the book home and try them. If it works for you, fine. If it doesn't, keep looking. It never hurts to keep our minds open and to see if there is indeed one more step that is possible for us to attain in our state of consciousness. What we are looking for is the direct experience with divine ECK, or Spirit.

Our name for Spirit is simply ECK. This ECK is what the Bible refers to as the Holy Ghost, the Comforter. This is the same manifestation that came to the apostles at Pentecost. They heard a sound like a rushing wind. This is one of the sounds of Spirit. There are many more, such as the sound of the flute; many ECKists have heard It.

Learning the Laws of Spirit

You get a little God-knowledge and then a little bit more. This God-knowledge can be brought back into your daily life and put to practical use.

The purpose of the Sound is to give purification to Soul as It strives for wisdom, charity, and freedom. The wisdom comes from the ability to travel into the higher states of consciousness, or heavens, that lie within. We call it going within. You get a little God-knowledge and then a little bit more. This God-knowledge can be brought back into your daily life and put to practical use.

Charity is what the Christian Bible speaks of as goodwill. We call it vairag, or detachment. When we see another person with problems and troubles, we can have compassion; but we understand that somewhere down the path these problems have come to him by his own efforts. We let him have the freedom to have his troubles. If he asks for help or compassion in one sense or another, we can give it, but we certainly do not interfere with another person's problem and take it on ourselves by saying, I'm going to pray for his healing. We learn the laws of Spirit.

There are violations of these laws. One of them is the misuse of prayer; that is, using prayer to change another individual's state of consciousness without his permission. A classic example is where the convict at the gallows is breathing his last breath. A priest runs up and elicits an eleventh-hour conversion. Everybody else feels good then—Ah, this man is saved for all time—but actually the priest caught the convict at a very vulnerable moment.

People who practice psychic healing may get away with it for years, because the Law of Karma is in no hurry. Spirit has plenty of time; It's in no hurry to collect the debt that a man has created. A psychic healer may be very good for ten, twenty, even forty years; but then his health all of a sudden may go bad. The karma has come home; it must be paid. He doesn't know what happened, only that he can heal others but not himself. Furthermore, he doesn't know why it happened. He has absolutely no understanding that he violated the laws of Spirit.

We come to understand the total responsibility that each Soul carries for Its own thoughts and actions.

We come to understand the total responsibility that each Soul carries for Its own thoughts and actions. In ECK we acknowledge neither sin nor the guilt that goes with it. The burden of guilt oftentimes is heavier than the passion of the mind that caused it.

We speak of these passions as attachment, lust, vanity, greed, and the big one—anger. Many of our illnesses are caused by anger. I won't name specific ailments, because if you have one and I mention it, you'll say, Oh no, I'm an angry person. Then I've put you in a little box, and I don't want to do that. All I want to do is give you information about the Sound and Light of Spirit.

There is a way to uplift yourself spiritually, to lift yourself out of materialism into the true spiritual reality.

There is a way to uplift yourself spiritually, to lift yourself out of the area of materialism into the true spiritual reality. I spoke of wisdom and charity. The third part is freedom. The freedom that we are looking for is the spiritual liberation which takes us out of the realm of karma, so that when it comes time for us to leave this body and go into the other worlds, we go into the regions beyond the scope of karma.

The Mission of Soul

The mission of Soul is to become a Co-worker with God. This is Its only purpose. This is not such a dreary thing, either. If you misinterpret it to mean wings and halos, where you flit about like butterflies around flowers for all eternity, you might say, Not interested. That's because most of us are interested in growing and expanding in some way. I'm speaking of those who are of the higher states of consciousness and are looking for some way to unfold themselves. It continues even after we leave the physical body.

We don't get planted in a hole six feet deep and then hope for the day when the body and Soul somehow will be miraculously stuck back together. If you were a sailor who got eaten by a shark, which later was eaten by other sharks that all swam off in a hundred different directions, you might wonder how you would ever get the whole works back together again.

Some of the religious teachings believe body and Soul are one and the same. We believe Soul comes in and takes on the physical body as a temple to use so It can move in this physical world.

We are looking for the liberation of Soul, where those individuals who wish to rise above the worlds of matter and reincarnation may do so—to take their rightful place in the spiritual worlds as Co-workers with God, both now and after dropping the physical body. And then you can volunteer for temporary duty somewhere. You can come back to earth if you want, but you don't have to; you have a choice. You may choose to come back as somebody's neighbor. You may not even know who you are for twenty or thirty years, until once again you are given the opportunity to open up to Spirit. Often people work unconsciously as vehicles for Spirit, many times carrying the Light of Spirit without even recognizing it.

PSYCHIC CURRENTS

We are interested in consciously working with this Divine Spirit. As Soul we are looking for total awareness. This means that we become aware of the subtle psychic currents which are always sweeping around us, which whip our neighbors and nations into an emotional frenzy about many things.

People are swept back and forth by political forces, by the politicians and others whose own purposes are served. Find a cause, gain a lot of followers to support the cause, and if you win the cause, you get reelected. I have no objection to that, but it is important to become aware of what we're doing and why, so that we can be a knowing cause or even a knowing effect. It makes no difference which, as long as we know what is happening to us. We owe it to ourselves.

One of the ECK Masters who worked here before Paul Twitchell brought out the ECK message in 1965 was Sudar Singh.

SUDAR SINGH'S SEARCH FOR TRUTH

One of the ECK Masters who worked here before Paul Twitchell brought out the ECK message in 1965 was Sudar Singh.

Sudar Singh lived in India around the dawn of the twentieth century. He was the son of a rich man; he could have taken his inheritance and lived very well for the rest of his life, but instead he wanted to know truth. One day he dressed himself in rags, though they were of a good quality of cloth—it's hard to be humble when you can afford better—and started out on the road to find truth.

He had heard about this Rebazar Tarzs, a teacher of some ancient wisdom who lived up in the Himalayan Mountains, and decided to make contact with him. Through inquiries, he was directed to one of Rebazar Tarzs's students who happened to be an important government official, so he set off down the dusty road to find him. Arriving at the man's home, he was invited in and spent the next week asking question after question of his host.

The servant assigned to wait on Sudar Singh happened to be Rebazar Tarzs in disguise, who was observing the seeker very carefully as he brought him food and drink.

The servant assigned to wait on Sudar Singh during his stay happened to be Rebazar Tarzs in disguise, who was observing the seeker very carefully as he brought him food and drink. Sudar Singh looked into the teachings of ECK, and after about a week he concluded that there was nothing in the teachings of Eckankar for him. Very sadly, he left. Rebazar Tarzs merely stood by to see in what direction he would go, giving him perfect freedom, perfect choice.

A year later, after looking into a number of other religious teachings and getting nowhere, Sudar Singh had come to the end of his rope. He wondered if there was anything left to live for. One day, wandering up in the foothills of the Himalayas, hungry and tired, he fell into a light sleep. He awoke suddenly, and there stood Rebazar Tarzs with a pitcher of milk to give him some nourishment. This time Sudar Singh recognized him, and from that point he began earnestly to make his own steps on the path to God.

THE ROLE OF THE LIVING ECK MASTER

What is the role of the Living ECK Master? Not to walk the path for you; not to be the intermediary between you and God. It's your path; you must walk it.

If you want a guide, if you want to ask for help, it's there. The Living ECK Master is empowered to work with you on the physical plane, but he also has the power to work on the inner planes. He works with you through the dream state as well as directly through the expansion of consciousness, which is sometimes known as Soul Travel.

It's up to you to find out the truth of this for yourself. The spiritual path is an individual undertaking. ECK begins to work very subtly after a while. I don't endorse the idea of the individual becoming a puppet of somebody who manipulates him by some inner strings. There's no reason for that. We look to make our own direction.

PARENTS AND CHILDREN

We talk about how we must become as children to enter the kingdom of heaven. This means childlike in our state of consciousness. This doesn't mean that children are always angels; sometimes they can be real monsters, because they haven't yet learned the social consciousness. They're completely at the mercy of the world, yet, on the other hand, the whole world revolves around them. Some are working with primitive instincts from birth. It's a good thing children don't become six feet tall right away, before they learn to fit into society and learn how to respect other people's psychic space.

As parents we have a responsibility to show our children how to fit in and understand the laws of Spirit as they go out and try to make their way in life.

As parents we have a responsibility to show our children how to fit in and understand the laws of Spirit as they go out and try to make their way in life. We have to teach them about their responsibilities. We show them how the Law of Karma works. In other words, they learn that you can steal if you want to, but you're going to have to pay the debt.

It is the responsibility of parents to show their child how to fit into this life, understand the spiritual laws, and stand on his own feet. This is what the ECK Master does, too—spiritually—except not quite as directly as a parent. A parent is required by law to make sure that the child steps out there and understands what's what and what's not, but the ECK Master can give help only if it is asked for.

Asking for Help

If you have any questions now, I'm willing to answer some.

Q: Do we continually need to ask the Inner Master for his presence and help, or just occasionally?

HK: One good technique is this: In the morning, using whatever wording you choose, you can say something like, I ask God to give me direction throughout this day so that all my words, thoughts, and feelings are done for the upliftment of all those whom I meet.

You can chant HU quietly within during the day. You can put your attention on the spiritual part of yourself.

It helps to put the pieces together as you start out the day. Or you can chant *HU* quietly within, as you run into situations during the day. You can put your attention on the spiritual part of yourself.

Q: Is the chanting an invitation for the presence of the Inner Master?

HK: Yes. If you ask for help, if you ask for truth, it will be given to you. When you begin seeing someone on the inner planes—and it may be Jesus or one of the other great leaders—if you feel comfortable with that leader, go with the teachings that he has to give.

SPIRITUAL TEACHERS

In the hierarchy, when the student has learned everything he can from one Master, he is passed on to the next teacher. There are none of the jealousies among the spiritual teachers on the inner planes as we have here; there's no reason for it. Each one works at a specific place in the spiritual hierarchy, knows his position, and works as a humble Co-worker with God. The petty jealousies that we know about down here on the physical plane are really caused by people who haven't had any spiritual experience, or by their followers who have had just as little.

The Sound and Light of Spirit comes and washes, or uplifts, Soul. As this occurs, your outer life changes.

Sometimes the only way they can claim their religious path is greater is by a show of force. It is not based on true spiritual experience where the Sound and Light of Spirit comes and washes, or uplifts, Soul. The vibrations of the Soul body are raised. As this occurs and you reach into another state of unfoldment, your outer life changes.

Many people are born in one state of consciousness, they keep it for their whole life, and they die with it. Their life is as easy to plot out as the progress of an aircraft flying across the country. Very predictable. But when you step on the spiritual path and you begin getting this Light and Sound in, your life is going to change.

KEEPING UP WITH CHANGE

I'm not saying this is the path of sweetness and light, because there are times it isn't. There are times when we spiritually have moved into a greater state of awareness, while physically, mentally, and emotionally we're lagging behind, holding back, hanging on to that which we were before. That's when the conflict comes, and that's when the sparks fly.

For those people who unfold and go with it, the laws change at every step. At each heaven or state of consciousness that we reach, the spiritual laws shift. What was true before may not be true now, or it may be more true than it was before. You, yourself, have to learn these new laws with the help of the Inner Master—find out what they mean for you and how to utilize them to make your life easier and better.

If you learn the laws quickly, it goes smoother; if you don't, it's a little harder. But it is an adventuresome path, because those of you who wish to find God or to realize God must be of a bold and adventuresome nature. The coward doesn't get there. God doesn't want the meek. Somebody made a joke once about the meek inheriting the earth. It's true, they will inherit the earth—but who would want it?

We Are Soul

Q: Is a medium who claims he's communicating with a former personality actually getting that entity's point of view?

HK: We recognize that Soul is eternal; It has no beginning and no ending. Therefore, when a person leaves this physical body, he continues to exist, usually on a higher plane of consciousness. Very seldom will the higher teachers come back down to help.

The spiritual exercises lift us up to meet these individual spiritual travelers, working in the Soul body.

This is the point of the spiritual exercises: You have to undergo the discipline to lift your state of consciousness to an area where these teachers are, where they can help you. In a sense, we are led to believe that the grace of God descends upon us, but actually we climb the ladder to God.

The function of the spiritual exercises is to lift us up to meet these individual spiritual travelers, working in the Soul body. It's not to work with people living on the Astral Plane as personalities. The personality is a fragment of the mind, which is not as high as Soul, and therefore it is subject to illusion and errors.

Q: When this kind of contact is made, is it only with part of an entity and not the complete spirit?

HK: You are looking at life as though "we are it, and we have a soul." I look at it this way: I am Soul, and I have a body. It's just a different point of view, but it's a little bit hard on communication.

When a person goes into the higher states of consciousness, he goes into the other worlds as a complete entity, because he is a complete entity here. Complete doesn't mean perfect—there is no such thing as final and total perfection.

There is always the plus factor, always one more step to heaven, one more step to unfolding. But it is the total consciousness of that individual who has dropped the physical body as a useless husk when he's done with it. The body is worn out, or he has finished his job here. But that Soul continues to exist as a complete entity and works in other planes of being.

What are we? Are we Soul, or do we have a soul? Spiritualism works along the lines of which you are speaking. If you want to, you might read *ECKANKAR—The Key to Secret Worlds* just to get an idea of the different bodies that make up man.

What are we? Are we Soul, or do we have a soul?

Q: When one reincarnates, does he bring back just a portion of the former personality, or does the complete personality dissolve and allow the spirit to continue on?

ADMINISTERING KARMA

HK: Well, here we get into karma and how karma is administered. As long as you're under the Law of Karma, that personality is very closely tied to

Soul. This is in what we call the lower worlds—the Physical, Astral, Causal, Mental, and Etheric.

But when you have the karma administered from the Self-Realization state, the Soul Plane, it changes. The personality is no longer tied in with Soul. You recognize it as a sheath; you recognize the body as something to be left behind. Soul goes to the different planes and picks up a body to operate there in the same way we must have a physical body in order to operate here.

There is a cleanness about working from the consciousness of Soul; whereas when you work under the Law of Karma and have yet to establish yourself with self-recognition, then there is still a personality hanging on as a sheath around Soul. It is part of that which has to reincarnate and which is carried along as a person moves his state of consciousness around in these various heavens.

Developing the Creative Imagination

Q: Could you tell us some more about the importance of our imagination?

HK: Imagination is the creative spark within us. It is that God faculty which we use in finding our way back to God. The imaginative faculty is developed through the creative techniques described in the ECK books.

We begin using our imaginative faculty to start creating the world as we would have it.

When we come into this world, we are given a certain amount of ability to maintain a status quo; in other words, to get us from birth to death with the usual life problems and situations. But if we want to step on the spiritual path and begin making our way back to God, we have to work for it. The way we work for it isn't by doing anything physical; rather, we begin using our imaginative faculty to start creating the world as we would have it.

Everything that we have today—from our preference in clothing to our position in the family where we happened to reincarnate—has actually been a result of our attitudes as they have formed over the centuries. So what we try to do is spiritualize our consciousness, and we do it by working with the creative imagination.

We know that we can shape our future. This is why I'm not all that concerned about reading the future. I did this at one time; I usually don't anymore, because the future is unformed. You can make it what you want, but first you have to be able to visualize what you want very clearly. Unfortunately, most people look for materialistic goals such as money, health, wealth, and companionship. But again I'm going to mention this: As Jesus said, "Seek ye first the Kingdom of God . . . and all these things shall be added unto you." Make sure that your goal is worth the trouble.

To develop this creative imagination, work with the Spiritual Exercises of ECK. Experiment freely with these techniques. What you're looking for is to have experience with the Sound and the Light, where you will have adventures in the other worlds.

Some of you won't have these kinds of experiences, because we are all different. Some people come directly to a perception of seeing, knowing, and being. They are working directly from the spiritual worlds.

Each of you has the means to develop this ability. It depends upon how much interest and effort you put into it.

Each of us is different. I can't say you will have Soul Travel experiences, because you may not. It might be that you won't want to work for it. Each of you has the means to develop this ability, and many of you are successful. Others have some success, then it stops for a while, and then you're successful again. It's like anything else in life: It depends upon how much interest and effort you put into it. I'd suggest you read *ECKANKAR—The Key to Secret Worlds* if you want to expand on this subject.

When someone asks about Eckankar, usually the easiest thing to do is just ask if they would like to read an ECK book. If they say yes, recommend one of the introductory ECK books. If they say no, that's fine.

The creative techniques would mean very little to someone who has not actually tried them. What I'm saying means more if you have a little experience and have experimented—whether you've succeeded or failed. You have put a little of yourself into it, and you will have a better basis for understanding. If you are only interested in ECK a little bit some of this may be over your head; so I'd just recommend you read one of the ECK introductory books. Take it home—nobody will bother you there. If you like it, look further; if you don't, give it away.

If you are only interested in ECK a little bit, I'd just recommend you read one of the ECK introductory books. If you like it, look further; if you don't, give it away.

Shaping Our Personal World

Q: You said that we should start thinking about how we want the world to be and use our imagination in that way.

HK: Our personal world, yes.

Q: I'd like to know how you would like your personal world to be.

HK: Well, I'd like to have a little happiness each day. There were times before I was on the path of ECK when I didn't have that. We can think of the big things—a good companion and all this; but there are also little things, like not having to do the laundry today because you already have clean clothes to wear to work tomorrow. If I'm going to do something in my life—whether it's a job or even just committing myself to a dinner engagement—I might as well try to enjoy it.

Q: That's a very day-to-day sort of approach. What about wars and other major issues? Or is that all none of my business—should I just be concerned with my own personal world and having a little bit of happiness?

HK: When we're a vehicle for Spirit, we do what we can wherever we are. We get involved, but we also recognize that this is a warring universe. There has been so much talk about peace. Most of it has actually come from Palestine and that region from which Christianity sprang. But they just haven't been able to live with each other over there so far, and it doesn't look as if they're going to do any better in the next two thousand years either.

When we're a vehicle for Spirit, we do what we can wherever we are.

We do what we can, because the destructions that everyone speaks of do not have to occur. It's up to us. If we're not able to pull it off and avert a crisis, we don't develop an emotional disorder because we failed. We recognize, as the ECK Master Rebazar Tarzs said, that earth is the ash can of the universe. Yet it's an excellent training school for Soul.

We do what we can, but we don't feel guilty and we don't let ourselves get out of balance. We work with other like-minded people to accomplish things; we don't sit back in life and just wash our hands of the whole affair.

In the United States right now the government is trying to enforce prayer in the public schools. As parents we don't have to just sit back and do nothing if we disagree with this: We do something about it. We talk with the school board, we elect officials, we vote officials out of office. But we do this as individuals, not as a group of ECKists. This is an individual matter—we don't want to use the spiritual works as a political arm for manipulation.

Leaving the Body

Q: What is the best way for me to try to leave my body? I've tried a lot of times. I'm sick of reading books, so what's the next step that I should take?

HK: Books won't get you God, but they do help give us direction. Begin to work in the dream state by keeping track of your dreams. You could start a journal and watch your dreams. But the Inner Master isn't going to let you go beyond the area in which you're capable of going, because it would upset you.

Keep a journal of your dreams, review it every month, and just watch and see what happens. You will see a change in your inner experiences if you're sincere.

Keep a journal of your dreams, review it every month, and just watch and see what happens. You will see a change in your inner experiences if you're sincere. If you would like to write to me and let me know what's happening—though I may or may not answer you in the physical—by all means do so. It's an exciting thing, but I don't want to go too fast with you.

Initiations

Q: I've heard the sound of the flute which one hears on the Soul Plane, but I'm not a Fifth Initiate. What does this mean?

HK: You see, when we step on the path, we go through the different planes. We go through the Physical, or the First, Initiation, and then the Astral Plane, or Second, and so on up. We can go to the Soul Plane as a visitor, but the point is to become established there. During the Second Initiation, a person is taken to a Temple of Golden Wisdom on the Soul Plane called the House of Imperishable Knowledge. We visit many times before we actually become established there.

Wherever you go, whatever you see and hear, is between the Inner Master and you. We refer to the Inner Master, this high state of consciousness, as the Mahanta.

A lot of times when we hear the music of the Soul Plane while still in the First, Second, or Third Initiation, we say, "Ah, I'm greater than it appears." We try to impress people. But it's simply that we have earned the right to be taken there to visit. If you were going to move to England, you might go there and visit a couple of times first to make sure you really wanted to leave everything behind and stay there. It's the same way on the inner planes.

You are taken on visits, and then, as you earn the right—when you have come through the Second, Third, and Fourth Initiation and have established yourself in each one of those planes—you then establish yourself on the Soul Plane as you get the outer initiation.

Sometimes the outer initiation may be preceded by the inner initiation by anywhere from a year to four years or more. The inner initiation is for the inner, and the outer is for the outer; but you need the outer initiation to complete the inner. So, when you hear the sounds on the Soul Plane or even beyond, it's for your own enrichment.

When you hear the sounds on the Soul Plane or even beyond, it's for your own enrichment.

HEALING

Q: Is it all right to use the healing techniques to help someone else?

HK: No. Then you start picking up karma. Even when Jesus was doing healings, he told others: "According to your faith be it unto you." In other words, it is as you have earned. When you've earned something, consciously or unconsciously, the gift has already been given and is yours to receive.

There are different techniques for healing, but it ought to be self-healing. As soon as you start healing someone else, you run into a lot of karmic problems—you take on the other person's karma. It's better to gain an understanding of why illness and other types of problems come to us. It happens because we have violated one of the spiritual laws. Sometimes we violate them with "fun things" like gossip and anger, and we learn that it's not so much fun when we have to pay back the debt.

Until you come onto the spiritual path, you generally have a lifetime or two behind you that you're paying off, so you can't make the connection between what you did wrong in the past and the payment that is now coming due. As you move along the spiritual path, the higher you go, the quicker it comes back.

If you do something that stands between another person and God-Realization, you very quickly find out that you have broken a spiritual law. It comes back sometimes within a week, a few minutes, or even seconds. It comes quickly enough so that you know: Ah! This pain is the result of a lack of understanding of that spiritual law.

As you go further on the spiritual path, it becomes more honest. You become willing to accept total responsibility for your actions.

As you go further on the spiritual path, it may become harder but it also becomes more honest. You now know exactly what you're doing. You become willing to accept total responsibility for your actions. You watch your actions much more carefully than someone who looks for the justification of their sins in the spilling of someone else's blood so many thousands of years ago. If you believe this, you might think you can live your life any way you want to, as long as you repent just before you go. And this is not spiritually honest.

Dropping the Mind

Q: What happens to your mind when you go into the higher spiritual planes?

HK: Your mind has been dropped already—one, two, or three planes earlier. The mind is not able to go into the pure spiritual worlds; it has to be left behind. In the higher worlds you operate with seeing, knowing, and being. You have a direct perception of what is, and you don't have to go through the laborious mental process. It's different. We can't really conceive of operating without the mind because conceiving, of course, is a mental function. There is a way you can go and have these experiences, but you have to drop the mind before you can go into the spiritual worlds.

Q: How can you know, without the mind, when this has happened?

HK: Something may register on the mind, which registers on the senses, so that you can become aware of it in the physical state of consciousness.

It's impossible for the mind to understand the things of Spirit, yet that's the area in which we work. That's why we write books. They provide a way to give techniques so that the mind will have something to work with as a tool to get close to that spiritual plane.

The Inner Master is able to help you into the pure spiritual worlds.

The Inner Master is sometimes able to help you into the pure spiritual worlds. It's different there and it's not really something I can explain with words. Words go only so far. It is something you have to experience, and you will when you're ready.

Jesus as a Spiritual Teacher

Q: Was Jesus Christ a Master?

HK: He was a spiritual teacher who was giving a message which was important for his times. He often said that the things that he did, others could do and more, and that they shall be as sons of God too. This is the nature of Soul; it is our heritage. But, unfortunately, these statements have been pushed under the rug over the centuries by those such as the Council of Nicaea, which also helped put Gnosticism underground, because the leaders had lost the ability to do the things which Jesus did.

Soul and the Mind

Q: When I see something on the inner screen during a contemplation, the image only lasts for a few seconds, and then it's gone. Am I imagining it, or is it real?

HK: Yes, it's real. Soul is looking, seeing, and perceiving instantly, but the mind is much slower than Soul. The mind has to go through the mental processes. To compare Soul to the mind is like comparing the speed of light to the speed of sound. The latter is comparatively slow, but things do register, and what you have seen is there.

Q: Can the mind help us to gain the ability to astral travel?

HK: Yes, if you want to astral travel, but it's a limited form of consciousness. You can develop it, but a better way is Soul Travel.

Q: Wouldn't it be better to start off a step at a time?

HK: Astral travel is so limited; it's hard to do and there are even dangers associated with it. If you are out of the body astral traveling and someone startles you, you could sever the silver cord. When you return to the body too fast, you snap back in like a rubber band; but in the Soul body, it generally doesn't happen like that. In Eckankar, as you work with the different states of consciousness, you have someone standing by to protect you and to make sure that this doesn't happen.

In Eckankar, as you work with the different states of consciousness, you have someone standing by to protect you.

Once while I was resting on an airplane, I took off to enjoy myself somewhere else. The lady seated in front of me for some reason chose that time to rummage around in the overhead baggage compartment. I was sound asleep, and my jacket suddenly fell down and hit me right in the face. I came back fast! If I had been astral traveling, at the least I might have had a very sore spot in the stomach, where there is a faculty that links up directly with the Astral body. It is safer to Soul Travel, which is actually the expansion of consciousness.

THE PRESENCE OF THE MAHANTA

Q: While studying the first discourse series, I've become conscious of seeing a gold disk. What is it? Is it the presence of the Master?

HK: Yes, it's the Mahanta, and it's different for everyone. Usually when the first step comes, you see the Light—the Blue Light, the Blue Star, or a globe or disk. That is the Inner Master. It simply comes first as Light: This is the initial step. Next, you'll generally be able to hear the Sound—one of the Sounds of God.

When you have the Light and the Sound, it is usually then that the Inner Master comes into your spiritual vision. By his presence, by seeing him, you have the Light, and when he speaks you have the Sound. It's all in one; he's actually able to communicate with you, and this is what we call the reality of ECK—where you have the inner communication.

The Blue Light of the Mahanta goes ahead to prepare the way.

Sometimes the ECK Masters begin working with people years before they step onto the path, and they might see the Blue Light of the Mahanta. It is that high state of consciousness which goes ahead to prepare the way so that when you actually are ready to step onto the path, the transition is very smooth and natural. Even then, you may have doubts, but it's still easier than if you didn't have any preparation.

BECOMING ONE WITH SPIRIT

Q: Can we become one with God?

HK: Well, actually you become one with Spirit, but never one with God. To become one with God means you would become God. That's kind of a self-canceling mental concept. We become one with Spirit and a Co-worker with God.

We can realize—or develop—the attributes of God, which are omniscience, omnipresence, and omnipotence. We can develop these qualities but we never become God. We can have these qualities as Soul, as part of Its expansion of consciousness to the total awareness state, and yet we aren't God. We become the spiritual traveler, and with this comes wisdom, power, and freedom.

We become the spiritual traveler, and with this comes wisdom, power, and freedom.

Soul and the Physical Body

Q: You have mentioned situations where a body can be brought back to life. If the Soul has left that body and then taken on another body, can someone else inhabit the dead body?

HK: Yes, it can happen. This is why the ECK Masters have their bodies cremated when they leave—so that no entities can get into them. They're done with them, and they don't want them to be taken over by somebody else who would then mislead a lot of people. Cremation is a lot neater too.

Some people would rather be buried because they are looking for that resurrection where the body and Soul again arise together. In a case like that, if Soul hasn't gone somewhere else and the body is still in good shape, It could conceivably come back into the body in the same way It decides to enter a newborn baby.

The baby form is just a vehicle. Soul looks and sees if the conditions are absolutely right, as far as It can tell in Its spiritual unfoldment, for that lifetime.

If any one factor isn't right, the Soul doesn't come in, and then you have a stillbirth. Sometimes the fetus is born and even begins breathing, yet Soul still might hover around and watch it for a while. Or It may go into the body for just a little while because It needs only a short experience, and then It leaves. The parents, not understanding the ways of Soul, are completely heartbroken and wonder how they failed or what they did to displease God. Nothing.

Q: Are you saying an entity could take over a body if the Soul has gone on to another body?

There are workers on the inner planes—kind of like police here—who don't allow things to get completely out of hand.

HK: Yes, it could, but there are also safeguards for something like that. There are workers on the inner planes—kind of like police here—who don't allow things to get completely out of hand. If someone opens himself to the negative, or psychic, forces, he sometimes attracts entities, becomes unbalanced, and has to go for professional help. This happens simply because that individual somehow has opened himself through the use of black magic or drugs. And this is why we discourage the use of drugs and alcohol. They open up the psychic centers; you open wide the doors to entities who are always hovering around.

DRUGS, ALCOHOL, AND CIGARETTES

Q: What actually are the effects of drugs, alcohol, and cigarettes?

HK: Cigarette smoking can cut off the protection of the Inner Master, but drugs and pot smoking do more. Drugs are particularly bad because not only do they damage the physical body for a long period of time, they open up the whole inner to invasion by entities. Many times people come to the path of ECK after they have been off drugs for as long as three, four, or five years, yet they're still carrying some of the karmic burden. They are still finishing up the karma that they have created. Now they have to work it out completely.

If there is too great a gap between where they are in their state of consciousness and where one needs to be on the path to God, sometimes I just ask them to step aside until they can get the proper medical help. They should at least try to establish some kind of footing with their mental health which will help to close up those psychic centers.

Q: Can opium smoking, such as is done in China, help the users to get out of the body?

HK: They get out of their body, but they don't go far. It's interesting that after the British introduced opium to the Orient in the eighteenth century in an attempt to make money, very strange things happened. The destruction of the British Empire was caused in part because they passed something of such a destructive nature to another people.

This is also what caused the downfall of the Roman Empire, but first they got into something different. They brought back the Oriental teachings of Manichaeism, for instance, which were very similar to Gnosticism. It was completely foreign to the tight, rigid control that was necessary to keep the soldiers all together and out there fighting. Then later they got into drugs and other vices too, and this was really the cause of the downfall of the Roman Empire.

Usually there is good karma and bad karma associated with any nation as well as with any individual.

This is what happens; it's national karma. Some of it is positive and some is negative, and that's the case in every country. Usually there is good karma and bad karma that is associated with any nation as well as with any individual.

MALE OR FEMALE?

Q: Why is God always spoken of as a male and never as a female?

HK: It has nothing to do with the feminist movement, but with the nature of how the inner worlds are set up. For example when a person sees one of the gods of the Astral Plane—maybe Jehovah, who is so many times greater in splendor than anyone we know in the Physical Plane—this god appears in the form of the male. That's part of the way things are. That's why the person brings back the idea of the male gender.

The gods who are in charge of the different planes throughout the lower worlds all appear as males, and this explains the idea that God is a man. But God is neither man nor woman; nor is Soul man or woman.

God is neither man nor woman; nor is Soul man or woman.

You get to the Soul Plane by balancing the positive and the negative parts within yourself; they come into perfect balance on the Soul Plane. From this moment on we have Self-Realization. This is the first step of what we are looking for. From that moment on, your life is different—you see through different eyes. Sometimes your whole life is turned upside down at this point, and you may not know what's happening. This is a spiritual transfiguration that occurs—you actually become a new person. You are now in the state of self-recognition: knowing who you are, what you are, and what your mission in life may be.

WORKING WITH THE MASTERS

Q: When a Master translates and leaves the physical plane, what happens with those people who have been initiated under that Master?

HK: If you are an individual who has been initiated by one Master, that Master will work with you spiritually until you are established in the God planes, if you choose to allow it. Yet, here on the physical plane we need a physical Master. When Paul Twitchell translated, or died, and went into the other planes, those spiritual students who were not able to get in contact with him because they had not raised themselves far enough were able to work with his successor on the outer.

On all planes, the Living ECK Master stands at the head of the spiritual hierarchy, because that is the function of that position, but the other ECK Masters may meet with you too. If you are on the Astral Plane, you may work with a certain ECK Master; on the Causal Plane you will have another ECK Master working with you, or there may be two or three on the Causal Plane.

It's like this: Go within and see who you feel comfortable with. You can work with Jesus or Buddha or anyone. Go to the temple within yourself and see who is there for you. What you see is merely Spirit manifesting these states of consciousness, and Spirit cannot be divided within Itself.

The face of the Master that comes is actually the high state of consciousness in a form you can recognize. It really makes no difference. You can work with that individual who comes to you, because sometimes we have an affinity with a certain ECK Master from being with him in a previous life. The ECK Masters interchange very freely.

Look to the Spiritual Exercises of ECK; try them out, and if they work, go ahead with the next step.

Spiritual Exercises

Look to the Spiritual Exercises of ECK; try them out, and if they work, go ahead with the next step. Read a book such as *The Tiger's Fang*. It describes a journey into the heavens which lie beyond the senses of the physical eyes and ears. You may think it's fiction, and perhaps for you it is, but read the book; try to go there. *The Spiritual Notebook* also lists some creative techniques that you can try. Experiment with them. These are your own worlds for you to explore.

Sydney Regional Seminar, Sydney, Australia, November 4, 1982

When you have the ECK coming in, you have to give something back to life, and sometimes it's just helping out in the children's seminar for a while.

5
Giving Back to Life

Yesterday we managed to check into the wrong hotel. The woman at the front desk who had been working with our reservations had us scattered throughout the hotel. When we asked for our rooms to be closer together, she had to start juggling the arrangements. She was very cordial about the whole thing, but she did say, "Some mornings it doesn't pay to get up."

Yesterday we managed to check into the wrong hotel. Funny things happen, and this is when we exercise patience.

A short time after we went up to our rooms, it was discovered that we were in the wrong hotel. We had to get all our luggage together again and go downstairs to tell the lady who had been at the desk earlier, but she wasn't there. It's possible she was out back crying. So with great fanfare we came, and with great fanfare we left—all within half an hour!

Funny things happen, and this is when we exercise patience. You've got to have a lot of patience and a sense of humor. Someone had once asked Paul what trait a person would need to be able to work with him, and he said, "A good sense of humor!" I could never understand that—Paul looked so stern that I often wondered, *Does he ever laugh?* Many people said he had a wonderful sense of humor, yet I got a lot of discipline when he was the Inner Master, and I hardly ever saw any of that humor.

Inflow and Outflow

If you do the spiritual exercises and get more of the Sound and Light of Spirit flowing into you, what are you going to do with it?

I would like to talk this morning about inflow and outflow. I've been putting a little more attention on service in ECK. I'm trying to point this out to people. If you do the spiritual exercises and get more of the Sound and Light of Spirit flowing into you, what are you going to do with it? Mostly people just like to contemplate, enjoy the inner experiences with the Light and Sound, and sit there like a bump on a log. They think this is all it takes. Sometimes they just keep taking in and taking in; and then all of a sudden things start going wrong, and they begin having problems. They may not have written to me for a year or two, and then suddenly I'll start getting letters about all their problems.

Giving something back to life when you have the ECK coming in is absolutely essential for spiritual survival.

As a First Initiate, I read the books and really stuffed myself. I just read and read, and took all the ECK discourses I could. At first our vessel is empty, and then the ECK pours in and fills it up. And It keeps filling it up until about the second or third year of study. Then it gets full—and we have to start giving back.

One way to notice it on the outer is at a seminar. At first we are satisfied just to sit and listen to every talk. We can't hear enough. Then at some point we find we become restless and are unable to sit through the meetings and talks. And sometimes we wonder: Am I losing interest in ECK? No. It's the ECK prodding you off your chair to give service. When people don't understand this, they think they have lost interest in ECK. But the ECK is actually trying to take you to the next level, that of service, which is the first step to becoming a Co-worker with God. Sometimes it's just helping out in the bookroom or maybe in the children's room for a while.

We get the First Initiation, and outwardly we learn the disciplines that are necessary to survive. Spirit comes through very fast at the next higher level, when the Second Initiation comes; we have more of this power, this Light and Sound, coming through. Now, what do we do with It?

The mind is a little bit slow in catching on. The mind with its routines and habits doesn't want to change what it has been doing. It wants to keep reading and enjoying itself. But Spirit moves on, and the mind and emotions and everything else move along. If we aren't willing to exercise this randomity that Rebazar Tarzs spoke of, we have a hard time through our initiations.

Going from one initiation level to the next ought to be a very easy and smooth transition. We have to be willing to let go of old attitudes and stay very open to Spirit as It tries to lead us into greater awareness. Once you have opened up to Spirit, the Inner Master will step in—as long as you give permission—and take you into the greater vistas. If Soul has given permission but the lower bodies don't know it, this is when you start saying you've got all these problems.

Now is the time to start giving of yourself, to begin giving back to life in some way.

Now is the time to start giving of yourself. It doesn't necessarily have to be within the ECK program, but you have to begin giving back to life in some way. Do this according to your own talents and interests. Some people like to give talks, others don't; they're petrified. If that's the case, then don't give talks. Some like to work with children, while others—maybe those who have been parents—may say, I've done my time; let someone else have a turn.

Measuring Our Achievements

There is a life of fulfillment and growth as you begin serving the ECK, and you'll find that your life will improve in all areas. That doesn't necessarily mean financially—I'll give you the promise of the gold fields of heaven but not of earth. But even if you find yourself out of work, it's not the catastrophe it used to be. Spirit is moving you into a different arena, to another way. You still have to go out and look for work, but you now understand principles that were dark secrets to you before, and it will become easier to put yourself in that place which has already been prepared.

There is a life of fulfillment and growth as you begin serving the ECK, and you'll find your life will improve in all areas.

There is always a place for us, because creation in the lower worlds is finished. You visualize it; you see and know what is already yours. You accept the gift because it is already given.

The works of ECK are lifelong. Too often we look for short-term achievements. Did I Soul Travel? Did I see the Mahanta in my dreams? Have I seen the Light or heard the Sound? If you don't get an answer instantly or within a year or two, you may think you have failed. Or all of a sudden you may get the experiences, but as you unfold and the manifestations of Spirit change and become subtler, you may feel something is wrong—it's not the way it used to be.

People who came to the path of ECK during Paul's time had their initial experiences from the first plane of initiation. When his successor came six years later, in 1971, they were no longer having the same experiences. When a new Master comes, then all of a sudden things are different outwardly, and you become very aware inwardly. They started wondering: Now what's happening? How does it compare with the days of the previous Master? And they noticed it was not the same.

Of course it wasn't the same, because *they* were not the same. They did not recognize that they had unfolded. They had gone to sleep—drifted along for a few years—and then, lo and behold, a new Master came in. This forced them to take a good look at themselves, and they found that things were different: they had unfolded.

Recognizing the Masters

Someone out in the hallway asked: "Why does Eckankar have all these pictures of the ECK Masters? What is the purpose of so many pictures? It seems a little bit like idolatry."

That's not it at all. There are many individuals who have yet to come on the path of ECK, who have seen one of the ECK Masters on the inner planes during the dream state or during a moment of expansion of consciousness. They've seen an ECK Master without knowing who it was and wondered for years about that individual who came to them. Gopal Das is an ECK Master who worked and served his term as the Mahanta, the Living ECK Master in Egypt about 3000 BC. He is often mistaken for Christ because he has long hair, but it's blond.

The pictures help in identifying these ECK Masters, and this is the point of having them displayed. The ECK Masters are interested solely in helping Soul find Its way back to God—if It wants to.

The ECK Masters are interested solely in helping Soul find Its way back to God—if It wants to.

Walking the Fringes

Every religious teaching has those who walk the fringes; they're neither here nor there. Anyone who has his feet on the ground really wants nothing to do with them, and this holds true for every organization. The bigger the organization, the more you have, because there is that percentage who are always walking the fringes of sanity. Some of them have been playing with drugs; others have opened themselves to the negative forces in a previous lifetime by playing with black magic in one way or another.

This happened to Milarepa, the Tibetan saint. He played with black magic and had quite a good time. He developed all the lower psychic abilities, learning how to levitate and do all those tricks, because he felt this was part of spirituality. But there came a time when he had to drop them because he realized they were standing between him and God.

Contacting the Voice of God

The Sound and Light are the twin aspects of Spirit. This is the Voice of God. There are three parts, actually, that we are interested in as we step on the spiritual path. First there is thought. We use our mind and the imaginative techniques in working with the Spiritual Exercises of ECK. With the Spiritual Exercises of ECK, we consciously try to make contact with this Light and Sound of God. It's a worthwhile goal to experience the Voice of God: It means we have contact with the Divinity.

It's a worthwhile goal to experience the Voice of God: It means we have contact with the Divinity.

Thought is the first part; Light is the second. With the Light, as we go further in our spiritual unfoldment, we find we have peace, wisdom, and bliss. All this comes from the Light. You can actually see It, usually as a blue light.

I answered questions after the talk in Sydney and found that there were quite a few people who hadn't ever been to an ECK function before. Yet they had contact with the Blue Light of the Mahanta. This is a high state of consciousness that goes beyond cosmic consciousness. One man said: "I've seen this disk of light—what does it mean?" He had made contact with the Light of God. Anytime you make contact with the Light, you become very aware of the power of God.

After the Light comes in, later comes the third part,

which is the Sound. The Sound of God can be heard as many different things, from a flute to the buzzing of bees. These Sounds and the Light are described in *The Spiritual Notebook*, which also has a chart called "The God Worlds of ECK."

We are interested in gaining experience in this lifetime in order to become a Co-worker with God. We gain experience by going through the troubles and the trials of everyday living. We want to go through this life conscious of the spiritual laws and the spiritual forces that swirl about and affect everyone. They are going to affect us too.

I'm not promising you that as you step on the path of ECK you will have no more troubles or that you will become independently wealthy. All I can promise you is that as you go along the path, you are going to become more aware of who and what you are and how you fit into the scheme of life.

As you go along the path, you are going to become more aware of who and what you are and how you fit into the scheme of life.

The Living ECK Master will never interfere in your life at any time, because your state of consciousness is like your home—it's a violation of the spiritual law for anyone to walk in without your permission. The troubles we have are of our own making, through our own ignorance of these spiritual laws. These laws are at work whether or not we are conscious of how they work.

Two lower manifestations of Divine Spirit are magnetism and electricity. Whether you believe in electricity or not, I can guarantee you that an agnostic, an atheist, and a Christian are all going to have the same experience if they grab a live electrical wire. Spirit is the same way. It doesn't care if you believe in It or not. It doesn't care if you're an atheist, agnostic, Christian, or ECKist. It's an impartial force; It is the Voice of God.

There are tried and tested ways of contacting this

Light and Sound of God, and we call them spiritual techniques, or the Spiritual Exercises of ECK. They work. They have worked for others, and they can work for you.

Blind Spots

When we have problems, we don't recognize that we have made them for ourselves. We are apt to point a finger at someone else and blame them for our troubles. We complain because we don't understand that we caused the problem in the first place. We're blind to our own shortcomings.

The path of ECK is designed to help you open your eyes to the ways of Spirit as It interacts and works in your everyday life.

The path of ECK is designed to help you open your eyes to the ways of Spirit as It interacts and works in your everyday life.

It's funny how people can have blind spots to their own shortcomings and inconsistencies. As we were just about to leave the hotel room in Sydney yesterday, we started talking with a housekeeper from Scotland, a delightful woman with a charming brogue. We had some food left over in the refrigerator that we weren't able to take with us, so we offered it to her. She accepted some of it but made a point to emphasize that she never eats meat. "No, I never touch meat," she said. "But I do like my liver and onions."

In Eckankar we realize that whether you put meat or vegetables in your mouth makes no difference in your endeavors on this spiritual path. What you eat is a purely personal matter. It has nothing to do with how you unfold. God doesn't care what you eat or whether it's broiled or baked. God is interested only in Soul, and Soul doesn't eat.

The housekeeper also told us about her eighty-four-year-old father back in Scotland, whom she had recently visited. She said he was as hale and hearty as when he had retired from the army many years ago. "He's a big man, over six feet tall, and his back is still as straight as a ramrod," she said. I asked her what he did to stay in such good health. Did he eat a certain way? "No," she said, "actually he drinks whiskey—a lot of whiskey. In fact, he jokes about it. He likes to say, 'I'm pickled in whiskey—that's what keeps me from aging.'" But just so we wouldn't think her father was a degenerate of some kind, she added, "But he doesn't smoke." And here again, she was leading us down the garden path. "He doesn't smoke," she said, "but he does like his pipe."

She was a wonderful woman; she was being herself in the purest sense, and there's no way you'd want to correct someone like that. They're just too much fun, and you simply let them be just what they are. As she walked out the door, she said, "Ah, me, here I am talking with you as if we've known each other for a whole lifetime," and she shook her head and left.

She is one of the people who someday will walk into a lobby and see one of those pictures of an ECK Master, and say, "Hey, I know that guy." She may even buy a book to find out what it's all about.

People often have contact with Spirit years before they hear about Eckankar.

It's best, though, to go a little slowly, read one book at a time. See if this is really what you're looking for, because it may not be. But people often have contact with Spirit years before they hear about Eckankar. Each spiritual path leads to a higher one. I don't care which spiritual path you're on—there is always one more step.

This afternoon someone asked me where Jesus stood in the whole hierarchy of things. He knew that Jesus had met one of the ECK Masters who was serving at that particular time. This was a man called Zadok. Jesus brought a message for his time and for his place, to uplift those individuals who were ready for another step.

When you have contact with a master of any path, whether outwardly or inwardly, if he is a true Master, he will pass you on to the next one when you've learned all you can from him. This contact often will be made in the dream state or during contemplation. This is part of the reality of the inner worlds.

If you have any questions, I'll be glad to answer some of them for you.

Outer and Inner Initiations

Q: What is the connection between the outer and inner initiations?

HK: In Eckankar you don't get an initiation as soon as you step on the path. It takes two years after you begin as an active student of Eckankar before you qualify for an outer initiation.

An initiation opens you more to the Light and Sound of Spirit. This uplifts and gives you even greater insight and ability to survive in daily life.

When you have an initiation, it opens you a little bit more to the Light and Sound of Spirit. This is why it's important. You have a greater flow of this power of God coming through you, which uplifts and gives you even greater insight and ability to survive in daily life.

The First Initiation comes anywhere from six months to a year after you begin the study of the ECK discourses, sometimes sooner. It will come in the dream state. The First Initiation takes place purely on the inner. You may remember it, you may not; some do, some don't. It's better if you can.

After two years of study, you can ask for the Second Initiation. People who have the Second Initiation often report that they have gone far beyond the Astral Plane and that they are conscious of experiences happening on the Soul Plane, which is the first of the true spiritual worlds. From that stage on up, there are many, many more planes, actually without limit. In the ECK writings we have listed twelve planes at the present time.

The different heavens that have been established

by the orthodox religions are still within the worlds of matter, energy, space, and time—the Physical, Astral, Causal, Mental, and Etheric planes. Many of the heavens are established on the Mental Plane; here you have the heavens of Christianity, Buddhism, Hinduism, and others. Spiritualism is on the Astral Plane. But there is always one more heaven.

The ECKist can be taken by the Inner Master beyond the level of initiation that he has earned on the Physical Plane. After an experience on the Soul Plane, he may wonder: Does that mean I am now an initiate of the Fifth Circle? No. It simply means you are a visitor to the Soul Plane. These visits allow us to become acclimatized, a little bit at a time, to that state of consciousness.

One may be taken to the Causal Plane while still a Second Initiate. The Causal Plane is the area where you remember your past lives. If you want to, you may develop the ability through the dream state to find out what attitudes and forces from the past have brought you up to the present.

You may develop the ability through the dream state to find out what attitudes and forces from the past have brought you up to the present.

The connection between the outer and inner initiation is this: When you get the outer initiation for any level, this establishes you on that inner plane. It brings the balance that is necessary between the inner and the outer, and this is the whole point of the outer initiation.

CAN SOUL BE DESTROYED?

Q: Can Soul ever be destroyed?

HK: No, It cannot be destroyed. As you begin to work on the inner planes, in the Soul body, you may have some real adventures with entities there who are misusing the forces through black magic. This happens in the lower worlds, not in the higher worlds.

Whether we realize it or not, we are operating in these other planes at the same time. Once in a while it looks like a scene from *Star Wars*, with everybody blasting away. But you develop the strength and the protection of Spirit where these things are no longer able to harm you. You become immune to psychic attacks, and the entities are no longer able to touch or harm you. But never is Soul destroyed.

Soul is the creation from the heart of God. While It is in the lower worlds, It may become extremely negative, but It can never be destroyed. It must go through Its experiences until It becomes purified and qualified to move into the Soul Plane and beyond.

Directions on the Inner

Q: You said that what we receive on the inner should stay on the inner. How does that square with the law As above, so below?

HK: I'm trying to give people a rule of thumb so they don't go out and do something strange based on what they see on the inner. People without the protection of the ECK Masters may come in contact with one of the rulers of the lower planes, such as the Astral Plane. Because this being has a lot of light and power, they'll think they have made contact with God. And what do they do? They go out and start their own group, do strange things, and become unbalanced.

The path of ECK is to lead an individual into a life that is spiritually uplifting and never degrading or depraved in any manner.

The path of ECK is to lead an individual into a life that is spiritually uplifting and never degrading or depraved in any manner. It's supposed to build. When you get something on the inner—a direction to do something—if it's positive and harmonious, then do it. If you feel upset by it or if it demands that you exercise power over another person—in other words, the command you get means someone else loses his freedom to act as he wants to—then don't do it. It's the negative power, and it can even take the face of the ECK Master. Why? For our experience, so that we learn how to challenge it with one of the sacred words of God, such as HU. You can chant this quietly, and you can have protection. It opens you for this protection from Spirit.

This is one of the functions of HU, and it's a very useful tool. You can do it at any time. If you need help—maybe somebody's gossiping or attacking you—you don't direct it at them but you just chant to uplift yourself spiritually so that you either gain an understanding or to protect yourself or whatever's needed.

Perhaps you have an experience which seems to suggest that you take certain action in the physical world. If it's an uplifting thing, keep your attention on it gently and work toward it as you can, very gently, without pushing, even if it takes five or ten years. Eckankar is a universal teaching and a way of life for all your life.

Action or Inaction?

Q: If there is an injustice, either to themselves or to another group, many people would feel some desire to do something about it. Is there some ECK guidance about our spiritual involvement in matters of great injustice?

HK: As an individual, do what you feel you want to do. If it's something that upsets you very much, by all means get involved. Do it as a private individual, not as part of a group of ECKists. Your ECK way of life is a personal thing. You act outwardly as you see the need: Get involved whenever you see an injustice and you feel you want to do something about it. It's your attitude that is important.

We do what we can to uplift according to our talents.

This is a warring universe and there will always be injustices, but it doesn't mean we have to just lie around doing nothing. We do what we can to be a vehicle for Spirit and uplift wherever we can, in whatever way we can, according to our talents. Not being revolutionary myself, I personally would act within the laws and guidelines of the government of the country. But it's a personal choice—whatever you want to do. By all means, it's better to do something than nothing.

By living life fully, we get the experience we need to one day become a Co-worker with God.

We are interested in learning how to live life fully, not how to contemplate and withdraw, or retreat, from life. By living fully, we get the experience we need to one day become a Co-worker with God. You need every conceivable experience. It's better to go out and do something that you would later find was wrong, than to do nothing. At least you learned something—even if it's only that you would never do it again—and you're smarter than you were before.

Doing the Spiritual Exercises

Q: When you have a job and other activities that don't leave you time to do the spiritual exercises regularly or at the same time each day, what should you do?

HK: You can chant your secret word or HU or one of the other sacred words quietly to yourself. Do this for a while during the day and as you go to sleep at night.

If your schedule is such that it doesn't allow the time for you to sit up and do the twenty-minute spiritual exercise, you can also do a technique that I have used fairly often myself. Just before you go to sleep, you can say to the Inner Master: "I give you full permission to take me to the place that I have earned or where I can learn something." Then you go to sleep and don't give it another thought.

The Inner Master will begin working with you in the dream state. Often you will find that as your consciousness changes, your outer circumstances may change too. It may take a couple of years. This is the physical world, and often it's very hard. But the Masters begin working with us where they find us. In the spiritual works, we begin at the point where we are. We can wish for all the leisure time in the world, but the fact is, we have to really look at where we are and then consider what we are going to do in our own circumstances.

The Masters begin working with us where they find us. In the spiritual works, we begin at the point where we are.

The ECK will take us one step at a time inwardly; and this will reflect outwardly in some way. Your life may not be easier, but it will certainly become more adventuresome.

Developing Self-Mastery

You develop a sense of humor, and as challenges come up, you begin to draw on your creativity. You find solutions that would never have occurred to you before. Life becomes more fun—you actually have a more adventuresome life. You get put into situations you would not have been in before, because you are going one step beyond yourself. And as you get yourself in trouble, you also have help to get out of it, because as you learn to work with your own resources, you are developing self-mastery.

This is what I'm interested in—that those of you who wish to make the effort can also attain this self-mastery in life. You do not come to the point where you begin to direct or control Spirit, because Spirit will not be controlled or directed. People who try to do this are using the psychic powers, black magic. Instead, you let Spirit flow through you without any blocks or obstacles whatsoever.

Eventually you become Its pure vehicle, as an ECK Master; and whatever It wants, you carry it out. When you get a direction on the inner planes, you immediately begin figuring ways to carry it out. Sometimes it may take a while. You pick priorities and begin working on them.

What about Extinct Species?

Q: Is there a spiritual answer to animals becoming extinct? Does Soul no longer need the experience of being a certain species? And does it come back?

HK: You're talking now about the nature of Soul as It comes into different life-forms, such as the dinosaurs of prehistoric times, where the whole species eventually became extinct. These life-forms run their course, and Soul doesn't need the experience of that particular life-form anymore. Though we may do what we can to preserve the whale and other endangered species, there comes a time when that species has run its cycle. Soul is not that life-form or that body. Soul then comes in through another doorway, into another flesh temple.

We don't have transmigration of Soul where you go from human to animal. Rather there is a natural progression of Soul through different life-forms.

We don't have transmigration of Soul where you go from human to animal. Rather there is a natural progression of Soul through different life-forms. In the lower worlds the peak is the human state of consciousness. Within the human state of consciousness there are two poles that go from the most negative all the way to the positive; those who are in the lowest areas of the human consciousness versus those who are working in the higher spiritual states.

The Search for Happiness

You'll find a wide range of consciousness within any city. There are people who like to spend their leisure time on the street corner with a bottle. It's the way they choose to be, and I won't compare such an individual with the man in a pulpit. As Paul Twitchell pointed out, maybe the man with the bottle is as spiritual as the man in the pulpit; each is trying to find God in his own way. The search for God is the search for happiness. While looking for it, sometimes one might think the only alternative is to be found in a bottle, so he uses it for a lifetime or two and pays the price. That's how it works.

We don't know our blind spots, and so we have to learn them. Pain is not all that bad—in a spiritual sense. The saying goes something like this: The sorrows of the body are the joys of Soul. If things were always happy and uplifting, there would be no motivation for us to even search for the spiritual path, to unfold, and to reach into the higher states of consciousness where we come to accept our heritage as one of the sons of God, as a Co-worker.

Taking Your Time

If you are interested in the works of ECK, take your time. There is an incubation period from the time you first come in touch with the ECK works until you actually take the next step, which means becoming an active student. This incubation period may take a year, two years, three, four, or five years; there is no need to hurry.

If you are studying Eckankar and your spouse is not, you don't have to try to convert them. Let them be. They have the protection of Spirit too, simply by being open to It; and if you're open to It and they are open to It, that's all that counts. And if they are not open to It, what's the difference? They are getting their own experience. Let the other person just *be*, as you also are being.

Let the other person just be, as you also are being.

The spiritual path is so simple that sometimes I don't even know how to begin putting it into words, and when people have complicated questions, the best answer really is: Go within. It's more honest to direct you to the Inner Master and not to my outer personality.

Anyone who tries to follow a personality is going to be sorely disappointed when the leader leaves, because their reasons for following him have been built on sand. When he leaves and a successor comes, those followers are in turmoil and have all these questions: Is he really my Master or isn't he? Is this guy as good as the last one? All those things that have nothing to do with anything.

The Sound and the Light come together and take the form of the Inner Master, and this is where you get your help.

The problem is that the attention was on the personality when it should have been on the spiritual side of the Living ECK Master, which on the inner planes is the Mahanta. This is the manifestation of Spirit as It forms; the Sound and the Light come together and take the form of the Inner Master, and this is where you get your help.

Thank you kindly.

Melbourne Regional Seminar, Melbourne, Australia, November 6, 1982

I could see the man's astral hand move out, reach into his pocket, and raise the vitamins to his mouth, but he didn't have the courage to do it in the physical body.

6
Truth Has No Secrets

There's a story about a young man who came to a great, wise teacher and said, "I want to follow you to find the way to God."

"Well," said the wise teacher, "you'll have to give me a lot of gold. If you bring me this gold, then you can be my disciple and I'll teach you everything you need to know."

"But I don't have any gold," said the seeker.

"Then go out and get it," said the teacher.

When the seeker felt he had enough, he took his gold and put it before the wise man's feet. "Now will you teach me?"

So the seeker went out and spent the next several years working until he had acquired a great deal of gold. When he felt he had enough, he took it and put it before the wise man's feet. "Here it is," he said. "Now will you teach me?"

"I have no use for this gold," said the wise teacher, "because I have the blessings of God in my lap anytime I want them. If you haven't learned anything from the experiences of life while you were earning this gold, then there is nothing I can teach you."

This is what the path of ECK is for: to go out in life and gain experience.

Soul Moving On

A young girl asked me the other day how I felt when Zsa Zsa, the cat I had as a boy, translated, or died. I mentioned this incident in *The Wind of Change*. "Well," I said, "I felt pretty bad about it." She said she had lost a cat a little while ago too, and although she felt sad about it, she realized that Soul doesn't die. It had left that particular body, but later It would come back.

We used to have kittens on our farm, and about every four or five years, there always seemed to be three new ones: one gray-and-white cat, one black-and-white cat, and one tiger cat. Life was pretty hard on the farm, so they usually translated within a couple of years or so.

Whenever this happened, it seemed that all of a sudden we'd find we had the same little group of three kittens back again. Soul took a body form, and when that body wore out, It would leave for a while and then come back in a new cat body—maybe because our farm had so many mice. I could tell they were the same friends coming back again, and that's why there was never any lasting sadness when one of the animals left its body.

When Soul is able to go into the higher states of consciousness, into the heavens, into the other worlds, It experiences a joy that is completely beyond the ability of the mind to understand.

The same is true when we have family and friends who leave. It's natural to feel sad for a while—there's nothing wrong with that. But when Soul is able to go into the higher states of consciousness, into the heavens, into the other worlds, It experiences a joy that is completely beyond the ability of the mind to understand.

Accepting Change

When I lived on the farm as a young boy, it was a real treat to go down the road to the cheese factory with my dad. He'd load the milk cans onto our truck, and we'd drive over to the cheese factory. I watched as the milk was poured into a big vat, then into these huge tanks where the cheese was made. Sometimes the owner would give us a chunk of cheese as we sat there watching, and that made it a double treat. These were precious times, and I used to enjoy just being along.

But times change. Soon businesses were forced to become more economical. The cheese man had to produce more business in order to make more profit, though I'm not sure why—he was already the richest man in our neighborhood. The farmers had to become more efficient, and eventually they could no longer afford to spend that leisurely hour or two delivering the milk every morning. They had to use the time to work harder on the farm just to make enough money to survive. The cheese man saw the direction of the changing times: Soon farmers would no longer bring the milk to the factory, which meant he would have to hire a driver and maintain a truck just to go out to the farms and get it. And so times changed.

It's a sad thing for a child growing up to all of a sudden find that the things he used to enjoy are now changing. But in ECK we don't look to the past. When today is different from yesterday, we accept it. This is called living in the detached state of consciousness. We accept what we have here in the moment, without any regrets for the past.

UNLOCKING TRUTH

The initiation gives us the ability to see the ground we have covered.

Truth is really never secret. The initiations which I spoke of yesterday are really a final examination, in a sense, for us to become aware of what we have learned from the things that preceded that initiation. The initiation brings the Sound and the Light, but at the same time it gives us the ability to see the ground we have covered.

Many of the different religious teachings have

initiations. The Masonic order speaks of the lost word. This lost word actually is the sound of HU, or the Sound of God. This is one of the sacred names of God, which is a charged word. Such a word—and this includes our personal word—does not have power in itself. The word which we are given during the initiation acts like a key to unlock the protection and the spiritual help that is available from the ECK, or the Mahanta. We chant or sing this word, quietly or out loud, whenever we have need of this help.

The teachings of truth are not secret. Someplace in this world they are in a written form. In Eckankar we have most of them put together in one place.

But just because the teachings are open to all does not mean everyone can see and understand them. It depends upon the state of consciousness of the individual. This becomes apparent when you read an ECK book such as *The Shariyat-Ki-Sugmad*, which is the ECK bible. You will read it the first time, and when you come back to it perhaps a year later, all of a sudden you find you have a whole new understanding of what's in the book. This is because your state of consciousness has been opened, and now you see it with a new understanding.

The spiritual truths are secret only until the state of consciousness becomes unlocked.

The spiritual truths are secret only until the state of consciousness becomes unlocked. The Living ECK Master, or the Inner Master, is able to unlock the consciousness a little at a time so that we can get the deeper understandings.

Sidelight Phenomena

There are phenomenal things that go on which may be a lot of fun but really have very little to do with spiritual truth and spiritual realities. For instance, after a talk that Paul Twitchell once gave, he asked for questions. No one spoke up. He then looked over at one individual and said, “I see a big question mark over you.” It turned out the person did have a question in mind, which he then asked. These are interesting little sidelights that some people may develop, but they have nothing to do with the spiritual life.

I don’t usually look at people to see what their motives or intentions are; I’d rather let them be. I don’t go scanning an individual to see what he is thinking or feeling. Frankly, most of us think and feel pretty much alike, and there isn’t anything that shocks me. So I know, in the spiritual sense, and who and what you are doesn’t concern me. All that concerns me is that the Soul that is willing to make Its way back home to God has every opportunity to do so.

Who and what you are doesn't concern me. All that concerns me is that the Soul that is willing to make Its way back home to God has every opportunity to do so.

At the World Wide seminar, I saw a fellow going up to the watercooler backstage. In his pocket he had a packet of vitamins. I watched him as I waited to go onstage. He approached the watercooler with his little paper cup, and all he wanted to do was take his vitamins. But there was a group of people nearby, and he was embarrassed—he didn’t want to look like a health nut. Finally he said to himself, I’m going to take the vitamins later.

But it was interesting: I could see his astral hand move out, reach into his pocket, and raise the vitamins to his mouth. This is what he wanted to do, but he didn’t have the courage to do it in the physical body. Usually I don’t say anything when I see something like this, but this time I said: “Well, what about your vitamins?” He kind of laughed and then reached into his pocket, got his vitamins, put them in his mouth, and washed them down with the water.

We may see something like this every few years, but again, it has nothing to do with the spiritual path. These things prove nothing. They are delightful, they are fun little phenomena that come as a sidelight, but don't let them cause you to make a detour from your goal of God-Realization. Keep your eyes on the high aspiration which Soul has taken the trouble to come into the lower worlds to attain.

Help with Unfoldment

If you would like help with your spiritual unfoldment and you're having a difficult time with this during contemplation, you may ask the Mahanta to help you in the dream state. An easy way to do the spiritual exercises is to just give the Inner Master permission to assist you, and then go to sleep.

In the morning it's helpful to start the day by declaring yourself a vehicle for Spirit. It can be done in a very simple way by saying: I declare myself a vehicle for the Sugmad, the ECK, and the Mahanta. Anytime during the day that you feel you want a little help, use this declaration again as kind of a booster. Then just forget about the outer methods for tapping into Spirit. Go ahead and do your work. A person who loves his work and has pure enjoyment from doing it, whether or not he is an ECKist, is already living the life of Spirit.

A person who loves his work and has pure enjoyment from doing it, whether or not an ECKist, is already living the life of Spirit.

Whatever path you're on, if you follow the disciplines of your path with detachment—as it is spoken of in *ECKANKAR—The Key to Secret Worlds*—you're going to unfold in a direct line. And when you have outgrown the path of your childhood, a new one will come up on the horizon. Take your time. Do not hurry.

I'd like to thank you all for coming. The love and the protection of the ECK are with you as you journey homeward.

Melbourne Regional Seminar, Melbourne, Australia, November 7, 1982

When you have a family, you have to find new, creative ways to be of service in ECK.

7
Service in ECK

It's important to understand why, when we're on the path of ECK, there comes a certain time when the Living ECK Master will say, "If you have problems, the way to get rid of them is to give something back to life in some way, in some service." It doesn't matter if it's within the ECK program or if you do it for someone else—but do something.

In the works of ECK, it's spoken of as the inflow when the ECK comes in, and what you do with It is the outflow. The human vessel cannot contain the enormity of ECK. It has to go out somewhere. You have to do something with It.

When you step onto the path and ask Spirit to come into your life and give you greater unfoldment, It will. The Sound and Light pour into you whether or not you're conscious of it. It will pour in for perhaps a year or two, sometimes longer; then when you get filled up, you have to learn what to do with It. This is the next step, this learning how to give in some way that suits you.

This is the next step, learning how to give in some way that suits you—something that is fun for you.

It won't be the same for any two people, nor will the way that you've chosen to serve hold forever. You will eventually outgrow it, and then you have to find a new way—something that is fun for you.

If you have any questions, I'll be glad to answer some of them for you.

Family and Children

Q: How can we teach our children about the importance of being of service?

HK: We have to work toward that goal of helping the children to become a part of the ECK life. When they get to be about eight or nine, they're at an age where they want to help you—they just love to help you—and we have to figure out ways in which they can.

When the ECK comes in, you find ways to give. I'd get a bunch of posters and have my daughter help me make them up. She enjoyed doing this.

At one point, I wondered if perhaps it had been a mistake to get married, and an even bigger one to have a child—I felt I was no longer able to give out the ECK in the same way I had before. But when the ECK comes in, you find ways to give. Being married, I found I couldn't just go out on the road when I felt the need to do something, so I worked locally and at home. I'd get a bunch of posters and have my daughter help me make them up. She enjoyed doing this.

We also plan weekend family outings about once a month when I'm not traveling. We drive to a town that we haven't visited before and stay in a budget motel. The family enjoys themselves while I go out and put up posters, and later we'll all go out and pick fruit or find something else that we can do together. We mix our family time with ECK time, and we know that when we go on the road, no matter what happens, our efforts are blessed.

It's best to work together, especially in a family where your spouse isn't in ECK, because otherwise they're going to feel that ECK is getting in the way. They'll think it's standing between you and them, and there will be resentment. But you can tie in activities where they can enjoy themselves and be included as you're doing your ECK thing—something affordable that you can do together.

A TYPICAL DAY

Q: Could you tell us something about a typical day in the life of the Living ECK Master?

HK: When I'm home and not traveling, the first thing I do when I get up in the morning is exercise. The body needs it just like Soul needs the spiritual exercises, just like the mind needs something to keep it stimulated—whether it's a class, job training, or what have you. The emotional body needs exercise, too: happiness, crying, whatever. So I exercise and then I get cleaned up and ready to work. Then I work at the desk for the morning.

Afternoons are spent going through the mail. There are lots of letters. Some of the mail, such as processing requests for books, is handled by the staff at the ECK Office. I work with the spiritual end of things. I'm not always able to answer you, but I do read your letters. Your answers will come to you on the inner. What I try to do is turn you and your attention to the Inner Master.

Your answers will come to you on the inner. I try to turn you and your attention to the Inner Master.

I work at this for several hours, and by that time my daughter comes home from school. If I can convince her to go out to the playground to play soccer or softball, then I can get some more exercise. But I make her think I'm doing it just for her.

Frequently someone will tell me, "All I do is give to other people." But when we give or do something for someone else, we are actually doing it for ourselves. And as we do this for ourselves, it can also benefit others. Sometimes a person will say, "I'm always doing things just for myself," and these people have to learn to give to others.

Sometimes after dinner or on the weekends we'll go out for a drive as a whole family. If your life is very busy, it can be difficult to keep the family together. You have your family life; you try to earn a living and get the ECK work done as you feel the outflow of Spirit coming through you. This means you must become an excellent administrator of your own time. If you don't, you get rolled under by life. But there is always a way.

If you can't handle the ECK workload, then find someone who wants to help out so that they can grow too. This is what I have to do. I have to delegate many things; as quickly as a new thing comes up, I delegate part of it to someone who is capable.

Spiritual Experiences

Q: It's very difficult to talk to others about spiritual experiences if one has not consciously had any of these experiences. Do you have any comments about that?

HK: It really is difficult. Usually we feel confident in speaking about a spiritual experience to others while it's still fresh. As an experience gets farther away, we remember less about it and may feel less qualified to speak about the path of ECK.

You are having inner experiences, though many times the curtain is pulled for your own benefit.

You are having the inner experiences, though many times the curtain is pulled for your own benefit. I know of people who wanted to remember past lives, for instance, but when they finally had the experience, they found it frightening. They never imagined that it might involve something of a negative nature. The things that happened to us in the past are responsible for the fears we carry today. I would rather you go slowly and not be too concerned about whether you remember or don't.

When a person wants to know about your experiences in ECK, you don't have to get into a big explanation. You can observe the Law of Silence and simply tell them, "It's not important what experiences I have, but what you have." Just give them an ECK book and say, "Try one of the spiritual exercises. If you find they work for you, great—the path has something to offer you. If not, then maybe it's not for you. But try it for yourself."

If they find something for themselves on the path of ECK, it's because they have earned the right. The spiritual exercises will work; they have worked for others, but they won't work for everyone. If someone is not ready, that's all right.

Anything worth learning, anything really valuable, very seldom comes easily. You may have success the first time, but it can take longer. Much depends upon the individual's reason for doing the spiritual exercises. What is his goal? The goal ought to be God. And, in a sense, it has to be a strong yearning for God. I know we speak about the desireless state—don't seek God because if you do, It retreats—but on the other hand, you must have this desire. It's a subtle balance.

The goal ought to be God, a strong yearning for God.

In the Bible it says to seek first the Kingdom of God and all things shall be added unto you. What counts is the individual's approach to God. Whether or not you've had conscious experiences is unimportant.

Suggest to the questioner that they go to the ECK discussion classes and learn more. When the time is right, the Inner Master will give them what they're ready for. But one shouldn't push it, because the curtain may be opened before he is ready. Then he goes into spiritual shock, and I have to come along and put the pieces together again.

THE DREAM STATE

Q: Sometimes I'm aware of having dreamed all night about Eckankar, but in the morning I can't remember anything. How can I get a better grasp of what is happening in the dream state?

HK: You do that with training. There are some people who don't even remember that they've dreamed, so you have made that step. You can develop this ability as a discipline; keep a notebook and pen by your bed.

The mind on the physical plane seems like it has a great capacity to remember. But there are a tremendous number of experiences happening above: It's just not possible for the physical mind to contain everything that takes place, even on just the Astral Plane. Soul is working on a number of different planes at the same time. You have all this pouring in and boggling the little physical mind, so you have to be selective.

You will have many different kinds of dream experiences.

You will have many different kinds of dream experiences. Some are routine, day-to-day kinds of things, which are not highly interesting. Others will seem disjointed and won't make logical sense. There are also the spiritual dreams, which are the important ones, and you can make a discipline of learning to remember these.

Being Active

Q: You mentioned in the past about using the active state of the inner consciousness. Since the inner emotional nature has an active side and a passive side, you said that it is necessary to know how to use the active side in the desire for God. Could you talk about how to balance the active and passive states in our daily life?

HK: The human consciousness has a natural inclination toward lethargy and procrastination. This is because of attachment, which is one of the mind passions. We learn to work with it. In your personal life you learn to set goals. Set little goals, any goals, just so that you do something. Soul is here to gain experience, and you're not going to get a lot of experience without doing something. Paul Twitchell and the other ECK Masters have always tried to get us to be active.

Make your goal as positive as you can. If you're not sure if it's positive or negative, rather than sit still and be in doubt, do it and find out. The law of life will tell you soon enough. But it's important to do something.

THE CREATIVE TECHNIQUES

The spiritual exercises themselves are different from meditation for the same reason. In meditation, as taught by some of the other paths, you go inwardly and try to become passive and still. This is a first step. But then we begin the creative techniques to try to reach a meeting with the Inner Master in some way.

Using the visualization technique, for instance, we may form a setting for ourselves: We'll see the blades of grass, the clouds, and the trees. We then visualize one of the ECK Masters coming along. We may do it night after night without success, but we keep at it; and eventually it may work so well that we can even feel the wind and smell the flowers.

We may do the visualization technique night after night without success, but eventually it may work so well we can even feel the wind and smell the flowers.

There's another, subtler technique that helps those who are afraid to go into the inner worlds through the regular spiritual exercises. Just before you go to bed you can give the Inner Master permission to take you to the Temple of Golden Wisdom that's right for you at this time or on some adventure in the far worlds of God. Then just go to sleep and don't worry about it. Keep a notebook and pen by your bedside.

You might also use a flashlight or something that doesn't disturb your mate. It doesn't pay to turn on the lights each night—pretty soon you may not have a marriage. If every time you have a dream you hit the ceiling lights so that you can record it, you're going to have plenty of experiences to write down, but they won't all be from the inner planes!

Working with Detachment

Q: I have a chance to take a job as a welfare assistant. I just wondered if it would mean taking on karma to go out and help people to budget their money or advise them on marital problems.

HK: No, not if you're doing it as a profession and with detachment. You give your full attention to the person who's in front of you, and when the next one comes along, you forget totally about the one who's gone. If you can do this from the detached state, then once they go, you let their problems go with them; you've done everything you can within the scope of your profession to help them. If you can let it go, it won't ever bother you.

Working in the detached state of consciousness has nothing to do with lack of compassion or interest. You do what you can to help them while they are with you, as a function of your job. But when the person leaves, you let the problem go too. As you're working, you can do everything in the name of the Inner Master, and this way you are always protected. This way you don't pick up the karma.

As you're working, you can do everything in the name of the Inner Master, and this way you are always protected. This way you don't pick up the karma.

Interpreting Dreams

Q: I have some of the most extraordinary dreams at times, and then I sit down and try to figure out what they were all about. I don't really know how to go about getting the correct answer. Could you help?

HK: Often the inner will bring an insight symbolically through a dream about something that is happening in your outer life. The Inner Master is trying to give you insight into something that affects your daily life. Other times, if it's a spiritual dream, then you have direct experience with the Sound and Light, and this needs no interpretation; it has nothing to do with symbology. It merely relates to the presence of the Voice of God, or Spirit, coming into our daily life. That's a spiritual dream, and it brings upliftment and the purification of Soul, so that Soul comes to an awareness of Its mission in this life. This is what we are looking for.

A spiritual dream brings upliftment and the purification of Soul.

Between the Inner Master and the physical consciousness is something called the censor. The censor scrambles the dream message. Most of the time it mistakenly feels that in your human consciousness you are not strong enough to take the pure message as it is coming from the Master. This is only an excuse of the negative power, yet that's what you have to work with.

As you reach higher levels of consciousness through the Spiritual Exercises of ECK, you work more directly with knowing what the inner experiences mean for you in your spiritual unfoldment. You no longer have to convert them from symbology. You find on the inner planes that you are working for Spirit as a Co-worker, in one way or another. You remember logically the beginning of an event, the middle, and the ending; and it all fits.

But as we first begin working with the Dream Master, the parts may be scrambled. The experience itself happened in the proper sequence, from beginning to end, but as we get it in the human consciousness, it seems as jumbled as a jigsaw puzzle thrown on the floor. The pieces are all over the place; the middle comes first, and you get fragmented pictures of what the inner experience meant for you in your outer unfoldment. Study the symbology. Pretty soon you ought to become very adept at understanding your own dreams. It takes practice.

Q: Recently I had a dream in which I woke up in my dream and knew that I was sleeping in bed. It was quite vivid. Then maybe a few minutes later I awoke in my own bed. I thought about it for a long, long time and came to the conclusion that the Master was trying to tell me that what I'm now doing in the physical actually is the dream state; that my life here is just a dream. Would that be a correct assumption?

You are beginning to see and work from the spiritual realities. This is a very good step on the spiritual path for you.

HK: Yes, exactly. You are beginning to see and work from the spiritual realities. When you do, this physical life becomes the dream and the inner is the reality. In the Bible it was also spoken of: "In my Father's house are many mansions." This simply means there are many different states of consciousness or heavens.

At a certain level in your study of the ECK works, you awaken on one plane and think you're in the physical—it's that real—and then you wake up again. Sometimes you wake up three times before you finally find yourself awake in the physical plane. By then you're not sure if you really are here or if you're going to wake up one more time somewhere else. This is because you are working as Soul at several different levels of consciousness at the same time or in a rapid succession.

It's a testimony to the eternal nature of Soul—that It has no beginning or ending. At the same time, It also dwells in the high planes of God. This is a very good step on the spiritual path for you.

Healing by the ECK

Q: When a person is under psychiatric treatment for an emotional disorder and is on a psychotropic drug, does that block out the ECK flow or the presence of the Master in that person's life?

HK: If the drugs are prescribed by a licensed medical practitioner, this is how the ECK brings healing. It doesn't block anything out. It's bringing about a healing in that person's own life at a gradual, steady pace, at a rate they can handle, so that they can learn from the healing as it occurs.

This is why when someone asks the Living ECK Master for a spiritual healing, it often comes in a subtle way—he may be given a book on nutrition or he may be led to a doctor. This is because the process of healing ought to be an education. We should come out of the illness and into good health with a greater knowledge of who and what we are.

Soul Travel versus Astral Travel

Q: Many of us hear about astral projection, whereas Eckankar speaks of Soul Travel. Could you clear up the difference between the two?

HK: I used to astral travel. The Living ECK Master of the times gave me the experience so that I could tell the difference. When going out via the Astral body, I found it difficult to get out of the Physical body. It took just about every bit of effort I could muster.

Soul Travel is actually the expansion of consciousness to higher states of awareness. It's very smooth and easy.

Soul Travel is actually the expansion of consciousness to higher states of awareness. It's very smooth and easy, and there are none of the dangers that can be connected with astral travel. Furthermore, using the Astral body to go to the Astral Plane limits you to that plane; the Astral body cannot go beyond that. It's not worth it when you consider all the effort it takes to learn astral travel.

Soul Travel can take you to the Astral Plane, then on to the Causal, Mental, Etheric, and up to the Soul Plane. When we reach the Soul Plane and become established there, we no longer Soul Travel. We move directly into the spiritual states of seeing, knowing, and being. Soul Travel is merely for the lower worlds, those that lie above the physical en route to the Soul Plane.

What about Astrology?

Q: Does astrology apply once one becomes an ECKist?

HK: Astrology readings depend first of all upon the reader; some are better at it than others. I've had people tell me that after they got on the path of ECK, astrologers could no longer do an accurate reading for them. In one particular instance, the astrologer had done readings for a woman for years and could always tell very specifically when certain crises or happy events were coming up in her life. Yet after the woman got on the path of ECK, it no longer worked. The astrologer was the first one to acknowledge this.

The reason is this: Astrology is tied into karma, which is in the hands of the Lords of Karma. As long as we are under the Lords of Karma we walk under a very tight hand of destiny. But as soon as we step onto the path of ECK, our karmic burdens are taken away from the Lords of Karma and taken over by the Living ECK Master. Astrology works under the Lords of Karma; ECK is a whole new ball game, a whole new arena.

ECK is a whole new ball game, a whole new arena.

Miracles of God

Q: Sri Harold, how can one who was initiated under a previous Living ECK Master be of help to the present Living ECK Master? Also, I have experienced in the dream state and in the spiritual exercises a changeover from a previous Master to yourself. Even when I try to keep him in my vision, it always changes to you. I'm somewhat intrigued by this. Could you help to clarify it for me?

HK: On the inner planes there is no separation of Spirit. Spirit is one. It generally takes the matrix of the Living ECK Master, but It may take the face or the form of an ECK Master with whom you have a rapport from another lifetime, or this lifetime, and work with you. But It is still the same ECK. On the outer, the Living ECK Master of the times carries out the duties here to insure that the chela continues with the spiritual disciplines, to keep that contact with the ECK and the Inner Master.

If you want to help out for your own spiritual unfoldment as an Arahata or an ECK leader, you will find there are many benefits. Frequently when people ask for proof about the power of ECK, they'll sit back awaiting a miracle without ever gaining the recognition that those who are willing to give of themselves, in service to Spirit, are the ones most likely to see the miracles of God.

Those willing to give of themselves, in service to Spirit, are the ones most likely to see the miracles of God.

Can We Control Our Mind?

Q: Do we get to the stage in our spiritual unfoldment where we have total control over our mind and negative thoughts? How can we work toward this?

HK: As long as we are in the lower worlds, we always have to pay attention to the five passions of the mind. They are always with us, and we have to keep a watch on them. But as we go along, we are not so interested in controlling the mind anymore. Instead we open ourselves as a vehicle for Spirit, knowing that whatever we do with a pure heart, and in the name of the Sugmad or the Mahanta, becomes a karmaless action. Another person may look at us and say, "He did something wrong," but the act may turn out to benefit everyone. However, we are always careful that our actions will never create an obstacle for a truth seeker on the path to God-Realization, because that act is wrong.

Explaining ECK

Q: Even if the rest of the family aren't ECKists, the time comes when they are more or less confronted with Eckankar. What's the best approach to help them understand what it's really all about and that it is not a cult?

HK: There is no easy way to explain the teachings of ECK and the truth contained therein. That understanding has to be an individual undertaking. The most we can do for our family is to ask for their goodwill in letting us study the path of our choice. Give them the same freedom and just enjoy each other as people and as loved ones. Sometimes we're able to work it out, sometimes not.

I really don't like the teachings of ECK to come between members of a family, and I certainly don't recommend anyone take the ECK discourses on the sly, such as through an anonymous post-office box. That's being dishonest. In the spiritual life you find you have to be honest. We don't look to ethics as our goal, we look to God-Realization; but as we gain in spiritual unfoldment, our ethics do become greater—more so than on any other path.

The best way to explain is to say the Master is merely a guide, a spiritual guide.

Q: How can one explain to a non-ECKist what the spiritual ECK Master is?

HK: The person who is not in Eckankar wonders if the Master is someone that the ECKist looks to and worships, and he is not. The best way to explain it is to say that he is merely a guide, a spiritual guide. Point out that each individual has to walk his own path to God. As the song says,

"You gotta walk that lonesome valley; you gotta walk it by yourself. Nobody here can walk it for you." On the path to God, it's an identical situation, but the Living ECK Master is the experienced Spiritual Traveler who knows the way. Yet he will never help or interfere unless you ask. His sole function is to help Soul find Its way back to God.

The Living ECK Master is the experienced Spiritual Traveler who knows the way. His sole function is to help Soul find Its way back to God.

A Skill to Remember

Q: Never being unconscious while you sleep is much easier said than done. What would you suggest?

HK: It's a skill you have to develop. Even so, no state of consciousness is held perfectly as long as you are in the lower worlds. For a couple of weeks you may remember everything, and then for a while you won't. It means you have to change your disciplines or your approach. This is where the creative part of the spiritual exercises comes into play. You have to experiment with them and work from another angle to keep it fresh, so that you can remember your experiences. As you move into other areas of being, you also have to find new techniques to keep up with the change, to tune you in to that particular plane of heaven.

ECK Masters Working Together

Q: Can you elaborate more on the ECK Masters working together on the inner?

HK: As I mentioned earlier, on the inner planes there isn't any distinction; there is no separation of Spirit. The individual who has that responsibility as the Living ECK Master will provide the ECK discourses, the outer teachings, and the books to anyone who wants to learn the ways of Spirit and the spiritual laws. On the inner planes, I will also work with you, but at times one of the other ECK Masters will take you under his wing at one of the Temples of Golden Wisdom.

At times one of the other ECK Masters will take you under his wing.

We work together because that particular Master has a certain way of teaching which is necessary for you at that time and which will open doors. All the ECK Masters have their own talents and skills. Many times the Living ECK Master will pair a student with another ECK Master so that the chela can gain the spiritual unfoldment that is developed at that particular plane. This, then, will propel him to the next level when the time is right.

Smoking and ECK

Q: I'm interested to know more about smoking. Does an ECK Master avoid being around someone who smokes, or just while they are in the process of smoking? I believe you still do work with people who smoke, because I think many in Eckankar go on smoking, sometimes for a few years after joining.

HK: It's an interesting thing about smoking. Our whole group went out with a couple of smokers recently. Spirit has a way with these things, and the conversation turned naturally toward smoking. Everything said at the table was about the evils of smoking, even though most of these people aren't the kind who would normally say this or that is bad. But they did it this time, and it took a while before they caught themselves doing it. In the meantime, the smokers were pretty well put on the spot.

What smoking does is actually close out the protection of Spirit. It means that smokers love a vice more than they do the journey to God-Realization, and so they still haven't given it up. They are given help, of course, but it's not the high degree of help that could be given if they gave up the habit. Yet the ECK Masters do work with them over time to help them break it. They are not abandoned.

PERSONALITIES

Q: Sri Harold, I've tried to contemplate with you on the inner screen, but I haven't been able to see you there. Instead, I get invisible ECK Masters. There's obviously a lesson in the fact that these Masters have no personality I can see, because I communicate with them even though they're there without form. Yet if I get a different Master on a particular evening, I immediately know. I can tell that they are different individuals. What is the lesson in the fact that these particular Masters have no personality that I can see?

HK: These ECK Masters are working in the high states of consciousness. Personality actually doesn't come from a very high state of consciousness. Too often a truth seeker will look to the personality of the Master when he ought to be looking to the spiritual side.

It's the duty of every ECK Master to turn the attention of the seeker toward the eternal within himself, the Divine Spirit, or ECK. One should not put too much hope or confidence in the outer form of anything, including the form of the Living ECK Master.

On the inner, it really makes no difference if you see one Master or another, as long as the instruction given you is positive and uplifting.

On the inner, it really makes no difference if you see one Master or another, as long as the instruction that is given to you is positive and uplifting. At no time do you carry out negative instructions or destructive actions of any kind simply because an entity on the inner plane told you to do it. If it's negative, it's wrong, and it's not an ECK Master talking to you. This is the negative power hoping to trip you up, because that is its job. There are no holds barred; anything goes. Pretty soon you become so spiritually experienced that nothing will shake you. Rebazar Tarzs, the great ECK Master, said that nothing should move the dweller in ECK. And he meant absolutely that.

Thank you for coming.

Perth Regional Seminar, Perth, Australia,
November 9, 1982

As Soul gets a little of this Light and Sound of Spirit, It is drawn on just like the honeybee to the flower.

8
The Search for Happiness

Often we look for a spiritual healing, feeling that it is part of the spiritual path. We hardly realize that whatever illness we have is of our own creation, and that the cure is often brought about by Spirit through natural means. This could mean the medical profession, natural healers, or whatever comes into our state of consciousness.

Greater Vision

This is what Soul is interested in: coming ever into the greater awareness.

A fellow told me recently about an experience he had when he got his contact lenses. It's an example of going beyond, into another state of consciousness. This is what Soul is interested in: coming ever into the greater awareness. After wearing glasses for most of his life, he decided to take the big leap. So he went to the eye doctor to get himself a pair of contact lenses. When the examination was completed, the doctor said, "Try these out. I'll put them in your eyes for you."

This individual was very squeamish about having something put into his eye. As the doctor was trying to insert the lenses, all of a sudden this fellow felt himself beginning to faint. Right there in the examining room, he passed completely out. The optometrist and his nurse didn't quite know what to do. They laid him out on the floor and tried to revive him, but he had left the body so completely that it looked as if he had left the physical plane and died—or translated, as we say in ECK.

While the doctor and nurse were frantically trying to figure out the next logical move, this man was in the Soul body watching the entire event from a point near the ceiling. Once an individual is able to move into this state of being, he finds it feels quite good, so the scene struck him as highly amusing.

The doctor came running in with oxygen, and slowly they were able to revive him. This whole scene had seemed so funny to him that he awoke laughing. The doctor and nurse were amazed at his reaction. "That was a very serious thing," they said. "You didn't even have a pulse!"

We learn how to move into the higher states of consciousness so we may gain confidence and know we are a spiritual being who survives beyond death of the physical body.

He had this experience so he could become aware of himself as Soul, the eternal being which has no beginning or ending. What we do in the works of ECK is learn how to move into the higher states of consciousness so that we may gain confidence and know that we are a spiritual being who survives beyond death of the physical body.

Do I Live Beyond Death?

When I first approached the path of ECK, I was in the military, stationed in Japan. I had finished preministerial training a couple of years earlier, still without answers to questions such as, Do I live beyond death? I had no knowledge of the attributes of Divine Spirit, known in the Bible as the Word.

This Word of God, called the Logos by the Greeks, can be heard as Sound and seen as Light. It is important for any individual who hopes to make any advancement on the spiritual path to have these two aspects, the twin pillars of God, in his life. In Eckankar we give specific techniques for the individual to practice, and we call them spiritual exercises. Some of these are found in books such as *The Spiritual Exercises of ECK*.

The ECK teachings have been here since the earliest times that man inhabited this planet. The ECK Masters first had to show man very basic ways of survival, such as how to work with fire. The Living ECK Master of every age works with the consciousness as he finds it. His goal is always to help Soul out of the worlds of materiality, into the pure positive God Worlds. The Living ECK Master of any era wants only to lead the individual to look within to the source of all knowledge, wisdom, and understanding: the place where one can move toward Self-Realization and God-Realization.

But these are just words. I can stand here and say a lot of words about Self-Realization and God-Realization, but they will have no more meaning to you than when a minister stands in the pulpit and speaks of salvation by faith. It means nothing.

What sets Eckankar apart from other religious teachings is not only the Sound and Light—which is shared in some measure by several other teachings—but the fact that we can reach the kingdom of heaven while still in the human body.

An ECKist found something that the tourist center never talked about: the Australian fly. He got to calling it the spiritual fly because of its benefits.

The Spiritual Fly

An ECKist went out to an island nearby to bicycle around and look at the marsupials. While he was there, he found something that the tourist center never talked about: the Australian fly. He got to calling it the spiritual fly because of its benefits. One is the prevention of sunburn if you happen to go out and lie on the beach. As soon as you lie down, all these flies come and land on you. The only way you can escape them is to get on your bicycle and start pedaling. If you pedal fast enough, the wind will be too strong for the flies to land on you.

Another benefit of the spiritual fly is that it prevents untimely death. It is so hot in the outback of Australia that the moisture just pours out of the body, and the weary traveler who's out there would like nothing more than to lie down and leave this world forever. But one thing keeps him from giving up—the same thing that prevents sunburn. As soon as he lies down, the flies land all over him.

This ECKist calls it the spiritual fly because it seems to zero in right around the Spiritual Eye while leaving the rest of the body alone. I know you've learned to laugh at the fly, because if you didn't, it would drive you crazy. Australians are known the world over for their ruggedness, and I suspect the fly has something to do with it.

You wonder what the fly has to do with the spiritual path?

You wonder what the fly has to do with the spiritual path? When we're in the lower worlds, we have to put up with trials and tribulations. We may resent them and wish we could get out of this world and go on to heaven, but as a man once said, as much as he'd dearly love to go to heaven, he didn't want to have to die to get there.

How to Visit Heaven

In ECK we have the opportunity to learn the expansion of consciousness which is often referred to as Soul Travel. Sometimes people mix it up with astral travel or astral projection; this is not what it is. With Soul Travel we are able to move into other states of consciousness. Although some of the experiences are similar to astral travel, we go way beyond the Astral Plane.

The Astral Plane is just one of the many heavens,

or worlds, of God. Beyond it, the spiritual travelers have recognized the Causal, Mental, Etheric, and Soul Planes. Some of the other religious teachings have called them by different names, but it really doesn't matter what the name is. What is of importance to the seeker is to find out how to get there.

There are places of wisdom and knowledge that correspond to that level we know of as the Astral Plane. These include a museum that contains the prototype of every invention ever to be discovered on the Physical Plane. Inventors go to this Astral Plane museum, as Edison did, and draw on it. Sometimes they remember, sometimes not.

A library is there also, which houses every master volume from which the writers here draw what they need in order to write their own books. Editors of large publishing houses are familiar with the phenomenon of writers from both ends of a continent, or even in different parts of the world, submitting very similar manuscripts. It's likely each of the two authors went to this same inner library, or maybe they had an adventure together and then came back and recorded it without remembering each other. Often they won't even remember that they were at this library.

Purpose of the ECK Masters

As we go on the spiritual path, we work with the Spiritual Exercises of ECK. There are people who have a difficult time with them because they are afraid. My purpose is to dissolve the fear so we can move into these other areas in the higher worlds with confidence and joy, get the knowledge we find there, and bring it back to be used in some way for our personal upliftment and for the benefit of all those around us.

My purpose is to dissolve the fear so we can move into these other areas in the higher worlds with confidence and joy.

There is little reason to learn how to move with the expansion of consciousness unless we are going to do something with it. Some spiritual seekers get a little bit of enlightenment, then go up in the mountains, into a cave or monastery, and spend the rest of their lives contemplating on the higher truths—without doing anything whatsoever to bring a little light to their fellow man.

In Eckankar we speak of God and we call It Sugmad. We also speak about Divine Spirit, the cosmic energy that comes forth as the Voice of God. This is spoken of in religious writings around the world, but very few of the followers of these religions are told the function of Divine Spirit and how It can help us in our spiritual unfoldment. The ECK Masters come to bring this knowledge to man. As we gain spiritual unfoldment, we gain the attributes of wisdom, power, and freedom.

Soul longs to return to God. The search for God is really the search for happiness, and vice versa.

Soul's Mission

Soul longs to return to God. The search for God is really the search for happiness, and vice versa. There is a great loneliness that some people experience—they look for a mate; they look for health, wealth, and well-being. This is Soul's desire to return to God as it manifests in the feelings that we carry here on the physical plane. We look for something from the Golden Age. Perhaps we enjoyed it during a past lifetime on the physical plane, or we're remembering the state of Soul as It actually existed on the spiritual planes before It was sent into the lower worlds for experience.

Soul's mission is to become a Co-worker with God. It is simply that and nothing more.

There are adventures waiting for those of you who wish to explore these worlds of ECK. The Temples of Golden Wisdom and how the Light of ECK manifests on the different planes are spoken of in the different books of Eckankar, such as *The Spiritual Notebook*.

Another area to study is the ECK-Vidya, the ancient science of prophecy. There is a great interest by seekers of truth to know about the future as well as the present and the past. This is an ability you can develop for yourself.

The teachings of ECK are similar to a college curriculum—you can study certain aspects of the spiritual life for yourself, whatever interests you. Some people don't care about knowing the future, others aren't interested in working with dreams. Many are interested in knowing and being aware of the love and protection of Divine Spirit that can come into our life through the use of the charged words, one of which is HU.

There is no hurry to step onto the path of ECK. We do not look for someone to become an active student the first time he puts his hand on a book. From the time one picks up a book until the decision is made to go further on the path is the incubation period; it may last anywhere from one to five years or more. Some people have read an ECK book as long as ten years ago, and they're still not ready—and that's fine. There is no hurry.

It takes a special effort to go beyond and reach greater states of consciousness. We can do this by direct experience with the Light and Sound of Spirit.

All paths to God are provided by Spirit for the express purpose of giving Soul in Its varying states of consciousness a choice in how It wants to return to God. Each path leads to another path, and then to another.

It is one thing to be born into a certain state of consciousness, but we owe it to ourselves to make the effort to reach higher and beyond. Upon birth, we are given whatever consciousness we need to get from birth to death; the kind that allows us to go to school, learn a trade or a profession, and make our way. But it takes a special effort to go beyond and reach greater states of consciousness. We can do this by direct experience with the Light and Sound of Spirit.

There is a Light that corresponds to each of the heavens found in the spiritual worlds. There is a Sound that can be heard which uplifts and purifies Soul.

Spiritual Yardsticks

There is a Light that corresponds to each of the heavens found in the spiritual worlds. It may be blue, green, pink, yellow, or even violet or lavender.

There is a Sound that can be heard which uplifts and purifies Soul. This Sound is actually the Voice of God. It does not come as a booming voice from the clouds, but as one of the sounds of Spirit. It may be heard as a flute, the buzzing of bees, the roaring of the ocean, or as stringed instruments.

These all are signposts and guides to show you where you stand at that moment in your state of spiritual consciousness. There are definite yardsticks so that you can know if this path is working for you. If you are looking into any path, I urge you to take your time, examine it carefully, and don't be in a hurry to step into something that is unfamiliar to you.

When I first approached the teachings of ECK, I found that the power of Spirit was cleaning my consciousness. Translated into everyday living, this meant that my stomach turned every morning for a while. I wondered why I was cursed with this eternal yearning for greater truth that twisted my stomach.

All I wanted was to enjoy life the way the other farmers did: work hard all week, treat myself to beer on weekends, and sleep it off in time to get to church on Sunday morning—knowing that would make everything all right for the next seven days—and then do the whole cycle all over again. My neighbors back in the midwestern part of the United States are still doing it. I went back to visit and found they were enjoying themselves quite well, and for them it's the right way of life.

But the stirrings of Soul would not let me rest. It's time to move on, It said. It's not necessarily easy, and yet we are pulled along. As Soul gets a little of this Light and Sound of Spirit, It is drawn on just like the honeybee to the flower or the moth to the light. Spirit will take us over completely.

Our Goal in This Life

Life becomes an adventure. We are opened to learning in a way we have never been before.

Our goal in this life is not to find out how to use Spirit in our life, but how to open ourselves as a vehicle for Spirit to use as It will. Life becomes an adventure. We are opened to learning in a way we have never been before. I won't guarantee that the path of ECK will be easy, but I will guarantee that it is going to be different from anything that you have ever done before. If we give up to Spirit as It leads us into greater awareness, we can build and expand into a greater life. It's when we hold back—when Spirit opens the door and we refuse to walk through—that we find life becomes difficult.

Periodically I am asked if I can speed up the spiritual path for someone. I don't like to do this, but I occasionally do. The individual can also ask that it be slowed down. I ask that such requests be made in writing so that one is very aware of the fact that their path is speeded up or slowed down.

You may spend a year or two on the path of ECK before you have any conscious remembrance of the First Initiation. This initiation comes in the dream state about six months or a year after you have begun the study of the ECK discourses. This is where the Inner Master takes you to some far region in the other worlds to give you a little experience.

Essentials on the Path of ECK

We recognize several essentials on the path of ECK: First is God, or Sugmad; then Divine Spirit, that Voice which comes out of God; and then the Living ECK Master, who is myself in the physical. The greater part of the Living ECK Master is the Inner Master, who can meet you in the regions that are approached through the Spiritual Eye and through the Spiritual Exercises of ECK. If a Master is right for you, you ought to be able to see him on the inner planes as well as on the physical. Most people find it easiest to approach the inner worlds through the dream state. If you do the spiritual exercises that are found in the books and if you are interested in looking further, you will begin having these experiences.

Some of you will see past lives. The only importance of a past life is, How does it relate to you today? Why are you what you are?

Some of you will see past lives. The only importance of a past life is, How does it relate to you today? Why are you what you are? You may also see the future, which is simply to show you how to direct your life, how to bring yourself into greater awareness. The past and the future are only to give an understanding of the present. The greatest thing we learn on the path of ECK is to live in the moment. This means that even though we may plan how to earn and spend our next paycheck, for example—once we've done the best planning we can—we put the rest into the hands of God.

I'll be glad to answer a few questions if you have any, since they do help to bring out specific points.

The Oldest Spiritual Teaching

Q: Eckankar states it is one of the earliest teachings, and so do the Sufis. What is the relationship between the Sufi teachings and Eckankar?

HK: The word *HU* is also found in the Sufi teachings; it comes from the same source. This goes back many thousands of years. You can find out more about this for yourself as you make a study of it through the inner communication. Anyone could sit here and make claims about being the oldest teaching, but what does that do for your spiritual unfoldment? It merely gives information to the mind. There's nothing wrong with that, but as we go further along, there comes a point where we have to give up the mind.

Those civilizations and cultures that put great emphasis on the mind often have a difficult time working toward the spiritual life. You'd think it would be easier, but it's not. The mind is always asking questions about the nature of Soul. Soul is beyond the realm of the mind, which is on the Mental Plane. We can only hint at the nature of Soul and the nature of God.

There is a history of ECK in *The Spiritual Notebook*, and if you're interested, you can make a study of it. You also can ask to be taken in the dream state to have a look at this. There are some who have gone back to Lemuria and Atlantis and learned their role there. More importantly, they found out how it related to their life today; for instance, why they had certain fears.

Some have gone back to Lemuria and Atlantis and learned their role there. More importantly, they found out how it related to their life today; for instance, why they had certain fears.

Often it is best not to look into the past, and so the Inner Master will draw the curtain. We look for the lives that were pleasant for us in the ancient civilizations, to learn about the teachings as they were being given at that time. It seldom occurs to us that we may have left some of those lifetimes under hardship or torture. When we go through the experience again, it's frightening.

I have my own war stories, as do many of the ECKists. We spent lives in which we didn't learn the spiritual law—and we suffered for it. I've done this, and so have you. We have come to the feet of a Master many times, we have run across the Living ECK

Master many times; but we weren't ready, and so we kept wandering in the lower worlds. You can find more about this in *The Spiritual Notebook* if you're really interested. You can make up your own mind, and you won't have to take my word or anyone else's for it.

Following the Disciplines

Q: I haven't done any of the spiritual practices of ECK. I'm interested in the effectiveness of transcendental meditation as compared with the spiritual practices of ECK. Can you say a few words about that?

HK: Some people can find spiritual advancement in transcendental meditation. Any path can be of help to you, no matter what it is, if you follow the disciplines of that path. Even in the orthodox religions you will find those who have made progress on the spiritual path. But the vast majority of people have not. It's a personal thing.

The Teachings of Jesus

Q: I was wondering if Jesus, in his day, was trying to give out some of the ECK teachings. His earlier teachings seem closer to the ECK teachings of today, whereas in modern Christianity there are very few parallels. Somewhere along the line, the Christian teachings seem to have undergone a change.

Jesus was acquainted with the ECK principles and the ECK teachings, and he carried these to the people of his time.

HK: There is a saying that there are really no secret teachings, that everything we need to know is available to us on an open shelf somewhere. But it depends upon our state of consciousness to accept it.

Jesus was acquainted with the ECK principles and the ECK teachings. He was exposed to the teachings of Spirit, and he carried these to the people of his time. The people during the time of Jesus were of a very low state of consciousness.

When he brought the basic truths of Spirit to them, in relation to their state of consciousness, it was considered a very great teaching. The teachings of Jesus were meant for his times.

The Living ECK Master will do the same thing in any era. He will try to approach the culture with the ideas that are of interest to them, with things which they admire.

The Living ECK Master will do the same thing in any era. He will try to approach the culture with the ideas of interest to them, with things which they admire.

During the time of Jesus, there was a Living ECK Master whose name was Zadok. Today there is an imperfect knowledge of what the teachings actually were in those days. Eckankar had been forced underground several thousand years before that due to the influence of astrology and the persecutions during the time of Egypt's prominence. The priestcraft found that they could manipulate astrological charts and give readings, but they had not learned the techniques of the ECK-Vidya, which is the ancient science of prophecy.

THE LIVING ECK MASTER

Q: How is the Living ECK Master chosen? Is it in the other worlds, or is it here?

HK: This is a little difficult to answer, but the information is available in *The Shariyat-Ki-Sugmad* as well as *The Spiritual Notebook*. Just flip through the indexes and look for the listings under "Living ECK Master" or "Rod of ECK Power." The individual who takes over this position is given the Rod of ECK Power, and he holds it until he passes it to his successor who has earned the right to carry it.

Q: Concerning the Living ECK Master of the times, I realize it's totally my decision whether to follow the teachings you give out. You speak of trying the spiritual exercises, yet what about the significance of meeting the Living ECK Master? Is that an important step?

HK: Outwardly it's no big thing, but inwardly it is. The purpose of the outer is to lead you to the inner.

Experiencing Other Planes

Q: You say that we can experience the Soul Plane while living on this plane. After we leave this Physical Plane, do we have to experience every other plane? If so, what is the point?

HK: If we've earned the Third Initiation, then when we leave the body, we go immediately to that place on the Causal world that we have earned. We don't have to go back to the Astral or to the Physical. If we reach the Soul Plane, we don't have to come back to the lower worlds if we choose not to. But many of the leaders in the ECK works do decide to come back as Co-workers with God.

It doesn't matter where you're stationed throughout the worlds of being. You have instant access to the high state of God-Realization, so what difference does it make where you serve? The wear and tear on the particular body that you use here in the physical or on one of the other planes doesn't matter, because you are giving pure service.

You are not just limited to one plane.

You are not just limited to one plane. You are actually experiencing the other planes now in the Soul form. What I am trying to bring about is a conscious remembrance so that you can bring that awareness back here and benefit your life now.

For instance, although you're here in the physical body on the Physical Plane, as you get the Second Initiation in ECK, this means you have become established on the Astral Plane. But this does not limit your inner movement to the Astral Plane. The Inner Master, at his discretion, may take you to the Causal, Mental, Etheric, and Soul Planes—and even beyond.

First you visit, like a tourist, in order to gradually become exposed to these different states so that when you get the outer initiation there will not be a great shock. This is necessary because when you become established on each succeeding plane, you will find sometimes that the spiritual laws change. It appears almost as if you retrogress and have to learn anew what the laws are on each succeeding plane.

As we try to pick up a smattering of what happens in the inner worlds and apply it in our daily life here, often we find our life is thrown into turmoil. This can happen when we don't surrender to Spirit as It is trying to lead us into a greater way of life. We have experiences on the other planes, but sometimes we have the benefit of this knowledge only by impressions.

There are many people who are vehicles for Spirit—in government, in education—and are not aware of it. We are interested in becoming aware of our roles, both here and in other states of consciousness, because Soul has the ability to be in the Physical body while simultaneously in the Astral, Causal, Mental, and Etheric bodies. It's mind-boggling.

Soul has the ability to be in the Physical body while simultaneously in the Astral, Causal, Mental, and Etheric bodies. It's mind-boggling.

DISADVANTAGES OF THE OCCULT

Q: Are the studies of astrology and other occult sciences an advantage on the path of ECK?

HK: They are generally a disadvantage. Astrology, numerology, and similar disciplines come from the psychic and occult teachings. Usually they are preliminary to the path of ECK. Initiations on any other path really do not help you on the path of ECK. You'll find as you get on the path of ECK that these earlier disciplines no longer work when it comes to projecting what your future will be.

On the spiritual path we are looking for self-responsibility. If we have created a debt, we're going to have to pay it back. It's the spiritual law. This debt is called karma. We pay off only as much as is necessary to gain an understanding of the spiritual law which we have repeatedly broken, whether in this lifetime or a previous one. When the lesson has been learned, not just at the mental level but deep down, then the Inner Master has the power to dissolve the rest of the karma that resulted from the particular negative attitude that caused the karma that caused the symptom of illness in this lifetime.

Healings

Many of the psychic healers are not able to look back into the life of the person and find out the real cause of his illness. So they are actually curing symptoms. And when they cure symptoms, it means they have taken on that karma, which is necessary if the healing is to occur. Then sometime, either later in this life or in the next life, they are going to have to pay this back.

The ECK Masters learn how to turn requests for healing over to Spirit, and then if Spirit decides to do something, It will.

The ECK Masters learn how to turn requests for healing over to Spirit, and then if Spirit decides to do something, It will. If the individual hasn't earned the spiritual healing, he may have to work through other more conventional means or be given the strength to bear what he must. If the experiences and hardships of life can bring you compassion, then you have gained; and it will be easier for you to live with your fellow man.

When Jesus healed someone, he didn't just look at people and heal them. If he healed one, he could have healed two; if he fed one person, he could have fed five thousand—and he did. Yet he could have healed all the people in the land of that time, but he didn't. Instead, he said, "According to your faith be it unto you." There is the matter of the individual state of consciousness involved in any healing.

It's not just given indiscriminately, nor will a healing last forever. If it did, we would have more than one Wandering Jew and they would all still be wandering around. Living forever in the physical plane is not exactly something to be set forward as a goal. The spiritual life is a spiritual liberation where we shed the karma when we're able to reach the Soul Plane. That is a goal worth attaining.

The spiritual life is a spiritual liberation where we shed the karma when we're able to reach the Soul Plane. That is a goal worth attaining.

ROSICRUCIANS AND ECK

Q: We have studied for a year in the Rosicrucians, and their teachings seem to have much the same as is found in the ECK teachings. What is the main difference?

HK: The Rosicrucians are a good step. I studied with them too, for a while. The main difference is that the Rosicrucian teachings go into the Mental Plane, but not much farther. If you find help there, by all means keep on with it.

Q: You mentioned something about the service of the spiritual leaders when they come back to earth. How would that apply to the many other disciples of the path? What is their service?

HK: Service on the path of ECK is an individual choice. When you become an Eighth Initiate in ECK, you have the choice of whether to stay here or go into the other worlds. And when this choice comes, you may have to make a great struggle to stay in the physical body. Or you can take the easy way out: go and enjoy the bliss of Spirit in the higher realms, if you want to.

It is written in *The Shariyat-Ki-Sugmad*, the

ECK bible, that if an aspirant who steps on the path of ECK could look ahead and see the disciplines he would need as a Sixth Initiate, perhaps he'd be discouraged from taking the first step. I'm not saying this to discourage you, but ECK is a path that is real. You ought to find out for yourself the reality of Divine Spirit as It works, as It helps in the purification of Soul. And as you learn the spiritual laws, then you can make this way very easy for yourself.

The spiritual path can be an easy one. It means giving up our preformed ideas of what spirituality is and what it is not. We have been given a lot of misinformation by religious teachers of different paths because of their ignorance. They have no knowledge or understanding of the Light and Sound of God. They speak of doctrines and salvation and what happens after you leave this body, but much of what they say is in complete error. I don't ask you to believe me or anybody else. Find out for yourself. This is what the teachings of ECK are prepared to help you to do.

I don't ask you to believe me or anybody else. Find out for yourself. This is what the teachings of ECK are prepared to help you to do.

Look into the ECK books; look to your dream state; look for the Light and Sound of God; look for the high spiritual goals of Self-Realization and God-Realization. The teachings are so simple that I sometimes wonder how I can stand here and talk about them for twenty minutes or an hour. The teachings are found within yourself.

Thank you.

Perth Regional Seminar, Perth, Australia,
November 10, 1982

Spirit will often use us in interesting ways, even if it means we lock our keys in our car, to quietly bring the Light to another person.

9
Contact with the Light and Sound

Talking about the Sound and Light of Spirit in our lives and how It works, I find that many of you have this contact inwardly with Divine Spirit. The teachings of ECK are simply for you, as an individual, to go to that temple inside yourself where you can reach that source of divine inspiration to give you the spiritual upliftment you have been looking for, perhaps for years.

The teachings of ECK are simply to give you the spiritual upliftment you have been looking for, perhaps for years.

How Spirit Uses Us

Last night we were at a restaurant, and one of the ECKists locked his keys in the car. This was the second time it had happened on this trip; the first time was in Australia, and he had vowed that it would never happen again. He tried to get into the car, struggling with a wire coat hanger he got from the waitress, while the rest of us stayed at the table and kept eating, very slowly and leisurely. We had been through this lost-key business before.

Here in Singapore, every place you go everybody knows someone else—a relative or friend. As we sat at the table with one of our friends who was translating for us, a lady walked in and said hello. Our friend mentioned casually, "The keys are locked in the car," and this lady turned around to a table where a Chinese family had just seated themselves and pointed to a man. "He can help," she said.

The man stood up, wearing a big smile on his face. We found out that he'd had a lot of experience with unlocking car doors, having recently locked himself out twice. He went outside, and in about five minutes, the car door was opened. The ECKist was so relieved that he started taking pictures of everyone, calling this fellow his hero, because without his help we would have had to leave the car there and take a cab back to the hotel.

Sometimes Spirit uses us in a way that appears as if we are making a mistake, yet we're not.

Sometimes Spirit uses us in a way that appears as if we are making a mistake, yet we're not. We do the best we can, and Spirit uses us. In the hour the ECKist spent out there trying to open the car door, he met with a lot of different people; a whole crowd had gathered around trying to help him. Spirit often will use us to quietly bring the Light to another person, to light up Soul. We might think we have made a mistake, such as locking the keys in the car, but that's how Spirit will sometimes work.

Who Are We?

The ECKist is the ideal citizen of whichever country he is a member; he lives according to its rules and regulations. We work as individuals in a spiritual sense, learning the laws of Spirit to make our life a little bit easier, to gain understanding, and to take away the fear of death.

This is something, at least in the Western world, that is of great concern to people. The orthodox religions give no assurance of what happens after one leaves the physical body. This is how it was for me as I grew up, and I was afraid. One of the purposes of Eckankar is to give us a spiritual understanding of who and what we are.

We do not try to influence other people. We don't go up to them and push Eckankar on them, because it may not be right for them. Each of us has an individual approach to our own God. All I want to do is show you how to go within through the Spiritual Exercises of ECK. You can experiment freely with them. The Spiritual Exercises of ECK, done for perhaps twenty minutes a day, are a lighter form of going within than meditation. We don't go out and push the teachings of Spirit on anyone, but we let the Light shine from within. People will wonder what we have that is special; they can tell that there is something.

We don't push the teachings of Spirit on anyone, but we let the Light shine from within. People wonder what we have that is special; they can tell there is something.

GIVING OTHERS FREEDOM

While we are in the physical world, the physical body needs exercise. I don't always get as much as I should, as much as I did before I started working in this job. But I like to play Ping-Pong. Around nine o'clock one night in Australia, we found out about a community center that was only six blocks from the hotel. We had just bought new Ping-Pong paddles and balls, so we walked over.

They were just closing, but we asked if we could stay and play for a little while, and they said sure. We talked with a few people after the game and asked them if they would like to read some of the ECK material we had with us. When they said yes, we left it with them as kind of a thank-you.

This is how we do it. We never push. We let other people be. If they have another way of believing, we let them have it. We give total freedom. If we want freedom ourselves, we must allow others freedom. To get love we must give love, and the same is true, spiritually, of freedom. To have freedom we must give freedom, and you find that the more you are able to give, the more you get.

The Cloak of the Master

Somebody mentioned earlier that he got goose bumps while doing the spiritual exercises. When you put your attention on the Inner Master or you chant or sing one of the sacred Sounds of God, it opens you to Spirit. With the love of Spirit coming in, you might get goose bumps, your face might become flushed, or there may be a feeling of warmth that settles over you like a cloak. This is the presence of the Master—the protection and the love to which you have opened yourself.

Some of you see the Blue Light or hear one of the sounds. Others may never see anything, but they have the assurance and the knowingness of the Master's presence. Another way of being in the life of ECK is to be able to see Spirit working with you in your daily life. The best way to have assurance that you have been touched by this higher power that you never had before is when you find that It smooths your way throughout the day, if you let It. It will make things go smoother for you and give you confidence and even happiness.

Throughout the day, if you let It, ECK will make things go smoother for you and give you confidence and even happiness.

Someone said he got headaches while doing the spiritual exercises. That may be from doing them too much. If that's the case, then back off a little bit. If one asks on the inner to slow the pace down, I can slow it down. Sometimes people do the spiritual exercises too often or for too long a time—morning and night, for an hour, two hours, or three hours—and then they get too much Light coming in. This can speed things up in the physical body faster than you can handle or grow into.

Take your time. You'll find how it works for you as you go. You might check with a doctor, too, since the headaches may be caused by a food allergy or some other reason.

HEALING

Spirit may give a miraculous healing at times; but It may not, because the purpose of life is to give you experiences. If an illness is taken away just like that, you may never gain a needed understanding about yourself. Every illness ought to teach you something you didn't know before. The spiritual path is just to bring you to a greater understanding of yourself and the spiritual laws. When illness comes, it means you now have come to a point of understanding a greater spiritual law.

Every illness ought to teach you something you didn't know before.

As you unfold, even your food habits will have to change, very gently and very gradually. Nobody else will tell you how to eat, but you will figure it out just by trial and error or maybe by going to a doctor or reading a book. You will find that your health is going to improve too: It has to, because this change in eating habits will reflect the change in your state of consciousness as you move along the path.

One should stay open to all kinds of information that may come, even down here in the physical. See if it gives an answer to what causes an illness, such as headaches. I'm not supposed to give health diagnoses or anything of this nature, but if one is looking for the cause, he will come to an understanding of it.

If you have any questions, I'll be happy to answer a few.

HOW TO SURRENDER

Q: If we want to create something for ourselves, do we visualize it and it happens, or do we just ask the Inner Master for it, or do we just surrender our will to the Master?

HK: We surrender our fears, our cares, and our worries. In the meantime, we plan our daily life. For example we might study if it is necessary for a better job. It's not enough to visualize something in the mental stream and then say, Now I can sit back and hope I get a better job, better health, or the proper mate. It doesn't work like that.

We visualize something on the inner, and then we set out to do whatever we can to bring that plan into being. There are many people who have thousands of ideas, but the truly rare person is the one who can figure out what he has to do in the physical world to make his dream come true. The inventor is actually the individual who not only has the great idea but figures out the technology to accomplish it. It takes actual work down here to manifest whatever shows on the inner screen, in the Third Eye.

We don't necessarily want to figure out how to use ECK in our life, but rather, how can ECK or Spirit use us?

We don't necessarily want to figure out how to use ECK in our life, but rather, how can ECK or Spirit use us? We want to become a vehicle for Spirit. To do this, we have to get rid of the fears or cares that constrict and close the line between Spirit and Soul. Our fears and worries are the things we give up, not our money or any of those things. If our goal really is God-Realization, the other things will come to us.

The Christian Bible says, "But seek ye first the kingdom of God . . . and all these things shall be added unto you." Too many people are looking to use Spirit for material gains; this is not the purpose of the high path of ECK. I know what you are trying to say with your question: How can we use Spirit? But what I'm trying to say is that it ought not to be for material gain, for power over anybody else, or anything of this nature. It is to open ourselves as a clear vehicle for Spirit, and then It will use us as It will. Sometimes we are conscious of It, often we are not.

What we want is to come to a conscious awareness of how Spirit is using us, no matter what It brings.

Q: If I want to have a Satsang class, should I use visualization to bring it about?

HK: What you can do is send out the invitation on the inner planes and then do what you have to do out here to reach people who might be interested. If you give an ECK book to someone who is interested, you can just mention to them that you might be starting a class or discussion group. But first send out an invitation on the inner planes: Ask God to bring those people who are ready to hear the message of ECK to the particular class that you have in mind, and then go about working with the area coordinators to form that class.

TAKE YOUR TIME

Q: I'm anxious to be a Fifth Initiate before I die. I don't want to reincarnate, even on the inner planes. Will the frequency and length of time I spend doing the spiritual exercises help the progress of my spiritual unfoldment? If not, what will lead to attaining the higher realizations?

There really is no hurry. The Inner Master will take you at the speed that is right for you.

HK: There really is no hurry. When you first begin on a spiritual path of any kind, you are so enthusiastic that you want to go as fast as you can. You're actually opening yourself to Spirit. If you open up too fast, you can cause many problems in your life: money problems, health problems, everything. This is why I generally encourage people to go slowly.

I am more concerned that you have contact with the Light and Sound in some way, that you see one of the ECK Masters in the Third Eye or at an inner temple. This is the ECK manifested as Sound and Light in an inner form. Then the Inner Master will take you at the speed that is right for you. It is something we don't want to force; this is a lifelong path.

This is a lifelong path.

The ECK-Vidya is a series of interlocking wheels like on the old time clock; and if one part speeds up, it can upset the movement of the whole clock. This could affect not just yourself, but from within yourself it could upset the greater circle of people around you—in business and everything else—because you're going too fast.

Spiritually, we must fit in harmoniously with whatever is around us. Whether you actually see the Light, hear the Sound, see the Inner Master, or feel Spirit in some way, once you have the Sound and Light then you are in contact with the higher source. It will take you as you are, according to your unfoldment. Going too fast causes so many problems, which later can slow you down on the path; it's better to go along steadily than to go fast and then fall back.

Fasting

Q: Is fasting necessary for our spiritual unfoldment? I am a doctor myself, and for the last ten years I have had to take medication. If I have stomach trouble, do I still have to fast in order to progress spiritually?

HK: No. When you are under the care of a doctor who has you on a certain program, diet, or medication, by all means take care of yourself as you have to. If the doctor says eat, then eat. Some people aren't able to do a total fast, and it isn't necessary; there are other ways to do the Friday fast.

As long as we're on the subject of Friday fasts, for those of you who may not be familiar with them, actually there are three different kinds of fasts that we can do. There is a total fast where you only drink water for twenty-four hours. Another is the partial fast where you may have one meal a day or just fruit or fruit juices. And then there is the mental fast, which means keeping your attention on the Inner Master as well as you can for twenty-four hours, or weeding out negative thoughts for twenty-four hours; you can do it that way too. So we have the total fast, partial fast, and mental fast. You choose the one that suits you, and even this may change.

Recognizing Our Progress

Q: By the yardsticks provided by you and in the ECK literature to measure our progress in the ECK spiritual exercises, I think I am hardly making any progress. In desperation, there were many occasions when I literally called to you for help, but you don't seem to be responding. What I'm wondering is whether or not I have any chance at all of making progress with the spiritual exercises?

HK: I might just ask you a few things here if you feel they are not too confidential. First of all, how long have you been in ECK?

ECKist: For about one year.

HK: What yardsticks are you looking for that you feel would be the first indications that you are progressing on the spiritual path?

ECKist: Even if it would happen rather occasionally, I'd be very contented with seeing the Light, for example, or seeing the Inner Master in the Tisra Til. That is the sort of yardstick I'm referring to.

We're making some progress here!

HK: Do you remember your dreams?

ECKist: There was one particular dream, come to think of it, in which you responded.

HK: We're making some progress here!

You've been in for a year, and you're doing well. A year is actually a short time. During my first two months in ECK nothing happened, and then I had tremendous experiences in the other worlds. Then I had nothing again for months, and those initial experiences began to wear thin.

I wondered about it, but I still knew that something was going on, even though I couldn't really remember what happened. Often the Inner Master pulls the curtain, because at that early stage, what we see would be too shocking.

All I'm concerned about is that the outer life stays in harmony and balance and that you don't go out there and do strange things all of a sudden—give up your job, take all your savings out of the bank, and go off to an ashram. That is not the spiritual life. The spiritual life is carrying out the duties that we have accepted, such as family and children, and figuring out ways to support them. This is where the challenge of life is today.

WORKING IN THE DREAM STATE

The dream state is generally a very easy way for the Inner Master to work with Soul because the fears are set aside.

Some people are very good in the dream state, and some are very good in contemplation. I can work with you in the dream state a little bit more. The dream state is generally a very easy way for the Inner Master to work with Soul because the fears are set aside.

The gentlest technique that I know is one that I used to use fairly often when I'd run up against a wall: I'd still do the contemplation every day, same as always, but before going to sleep at night, as an inner thought I would just give permission to the Inner Master to take me to the place I had earned. I'd say, Mahanta, I give you permission to take me to that world or to that Temple of Golden Wisdom which would be for my benefit. Then I would go to sleep and not be concerned about it. Next day, I'd see if I remembered something.

So often when we first wake up, the inner experience is fresh, but the reason we forget is that it is so commonplace. If you can develop the discipline to write down whatever happened in the dream state immediately upon awakening, then within an hour or two you'll be quite surprised at what you find written in that notebook—and much more so after a month. Then include these dream experiences in your monthly initiate report.

If you can develop the discipline to write down whatever happened in the dream state immediately upon awakening, then within an hour or two you'll be quite surprised at what you find written in that notebook—and much more so after a month.

When we travel in the physical, we're in a greater state of awareness than usual; everything is strange and different enough for us to take notice. But at home things are more commonplace. We follow the same routine for so many years: get up at a certain time, shave, stumble out the front door, and go to work. If somebody were to ask you to describe the house on the corner of the third block from your home, you probably couldn't do it. It's too commonplace; there is nothing to strike the mental screen to make it stand out and cause you to remember.

It's the same way with the inner. Many people fail to remember experiences on the inner because when you're there, it is so natural that the inner and outer blend into each other. As you wake up and become conscious, you figure it's not worth the trouble to record the dream because it seems like something you always do. By the time you're finished shaving, you've forgotten. If you can just get down a few notes, maybe two or three sentences to trigger the memory, to give you a key, this will provide a focus so that during the day you can try to recall what happened there.

Initiate Reports

ECKist: Sri Harold, can I conclude that if we would proceed with the spiritual exercises, we would be successful?

HK: Yes. This is also the point of the monthly reports. If you feel you don't have contact with the Inner Master, then write an initiate report and send it to me. If you are having contact with the Light and Sound and the Inner Master, write the initiate report anyway; but you don't have to mail it. It's simply for your own benefit to see what has happened during the last month.

In my own unfoldment, if I had contact with Spirit once or twice a month in any way, I used to consider that everything was all right. Every month I liked to have some indication that there was this inner connection. It doesn't have to be every moment or every day; that might be too much for us. It might unbalance us to the point where we would become unfit to live among people.

Q: Insofar as the initiate report is concerned, that is only a requirement for those who have received the Second Initiation. Are those who have just gone through the First Initiation also asked to write initiate reports?

I open the door for you if you want a little help here.

HK: If you want to. I open the door for you if you want a little help here. If you like, you can just write *Initiate Report* or *IRO*—which stands for *Initiate Report Only*—at the bottom left-hand corner of the envelope. It helps in the mail sorting at the office. It helps me to get through my work a little faster.

Singapore Regional Seminar, Singapore
November 13, 1982

While washing dishes, the woman saw into a past life which helped her understand her strong attachment to her son.

10
Eckankar—a Direct Path to God

I'd like to welcome you. For those of you who are new to the teachings of Eckankar, the purpose of this path is simply to get in contact with the two aspects of God: the Light and Sound.

The Benefits of ECK

It's difficult to put into words the benefits of ECK in your daily life. There comes a time when life's problems weigh us down to the point where we may feel that we could be crushed at any time and never arise to face tomorrow. No matter what path you are on, there is always the straw that can break the camel's back. But it depends upon our understanding: What are we expecting from this experience of living? If we expect a life that will be constant happiness and joy, day after day, we're going to find ourselves deeply disappointed when it doesn't happen.

What are we expecting from this experience of living?

What we are looking for on the path of ECK is the understanding that when life leans heavily upon us, we have the strength to get up.

We speak about God—Sugmad, as we call It—the divine substance from which Soul has sprung, and about the contact we have with this Divine Source. This contact comes through Spirit, the Ocean of Love and Mercy. Spirit can be heard as Sound and seen as Light.

What is the purpose of the Sound and Light? There are stories of saints who have had experiences with this Light of God. There was the mystic cobbler Jakob Böhme, who experienced being enveloped by a pink light. He tried to tell other people about the spiritual insights that had come to him so that perhaps they, themselves, could learn how to reach a greater understanding of their purpose here—why it is worth the bother of getting up in the morning.

Necessity Has No Laws

When I was in preministerial school, I was forced to take a Latin class as part of my instruction. I didn't have any use for Latin and did very poorly most of the time, except when I was about to fail the class. That would have meant I'd have to leave the school—quite a disgrace for my family—so I would study hard and do just well enough to stay in school. I had the ability but not the interest to succeed. I've forgotten almost everything in Latin except for one or two sentences. One is the saying *Legem non habet necessitas* which means "Necessity has no laws."

When we have contact with the Light and Sound, we find we have alternatives whenever obstacles confront us in our daily life.

When we have contact with Spirit in the form of the Light and Sound, we find that we have alternatives whenever obstacles confront us in our daily life. Somebody told me the other day, "When I have a problem, I now consider it a stepping-stone, a building block in my life. If I can meet this obstacle, I can be more sure of myself, not just physically but spiritually. I will have more confidence because I have overcome an obstacle in life."

Far too often we ask God, "Please take away my sorrow and trouble," and we overlook the reason for the problem. The purpose of difficulties is to make us strong, to give us experience. Experience for what? The mission of Soul. The mission of every Soul, whether It understands this or not, is to become a Co-worker with God.

The other Latin saying that has stuck with me is *Barba non facit philosophum*. It means "It is not the beard that makes the philosopher." A person's philosophy has little bearing upon anyone else if the other people haven't experienced it themselves. There are certain things we can learn only by putting in our time. A child might be very smart, yet there are some things that only an older person can know. Certain things come only with a little hard learning, and it's probably the hard learning in life that makes our hair gray.

Spirit wants to uplift us so that we develop what we call the spiritual consciousness, or Self-Realization. This is the self-recognition of truth: to know who and what we are and what our mission in this life may be. When we have achieved this state of consciousness, then our next goal is God-Realization and reaching the kingdom of heaven in this lifetime. This is when we are able to break free from the wheel of karma, the chain of events that has held us here in the physical body for so many lifetimes.

Recognizing the ECK at Work

There are some of you who subscribe to reincarnation, while others do not; whatever you believe really is not of major importance. My interest is in helping those of you who have had spiritual experience with the Sound and Light to become aware of how ECK works and to recognize It working in your lives.

The Sound of God is contained in the word HU, a secret or sacred name for the Sugmad. This word can be used quietly at work, at home, or anytime you face a crisis.

The Sound of God is contained in the word *HU*, a secret or sacred name for the Sugmad. This word can be used quietly at work, at home, or anytime you face a crisis. After you have done everything you can do, you sing this word quietly, and then stand back and let Spirit take charge.

We expect too many miracles. We expect that if a boss is really bothering us, Spirit will come in and do something dramatic—make him go up in a puff of smoke or something like this. But Spirit works in quiet, indirect ways; It is frequently so subtle that we never recognize Its ways.

Those who have earned the higher states of consciousness have a protection from Divine Spirit that is unknown to the average person.

Protection

Those who have earned the higher states of consciousness have a protection from Divine Spirit that is unknown to the average person. When anger or mockery is directed against one of these individuals—whether a member of the Christian, Hindu, or Buddhist faiths, or of Eckankar—there is a white light that surrounds this person and gives protection. The negative thoughts which are directed toward him, like darts or arrows, can only come back upon the sender. The individual who sent the thoughts will suddenly find himself with all kinds of problems in his daily life. This keeps him so busy that he no longer has time to think negatively about the other person who was protected.

This has happened many times in my own life. In one particular case a number of years ago, I took a job in the printing department of a large hotel in Las Vegas. The man who hired me had a reputation for firing people. I needed a job, but I really didn't know the work very well: I worked in printing as a cameraman at the time.

There were only five of us in that little shop, including this manager. He would fire people on any excuse whatsoever. In fact, when a labor union came in just before I left, it was revealed that he had fired fifty-one people in only a year. There was a tremendous turnover, and I knew I didn't have much of a chance to stay there.

But I didn't just leave it up to Spirit to hold my job for me. I put my trust in Spirit and worked as hard as I could to learn everything he threw at me.

I put my trust in Spirit and worked as hard as I could to learn everything this manager threw at me.

One of the pressmen started to get on my case, then another pressman. It got to be very much like animals in the wild—when they find one of their kind who's weak and hurting, all the stronger ones will attack it. It's survival of the fittest. If you're the weak one, you find the whole crew is after you. I didn't know what to do, so I turned it over to Spirit. I simply said, *I turn this over to Spirit.* And then I did my work just as carefully as I could. Any instructions that my boss gave me were carried out to the letter, and everything was done right the first time.

Then an interesting thing happened. One of the pressmen who was after me had a truck that he spent a lot of time waxing and polishing. One day somebody ran into it for no apparent reason. The other pressman was fired while I was still there.

In the end, I was able to leave under happy circumstances: I got married and moved to California. My boss and I parted on a pleasant note. At first he seemed happy to see me go, but then he began trying to convince me to stay. I had turned into a pretty good worker by that time. Just to survive, I had done everything possible to become a very good worker.

The point of Spirit in our life is to lift us up spiritually. We look for several things in life: mainly to find an individual who can open us up to Spirit in the form of Light and Sound. This Light can be seen in a number of ways, one of which is the six-pointed star; we speak of this as the Blue Star of ECK.

The Spiritual Exercises of ECK are the key to the ECK works. Each day you shut your eyes and go into a light contemplation for twenty minutes or so—not very long. Putting your attention on the

Spiritual Eye, you may chant *HU*, a sacred name for God. The true function of this word is to open us as a vehicle for Spirit. Most individuals have some success within a year—sometimes within a day, a couple of weeks or months. They begin to see this Blue Light that forms in the other worlds.

Being a Co-worker with God

When I first began to explore the different paths to God, I never wanted to be a Co-worker with God. It seemed to me a very boring and uninteresting way to spend this life or the next one or whatever came after that. Being a Co-worker with God, as we have been led to believe from some of the medieval paintings, usually depicts someone with wings and a halo who just sits around in pure bliss. I don't know how I could enjoy pure bliss with nothing to do for the rest of eternity.

Yet there are those who spend a lot of time in the different heavens, some of which actually offer this kind of lethargic bliss. The people there are very happy; but there comes a time in the spiritual works when we realize that there is always one more heaven, there is always one more step.

No matter what anyone says, there is no such thing as a perfected man walking the earth today. None of the ECK Masters make this claim.

No matter what anyone says, there is no such thing as a perfected man walking the earth today. None of the ECK Masters make this claim. They know that those who have walked the earth before are still moving onward in their spiritual unfoldment even though they are now working on some of the other planes or heavens of God.

The training I got in religious school spoke mainly of this present life and the life hereafter, known as heaven, and claimed the only way one could get there was by dying. A man once said he didn't mind going to heaven, but he didn't like the idea of dying to get there. If he had to die to get to heaven, he would rather not go. I know many who express that sentiment. So we have the Spiritual Exercises of ECK, which are simply to help us begin working in the Soul body.

We are Soul—you, me, and every individual, every embodiment. We are Soul; we take on a physical body, and this body goes through the experiences of infancy, youth, middle age, and old age. We go through all these experiences, and then the body is dropped, or dies, because it's worn out. But Soul is eternal; It has no beginning or ending. This is the message that I'm trying to bring to you today. You are Soul; this is the high being that you, yourself, are, and you can enter the kingdom of heaven while still in the physical body.

The Spiritual Exercises of ECK are simply to help us begin working in the Soul body.

The Light of God

The spiritual exercises bring the Light and Sound of God to us. Usually the color of the Light is blue, and It can be seen as a blue star or a globe. The color blue denotes the state of consciousness that we are looking to, the Mahanta Consciousness. This is the Inner Master, that high state of consciousness which is beyond the cosmic consciousness and the Buddhi and Krishna states of consciousness.

When that Blue Light appears in our inner vision, It will be seen very clearly. It won't be mistaken for imagination. This means simply that we have made contact with the Light of God which is part of the Sound Current. The Light and Sound are the Sound Wave that carries you back to God, that spiritualizes your consciousness as Soul. When you see this Blue Light, it means that the Holy Ghost—Spirit, Nam, or the Voice of God—has taken you in tow. It is bringing you those life experiences which are for your enrichment and show you that direct path home to God.

I don't say that Eckankar is the only path to God, but I do say that it is the most direct.

The Sound Current

The other aspect of Spirit, even more important than the Light, is that which we know as the Sound. This Sound Current is actually the Voice of God, spoken of in the Bible as the Word: "In the beginning was the Word. . . . And the Word was made flesh, and dwelt among us."

This Voice, the creative current which comes from God, has created the lower worlds. It comes out like a radio wave from a central broadcasting station. It's like a pebble thrown into a quiet lake, causing ripples to go out. These waves go out, but they must always come back to the center; it's the returning wave that we are interested in. This is what Soul is looking for: to return to the God center. When It returns to the God center, we call this God-Realization, or the God Consciousness.

This is what Soul is looking for: to return to the God center.

There is no way I can prove a state of consciousness to you, whether it's cosmic consciousness, Christ consciousness, or the Mahanta Consciousness; there is no one who can prove this. All too often an individual meets someone who has had one of these states of awareness, and the seeker will say, "All right, prove it to me—do a miracle. Make the table float around the room." If the man did this, the next question would be, Well, how can I be sure this is the positive force and not the negative? One question always leads to another.

The proof that the questioner is seeking will never come, because he won't accept it. There is a spiritual law that states: No Master can gain converts by using miracles.

The Nature of Truth

The teachings of ECK were brought out to the public in 1965 by Paul Twitchell. He was an author and a newspaperman. There are a number of ECK Masters who work quietly in the background, and then there is the Living ECK Master. He goes out in public to see if there are any individuals interested in learning about their own spiritual nature. He gives the outer works and the outer teachings to these individuals so that they can find the Inner Master and become their own authority about the nature of truth.

My purpose is to link Soul up with the Sound and Light of God. As you get this linkup, you become your own authority about what is truth and what is not. No longer do you have to listen to a man in a pulpit or even to myself standing on a stage and telling you about truth. Truth is not the same for any two people. No two people have exactly the same outlook on life. Each one of our experiences is unique; Soul is unique.

My purpose is to link Soul up with the Sound and Light of God. As you get this linkup, you become your own authority about what is truth and what is not.

The Bible has truth for many people if they use it and the laws found therein. One example is the Golden Rule: Do unto others as you would have them do unto you. That law, if used, would give spiritual upliftment to many people. Regardless of what religious belief one follows, there are always those who are "Sunday morning Christians." They follow their religion once a week: just long enough on a Sunday morning to make themselves feel less guilty about drinking on Saturday night. I have no objection to that: Soul is getting experience. We have this type even in Eckankar.

You find when you overstep a law of life, life has a way of putting the law into action and bringing it back to you. We know this as the Law of Cause and Effect. Saint Paul referred to it in the Christian Bible when he said, "Whatsoever a man soweth, that shall he also reap."

THE RAZOR'S EDGE

When one has not attained the high states of spiritual consciousness, this Law of Karma does not come back immediately. The higher you go in your awareness, the quicker the law comes back. That's good in one way and bad in another. I'd say overall it's good because as soon as you cheat someone, for instance, the law strikes and you get the karma over with sooner. The higher you go, the narrower becomes the path. Some call it the razor's edge.

People who do not really have any regard for the spiritual law may just be learning life, taking it as they find it, cheating, robbing, and having a good time. The law does not demand its payment sometimes for two, ten, twenty, or thirty years, or maybe not until the next lifetime. When the payment doesn't come due as soon as the violation of the spiritual law is committed, the person thinks he's getting away scot-free. But there must be full payment in the true coin for every action.

The only thing that I consider wrong is any act that stops another person on his way to God-Realization. The rest is purely experience; we learn by our own mistakes. I have no argument with anyone unless he wants to violate my freedom. I call this getting into my psychic space, and here I'll draw a line.

The Sound may come as a flute, as the chirping of crickets off in the distance when there are no crickets around, or as a humming sound, like atoms rushing.

Walking the spiritual path does not mean we become sheep. In Eckankar we never talk about the leader and his flock; we talk about the individual. I'm not interested in sheep; sheep are meant to be shorn, and they often are—that's their purpose.

The Inner and Outer Work of the Master

Soul, as the individual, is the aspect of you in which I am interested. One way that the Inner Master is able to work with you is when you begin to see the Light. Then you may hear a sound. The Sound may come as a flute, as the chirping of crickets off in the distance when there are no crickets around, or as a humming sound, like atoms rushing. These various Sounds of God really are the whirring of the atoms in the spiritual planes. The different Sounds you hear are guideposts to the state of consciousness you are in at that moment, which brings a certain degree of purification.

When you step on the spiritual path, the karmic patterns of your life will speed up. All of a sudden your life becomes very active and very interesting, and you can't put your finger on the exact cause of it. I won't necessarily guarantee you a life of ease and happiness if you look into the teachings of ECK and begin to follow the path with sincerity, but I will guarantee you that things are going to be more interesting than they were before.

We learn how to work with It, with Spirit, to let things be. Even when we give blessings on this path of ECK, we don't say, I bless you; instead, we say, May the blessings be. This gives the individual the choice and freedom to accept the blessing or to reject it. And we all should have this choice.

We don't say, I bless you; instead, we say, May the blessings be. This gives the individual the choice and freedom to accept the blessing or to reject it. And we all should have this choice.

Usually I work with you in the dream state. The true test of a Master ought to be that he can not only work with you outwardly and physically, but also inwardly. There are few individuals who have this power. Even in ECK there are some students who aren't conscious of this inward help. The best I can say is: Be patient. I am happy for those who have experiences with either myself or the other ECK Masters. Spirit is not divided; these ECK Masters are merely the manifestation of Spirit on a certain plane of the inward heavens.

UNDERSTANDING PAST LIVES

I will work with you at times to open up past lives when you are ready. An individual who had great love for her son also had the fear for many years that he would unexpectedly die. This feeling was with her long before she got on the path of ECK, but she had never understood the reason for it. It took eight years before she built up enough stamina so that she was ready to see the cause of this fear.

Every time she looked at her son, she would wonder, *When is he going to die?* It was a terrible burden. Then one day, eight years after stepping onto the path of ECK, she was washing dishes and looking out the window. All of a sudden the Inner Master opened up a past life for her to view.

She had now developed the spiritual stamina to understand what this past experience meant. She saw that her husband in that previous life had injured and killed their child in a most horrible, brutal way. After the whole experience passed, she was able to see why she had this fear, and for the first time she was able to confront it and understand it.

Once we gain an understanding of our fear, it will begin to dissolve.

The fear didn't go away overnight, but once we gain an understanding of our fear, then it will begin to dissolve. It's important to dissolve these fears one by one. As this happens, we open ourselves to a greater amount of this Light and Sound of Spirit, which always brings us into a greater awareness and consciousness of those circumstances that constantly swirl about us.

Using Obstacles as Stepping-Stones

As far as an onlooker could tell, we may have the same problems as our neighbors. What separates us is our understanding of the purpose of these problems. We can use the obstacles in our life as stepping-stones, whereas these same stepping-stones in the life of a person who isn't unfolding himself spiritually could be the blocks that crush him.

Necessity has no laws. You can experiment with this Word of God—HU—that we sang earlier. You can try it out. I'm not asking you to believe anything just because I say it; try it out and see if it helps you. You may sing it right before you go to sleep, just for a few minutes, and see what the Inner Master has for your instruction.

You may sing HU right before you go to sleep and see what the Inner Master has for your instruction.

If you have some specific questions about the path of ECK, its origin, how it can work for you, about the manifestations of Light and Sound, or anything of this nature, I'll be happy to address a few of them.

The Meaning of Eckankar

Q: What does the word *Eckankar* actually mean?

HK: It's an old Pali word which means Co-worker with God. Eckankar is not the same as ECK. Eckankar is the name for the outer teachings, the books and discourses, which lead one to Spirit, or ECK. ECK is the inner consciousness that we attain. We start with the outer teachings, and then we become the Co-worker. ECK is not just a nickname for Eckankar.

Out-of-Body Experiences

Q: I would like to know if you have ever had an out-of-body experience or done astral projection. Is it something that happened to you willingly or unwillingly, and is it possible to explain the steps or procedures that it actually takes to do it?

HK: I don't want to go and give a long list of stories about what I have done. If you talk too much about your own program, people will say, "Oh, sure." It's not something I can prove to you, anyway. Each individual has it programmed out for himself, in his own way. It's an individualized training program on the inner planes.

In ECK, we speak of Soul Travel and use the

Spiritual Exercises of ECK. This is the expansion of consciousness, that aspect of the teachings that is perhaps the heart and the life of ECK. I have found it highly informative and enlightening for myself.

I have found Soul Travel highly informative and enlightening for myself.

The book *In My Soul I Am Free* includes a story about me while I was stationed in Japan. This was in 1967. Paul Twitchell had just brought the ECK writings out in 1965. No one really knew much about Eckankar, but I found a little ad in *Fate* magazine and sent for the discourses. I had just started two months earlier with the Spiritual Exercises of ECK, when I had an inner experience where I was taken back to our farm in Wisconsin.

But talking about Soul Travel is one thing, practicing it is quite another. To me, the practice of Soul Travel, actually being able to have these experiences in the other realms, is the whole key to the spiritual works of ECK. There are individuals who have had these experiences naturally. Sometimes a person goes out of the body during illness, but they may never find a way to have that experience again.

Try the spiritual exercises. There are several given in *ECKANKAR—The Key to Secret Worlds*. You may be given an experience just to teach you about the reality of ECK and of this path, or you may begin working in the dream state. You can try them out and see if they work for you.

The ECK Masters before 1965

Q: Was there a Living ECK Master before 1965?

HK: Yes, there was. This was Sudar Singh, from India, who died in the 1940s. Then Rebazar Tarzs, the torchbearer of the leadership of ECK who had been the Living ECK Master some time before, came in. He took the leadership until 1965, when Paul Twitchell had earned the right. Paul

Twitchell had to earn it, as did all the others. There has been an unbroken succession of ECK Masters that goes quite far back. Some of them are described in *The Spiritual Notebook*.

At different times the ECK Masters have worked quietly in the background. Up until 1965, most of the teachings were given on a one-to-one basis because of persecution. And as I said, these Masters were not interested in doing miracles for followers or in being out front and taking credit for a lot of things, either.

Yes, there have been a number of Living ECK Masters leading up to the present, and there will be others after me. I'm already working to get myself to the next position. That's what we always do: work ourselves into the next step, whether it's in our job or in our spiritual life.

Masters outside of Eckankar

Q: Do you recognize masters outside of Eckankar?

HK: Yes. Every path to God is valid. We are all different; we have different states of consciousness. And yet there are some people who have similar ideas—you might call them ideological backgrounds for lack of a better phrase. Those who are similar in their spiritual unfoldment may group together and become known as the Baptists, as the Anglicans, or as ECKists. But within each group you will find those who stand higher, those who stand lower, and those who walk the outer fringes.

Every path to God is valid. Each is needed as a stepping-stone.

Each religion has been established by God to fit a certain level of consciousness, and each is needed as a stepping-stone. Just because we may have outgrown a spiritual path does not invalidate it for another person. If I have left a certain religion and moved on to another one, it wouldn't be right for me to say, Now that I've outgrown it, anybody who stays there is a fool. That path, that religion and its teachers, is still provided by God.

The high spiritual Masters always work together. It's only their followers who set up distinctions such as My Master is greater than yours. On the inner planes the master of one path will turn the true seeker over to the next master in a very natural way. Even on the path of ECK we have a number of ECK Masters who work quietly here on the physical plane as well as those teaching on the inner planes.

When you have learned what you need to know at a certain place, then you are graduated, in a sense, from this grade or class to the next. It's a very natural process.

Masters never shake their fingers at each other and say, You're less spiritual. They all know their place in the spiritual hierarchy, and they are all unfolding.

Giving of Oneself to Life

Q: From what I've read of the ECK works, there seems to be a very strong element of self in it and not so much emphasis on helping the other person. Wanting to get the self into another plane rather than helping someone else to get there seems to be a slightly different approach.

As you gain in spiritual unfoldment, everyone in your circle of acquaintances is benefited and uplifted.

HK: There's a reason for this. So many people who step onto the path want to help the whole world, but often you'll find that they are barely able to make their own living. It's an ideal which is great but not practical because they haven't got their own house in order.

As you gain in spiritual unfoldment, everyone in your circle of acquaintances is benefited and uplifted.

We are working in the spiritual consciousness, not from ego or vanity, and we recognize the right of every person to have his sicknesses and his problems. The ECK Masters never interfere in another person's state of consciousness without his permission. I hold your personal life sacred and won't intrude in any way, even in the dream state, without your permission.

There are always do-gooders who want to dry out the drunk, when maybe the drunk doesn't want to be dried out. Or they want to save the soul of the man who has committed a crime and is on his way to the gallows. We really don't have that right. Soul must have the freedom of Its own state of consciousness.

One is required to pay the price for breaking the spiritual laws even though it is done in ignorance. This is the highest law. "Do unto others as you would have them do unto you" really means if I don't want people meddling in my life without permission, then I ought to extend that same privilege to others.

But yes, we do have compassion, and we do go out in life to be of service as individuals. If we get this Light of God coming into us, we can sit around and talk about it, or we can give It back in service—in quiet service—perhaps in the form of a good deed a day. Because as It comes in, we must give It out. But we don't brag about it or tell anybody why we are doing it. We give service because it's a necessity; when we don't give, all of a sudden we find things going wrong in our life.

The first step is to get this Light and Sound flowing into you. Once It comes in, you're halfway there: now you have to learn how to give It back out.

The first step is to get this Light and Sound flowing into you. Once It comes in, you're halfway there: now you have to learn how to give It back out. This is where the selfless giving of oneself to life takes place, whether it's pushing a child on a swing or listening to a person who has problems. This is how the spiritual life works. But we have to become strong and be able to help ourselves before we can help anyone else.

Hong Kong Regional Seminar, Kowloon, Hong Kong, November 17, 1982

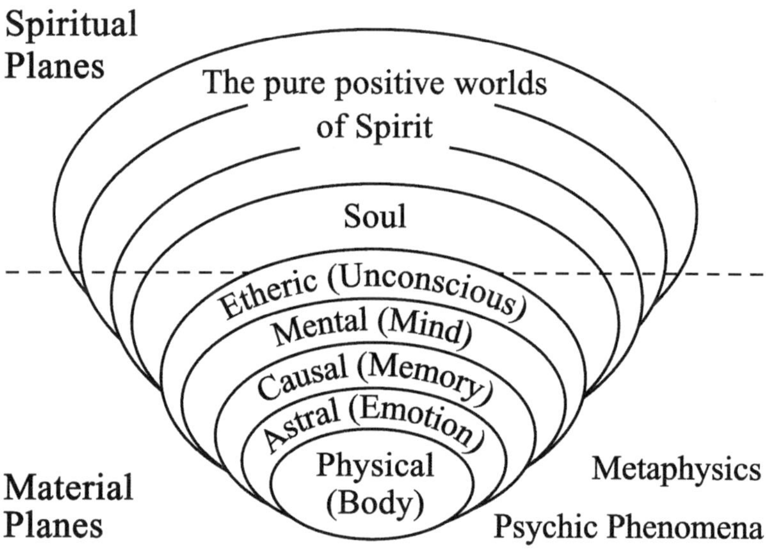

In the ECK works there are descriptions of the various heavens as guideposts that you can look to.

11
The Lost Key

I would like to welcome you this evening to Eckankar. Some of you have traveled a couple of miles, others of you have traveled many lifetimes.

Experience with the Light of God

I just had an interesting conversation with an individual I first met about three or four years ago. As we talked about various things, he mentioned an experience he'd had with the Light of God. It flowed into him in such a clear way that he wanted to spend the rest of his life having nothing more than this Light coming in. But after that experience he had no more for a long time, and he wondered why.

The Living ECK Master will not allow those who have put their spiritual life in his hands to become useless to society.

The reason is this: When we get the Light of God coming in, It can burn us. The Light is so pure that Soul desires nothing more than to exist in that Light for all eternity. While this in itself would sound commendable, like something we would all look forward to, the Living ECK Master will not allow those who have put their spiritual life in his hands to become useless to society.

After getting a little bit of this Light, many of the holy men who have been set up as saints by the different orthodox religions decided to isolate themselves from people and go off into the wilderness. Theirs became a selfish existence in which their enlightenment did nothing for their fellow man in any way.

When the Light comes in continuously, It can burn the individual. Therefore, we look to the second aspect of God, the Sound. There is actually a third aspect we look for on the spiritual path: the Master who can work with us to make contact with the Sound. This is the Audible Life Stream, also known as the Word of God. In the Bible, It is referred to as the Holy Spirit, the Holy Ghost, or the Comforter. Once this contact is made, this Voice of God takes us back on a spiritual wave toward the God center, back to God Consciousness.

Spiritual Liberation

This is what we are looking for. It's called spiritual liberation. Spiritual liberation actually comes at a point we call Self-Realization, which means that we have been freed from the cares of this world. I'm not saying that we no longer have problems, but we now have an understanding of those things which come into our life that must be faced. We see where they came from, how we caused them, and what to do about them so that we can live a life of greater happiness.

We develop a sense of humor and tolerance when things don't go the way we've planned.

As we have these experiences with Spirit and begin developing an understanding of what is happening in our daily life, we also ought to be able to develop a sense of humor and tolerance when things don't go the way we've planned. Too often our reaction is anger—I know my own used to be. If I planned something and it went wrong, I'd go into a black mood. That's just human nature.

We enjoy the low currents of human nature, usually because we do not realize that there is a way to pull ourselves out of this state and that the problems and troubles that we have are of our own making.

Giving Up Attachments

As the Light and Sound of God come in, we experience a spiritual upliftment that takes us above materialism. This doesn't mean that now we are willing to give up our material possessions, but it does mean giving up our undue attachment to these material things. We do not stop loving our family and friends, but we do give up the undue attachment to them.

On the path of ECK the Outer Master, which is myself, is established here only to show you how to reach the inner temple and the Inner Master. This is the basis of the teaching of Eckankar: to go to the inner temple and have direct experience with the ECK. Only in this way can you find out for yourself if there is such a thing as the Light which we see as a blue star, blue globe, or blue sphere or disk. It may be anything along these lines.

The Funny Side of Life

Last year the fellow who was traveling with us dutifully lost a key every once in a while—as if it went with his job.

When you're working for ECK, many things come into your life. I won't say it's going to be an easy life, but a lot of different things will happen. You learn to see the funny side of it.

Three of us were traveling together in Australia recently, and it seems whoever travels with me lately always loses an important key. Last year the fellow who was with us dutifully lost a key every once in a while—as if it went with his job. One time it was the key to a safe-deposit box, and when the clerk said, "If you don't find it, there will be a seventy-five-dollar charge to call in a locksmith," he started doing a very thorough search through his suitcase.

This year the key that kept getting lost was to the different rental cars we had. The first time it happened, we were trying to get to a meeting by seven o'clock. At about five to seven my friend called and asked where the driver was. He had lost the car keys and didn't find them until the last minute. We figured that was the end of it; certainly anybody who loses the car keys once shouldn't do it again—right?

Certainly anybody who loses the car keys once shouldn't do it again—right?

Two days later, after all of the talks and meetings were finished for the day, we went out to eat at a Chinese restaurant in Singapore. Halfway through the meal, our friend started patting his pockets again, wearing a wonderful expression on his face that meant he had lost something important. "I believe I've locked the keys in the car again," he said.

We just looked at him.

Well, Spirit will use you no matter where you are. Even if it looks as though you're making a mistake, you really are not. It will use you to spread a little of the Light and Sound that's coming into you as a result of the spiritual exercises. You may or may not be conscious of this Light and Sound of God that is coming in, but you find a way to give It back to other people. This doesn't mean talking their ear off and telling them all about your great experiences. You simply give back some service of love to the world, to your friend, your neighbor; and it may be simply by doing a good deed every day that no one ever knows about.

So this fellow went out to the parking lot—it was dark, hot, and sultry in Singapore that night—and started fiddling with the lock, using first a wire and then a screwdriver. Forty-five minutes later, he had a whole gathering of people around him.

Just when it looked as if we were going to have to forget the car and take a cab back, an acquaintance of the ECKist who had invited us out to dinner walked past. When our friend told her what happened, this lady immediately pointed to a Chinese gentleman who had just sat down behind us with his family. This scholarly looking man with glasses said he could help.

In just a few minutes he had opened the car door. "Now, did you pay close attention to how he opened the door?" we asked our companion. "No," he said. "It was dark, and he worked so fast that I didn't have a chance to see how he did it."

When there is a need, you find that Spirit will bring help if you just stay open and remain patient.

KEY TO THE SPIRITUAL WORLDS

Often we look for the key to the spiritual worlds and wonder where it is. We're too busy to see that the temple is actually within us.

While we're on the subject of keys: Often we look for the key to the spiritual worlds and wonder where it is. Many times it's so close—right in front of us—but we're too busy traveling thousands of miles to visit a guru here, there, and everywhere to see that the temple is actually within us.

There's an old story that when God made this world, man, and all creation, He said, "But Soul is a precious thing, and I want to put It somewhere safe. I believe I'll just put It in the heart of man; he'll never think to look for It there."

The third time we lost a key, it was late at night, and we decided to park the car in the underground garage of a hotel and go upstairs to the restaurant for a snack. We were hesitant about shutting and locking our doors, so we said to our friend, "Do you have the key?" He didn't answer but just slammed his door, and we took that to mean, Of course! Don't keep asking me if I have the key. That's what we thought he meant, but as soon as we slammed our doors shut, he started to motion wildly. "Oh, no!" we said. "Please tell us you're just joking." He said, "No, I'm not joking."

It was hot and muggy, and the smell of carbon monoxide was quite overwhelming in that underground garage. He suggested we go up to the air-conditioned lobby and browse through the shops while he got the door opened.

First he tried calling the Automobile Association of Singapore, but the twenty-four-hour-service number wouldn't answer. Then he talked to the bellman, who happened to spot a mechanic walking by. So the fellow who was with us, the bellman, and the mechanic took off for the garage. I believe they spent another forty-five minutes down there before they finally gave up and came back upstairs. We all sat up in the restaurant and had ourselves a nice little midnight snack while figuring out what to do; then he decided to try one more time.

We went down to the garage to watch him fiddle around with a piece of wire and demonstrate how far the state of the art of breaking into a car had come. After a while, I figured out how to make a special double loop in the wire. I wiggled it through the top of the window until finally I hooked the lock, pulled it up, and opened the door. This brought a lot of cheers.

With the life of Spirit an apparent problem comes up so that we can be thrown in with other people.

The Life of Spirit

This is the kind of thing that happens with the life of Spirit. An apparent problem comes up so that we can be thrown in with other people. This fellow was thrown in with mechanics. He may or may not have spoken the word *ECK* to them, but it isn't important; just being with others is a way of passing the Light and Sound along. At the same time, he was getting his own experience. In his defense, the travel schedule was rough, he had been going for many hours, and he was so tired that he really couldn't see straight anymore. After that, I tried to slow down the pace a little bit so that he could get some rest.

Just being with others is a way of passing the Light and Sound along.

Spirit will use us in this way, through ordinary, everyday living. You might say it's no great miracle to break into a car until you consider the fact that the person who sits down at the table behind you happens to be an expert at it. Each time something happened, we were able to figure our way out.

One of the spiritual principles that I have learned is that there is always a way, no matter what. If we have a health, financial, or some other kind of situation—there is always a way out.

Following Out a Cycle

Speaking about cars, another fellow had an interesting experience here in Hawaii just recently. Every time he got a rental car, there was something wrong with it. In just a day and a half he went through five cars, each with something seriously wrong with it. If you're on the path of ECK, you simply know that you have to follow out that cycle and not let it devastate you or get you so angry that it ruins your whole day.

The first time, he asked for a car but instead got a jeeplike vehicle with no window glass. "Where are the windows?" he asked. The man at the rental agency said, "There are windows for it, but we don't have any at the moment."

"Well, then, how do I lock packages up in it?" he said.

"You don't," said the rental agent.

The outside of the jeep was so rusted and battered that he was ashamed to drive it, so he said, "This won't do. You've got to get me something else."

He got another car, and when he and his wife got in and drove off, it seemed to handle OK except that it steered funny. It would just drift off the road. The next one had a muffler that clanged loudly because of a loose mounting; there was also an unidentifiable smell in the car. It was so bad that they had to buy a can of air freshener and spray it all around. It didn't help. Soon the smell was in their clothes, and it spread, getting worse and worse.

The last car seemed to be OK, if you could overlook the fact that it was covered with dents—the trunk, the roof, everything was dented. And if you happened to be in the backseat on the left side, you couldn't open the door to get out. I know because I tried. Someone had to go around the outside and open it. Still, this car seemed to run OK until yesterday; all of a sudden steam was blowing all over because the radiator had sprung a leak. The last thing I heard was that he planned to take it back and exchange it for another car.

What we learn out here can be taken inwardly; what's in there can be brought out here. We can learn from both states of consciousness, the human and the spiritual.

Understanding Our Inner and Outer Life

Life is like that when you get on the path of ECK. Things will begin to happen. You may not be aware of anything happening on the inner planes, but you definitely will notice that something is changing. Things will speed up in your common, ordinary, everyday life.

Our duty is to take what we see on the inner planes and use it to gain an understanding of what is happening out here. What we learn out here can be taken inwardly; what's in there can be brought out here. We can learn from both states of consciousness, the human and the spiritual.

All too often one has unrealistic dreams of what he is looking for in a spiritual sense, expecting a leader to do miracles. It's against the spiritual law to perform miracles to gain followers. This is a law that the spiritual travelers, or the ECK Masters, abide by very carefully. To violate it means that the individual who did so must suffer.

When you come to the state of self-mastery, it does not mean that you now have license to live life doing whatever you please. It simply means that now you know and understand the laws of Spirit as they apply to you. You know the things you can do and the things you cannot do. And while you make your way through life with these guidelines, you also are being a vehicle for Spirit.

THE KEY TO THE PATH OF SOUND AND LIGHT

The Spiritual Exercises of ECK are the key to this path. We want to see the Light and hear the Sound.

There are a number of ECK books that give some of the Spiritual Exercises of ECK. These exercises are the key to this path of Sound and Light.

We want to see the Light and hear the Sound. The Light may show up in a number of different ways. I've mentioned the Blue Light of the Mahanta. The Mahanta Consciousness is beyond the Christ state, the Buddhi state, and also cosmic consciousness—but there is always one more step. No matter what state of consciousness we look to, it will take us so far and then there is another that will take us beyond.

We look for heaven, but even in the Bible it is mentioned that, "In my Father's house are many mansions. . . ." Also, Saint Paul spoke of a man who had been caught up unto the third heaven. This is important because it presupposes heavens one and two.

In the ECK works, such as *The Tiger's Fang*, there are descriptions of these various heavens as a guidepost that you can look to. When you do your spiritual exercises and visit these planes, you may see the planes themselves or you may see the Light or hear the Sound that corresponds to that plane.

This Light and Sound is important for Soul. It is direct communication with God. This is how God communicates—through Divine Spirit, also known as the Holy Ghost, Comforter, Nam, or whatever you want to call It. This is something that is not understood by many religious teachings.

I don't ask you to believe me. I won't say that each of you will have the same experience, because you won't; Soul is an individual and unique entity. Each of you has had different experiences up until now, so each of you is going to have different experiences in the future. This is how it must be.

I'm not saying that this path works for everyone, because it doesn't, so we have a two-year trial period. First you can read the ECK books. Try the spiritual exercises that you find in *ECKANKAR—The Key to Secret Worlds*. There are several listed there, including the imaginative technique. There are over one hundred techniques given in *The Spiritual Exercises of ECK*. Try these techniques and experiment freely; you will have protection from the Inner Master. I can also work with you in the dream state.

Try these techniques and experiment freely; you will have protection from the Inner Master. I can also work with you in the dream state.

One of your tests of the individual who is going to be your spiritual guide ought to be: Can he help me on the physical plane as well as on the other side? Can he help me as the Inner Master, either through a contemplative exercise or in the dream state? Another method is being aware of the ways of Spirit: Can you see the workings of Spirit helping you in your daily life, even in small things?

This is my only purpose: to give those of you who are ready, who want to begin working your own way back to God, the opportunity to do so. I can't walk the path for you, and I won't. I can help you with some of the burdens, but I won't take them all from you. A debt to God that has been created must be repaid by the one who incurred the debt. This is the Law of Life: Whatsoever a man sows, that also shall he reap.

You are going to know for yourself from direct experience with the Light and Sound of God.

Of course, there is an even greater law, and this is the Law of Love. This is the Law of Spirit, the Light and Sound of God. You can bring It into your own life, and when you do, there will be no one who can take It from you or tell you this or that way is right for you. You are going to know for yourself from direct experience with the Light and Sound of God.

Hawaiian Regional Seminar, Honolulu, Hawaii, November 20, 1982

A marriage in the dream state means a closer marriage with Spirit and with God.

12
The Far Country

In the spiritual works, we put a lot of attention on the different planes that lead up to the first of the pure spiritual worlds, known as the Soul Plane. The orthodox heavens lie in the Mental Plane, which is on this side of the Soul Plane. What we are looking to do is visit the different regions—the Astral, Causal, Mental, and Etheric planes—leading to the Soul Plane, the first of the spiritual worlds. In this way, we can know and understand the different aspects of Soul to which these various planes of the God Worlds correspond.

The different planes that lead up to the Soul Plane are more like countries, or states or provinces within countries; and each has its unique way of approaching life.

Thinking in Parts or the Whole

In the lower worlds we have what you could call "thinking in parts." We know that the Astral and some of the other planes have over a hundred different regions. The planes are not stacked on top of each other as you will see illustrated in *The Spiritual Notebook*. They are more like countries, or states or provinces within countries; and each of these regions has its unique way of approaching life and expressing the state of consciousness of the inhabitants there.

For instance, in the United States you have the very easygoing way of life in Hawaii, and on the other hand you have the hustle and bustle of New York City. If a visitor from another plane saw life on a remote Hawaiian island while another visitor ended up in New York City, they could get into a real dispute with each other about who had *really* been to the Physical Plane. On the other hand, someone who has been to both locations, as well as other areas, would know that each visitor had been to the Physical Plane, but to different regions within it.

This is why those who have experiences on the inner planes, perhaps only on the Astral, can often run into problems. They go to a certain region, have experiences there, see certain entities, and then come back and say: This is it; I have seen the true reality. If they meet one of the gods established there, such as Jehovah, they might say, I have seen the Supreme Deity—now I will devote my life to God. Then they go out and start their own little group.

Beyond the Soul Plane in those worlds of Spirit, we begin to work in the whole. There are no regions or planes that we know of; it is simply one world of Light.

Beyond the Soul Plane in those worlds of Spirit, we begin to work in the whole. There are no regions or planes that we know of; it is simply one world of Light.

In the lower regions where we exist now, something can be known only by its counterpart—truth by untruth, light by darkness. At the Soul Plane, as this ECK Stream, or Spirit of God, comes down from the God center, It splits into two parts: the positive and the negative. We have manifestations of this split, and though we take it for granted, it shows up all around us. If you want to iron, you first put the plug into the wall outlet, and this uses alternating currents—the positive and the negative. We see the height of the mountains and the depths of the valleys, because the only way anything can be known in these lower worlds is in comparison to its opposite. We're always thinking in parts.

The Greek philosophers came close to having the spiritual viewpoint. They tried to have an overview when they looked at life as it existed here, and they would address it from the whole. In the West, we fragment it—man and woman, happiness and sadness—and generally view life in its parts.

Visiting the Other Planes

When we begin a study of the creative works, and as we do the Spiritual Exercises of ECK, we find that the creative aspects within ourselves begin to speed up. Inventors usually work with this creative aspect, even though they may never have heard of ECK. They may get the ideas for their creations on one of the other planes, generally the Astral Plane. Those of you who have read the ECK works are familiar with the astral museum, which has the prototype of every object ever to be invented.

Each of the planes has a sacred word you can sing or chant if you would like to visit there.

Each one of the planes has a sacred word that you can sing or chant if you would like to visit there. This applies to all of the planes in the lower worlds—the Physical, Astral, Causal, Mental, and Etheric Planes—and the Soul Plane. If you would like to visit one of these planes in the dream state, you can sing the word for that plane found in *The Spiritual Notebook*. Simply sing it for about five or ten minutes in a very quiet way, and then go to sleep. Because of the unique nature of Soul, some people have success sooner than others; you may not notice anything for a day, a week, even a month or more.

Beyond the Soul Plane there is another world known as the Invisible Plane. Beyond the invisible plane you come to the Endless world, known by that name because the space is so boundless. I say *space*, but really at that point we exist in realms that are beyond matter, energy, space, and time, which constitute the lower worlds. I don't speak much of the higher planes because, frankly, they are beyond description.

We gain the state of consciousness that comes in those realms, and the higher we go, the more difficult it can be to live here in the physical unless we bury ourselves in the activities of daily life. We get our experiences and grow here, enjoying people and the lessons of everyday living.

Gaining Experience

We recognize, or come to an understanding, that there is a purpose for living here in the physical body: We are Soul, and we are here to gain experience. For this reason we don't try to make a hasty exit through self-destruction. This includes things such as the abuse of alcohol, which actually is a subtler, slower form of self-destruction.

We ought to be able to lift ourselves into a higher, better state of consciousness. We do this in ECK through the spiritual exercises.

Often the way we gain experience is through pain and hardship, but not always. We ought to be able to lift ourselves into a higher, better state of consciousness. We do this in ECK through the spiritual exercises.

One of the things we encountered in our recent trip to Australia was a phenomenon called the Australian wave. At the airport, I saw a huge picture of a sand formation that looked like a big wave, as though one of the ocean waves had been taken and cast into sand. I thought, That must be the Australian wave I've heard about. It's not.

They have a fly there, the pestiest thing you've ever seen, that doesn't bite and is harmless except for one thing: It needs moisture because of the dryness in Western Australia, so it goes for the eyes, nose, and mouth. As a result, the people are forever waving in the air. Yet they do laugh about it and call it the Australian wave.

This is the kind of thing we contend with; it's part of our education. And since the people there can't get rid of the flies, they've developed a sense of humor about this rather negative thing. The fly itself is harmless, as I said, but it stays with you constantly. When I studied all the tourist brochures, they talked about the lovely sand and the beaches, which are just beautiful, yet for some reason not one of them mentioned the fly or the Australian wave.

One of the benefits of the path of ECK is that much of our karma can be worked off on the inner planes so that we don't have to go through it here.

As we go through the lower worlds and have experiences on the inner planes, such as the Astral Plane, we may not remember them. One of the benefits of the path of ECK is that much of our karma can be worked off on the inner planes so that we don't have to go through it here. If we've created debts, they must be repaid to God. But on the path of ECK we have this advantage: They do not always have to be worked out here on the physical; they can be worked off on the inner planes in the dream state.

UNDERSTANDING DREAMS

The dream state is interesting to work with. Every so often someone will report having a dream about a wedding. If it's a man, he might say, "I dreamed of marrying a certain woman." Then he forms the mistaken conclusion that it means they are Soul mates. There aren't Soul mates in ECK; that is an occult concept.

Each Soul is an individual and unique being. In the lower planes we have the two parts of our lower nature: the positive and the negative. When we get to the Soul Plane, we find that these two parts become one. This is called the self-recognition state, what the Greeks referred to when they said, Know thyself. Up until this time, knowing the self has meant merely knowing the ego, or the little self, rather than our true spiritual nature. Our consciousness changes when we reach the Soul Plane; we now have an outlook on life that is balanced.

In the dream state, marriage simply means that

Soul is having an inner initiation where the two parts of Itself are drawn a little closer together. We are looking for the linkup of Soul with the ECK, this Divine Spirit which comes from God. Each time you see a marriage on the inner planes, regardless of the personality you perceive as your mate, it means a closer marriage with Spirit and with God.

Too many misunderstand this and pester the other person on the physical plane: "I know we were meant for each other. All I have to do is be patient and wait until you know it too, and then we'll be married and live happily ever after." You lay all kinds of subtle traps to try to catch that person, and then when you finally have your way and get married, you find out who really got trapped.

Giving Others Freedom

Marriage is a funny thing. Nobody likes to admit it, but sometimes one gets married and puts their best face forward for a couple of months with the idea that you'll change your spouse later. If he drinks a little now, you'll think you can get rid of that habit later. We really don't change anyone. We shouldn't even try. The hardest part of a marriage, once you find someone you feel you can live with, is to let your mate be just the way he or she is.

As you come to the path of ECK, there are going to be changes—but they are not going to come about through nagging. The Living ECK Master won't nag you or say, Give up smoking and alcohol this instant.

As you come to the path of ECK, there are going to be changes—but they are not going to come about through nagging. The Living ECK Master won't nag you or say, Give up smoking and alcohol this instant. One person I talked to wanted to find out more about Eckankar, but he hadn't been willing to step onto the path because he misunderstood one thing. He thought if he got on the path of ECK that meant he had to drop smoking and drinking right away. He wasn't ready to quit. He thought somebody would say, "Don't do it."

Of course, I expect more from the leadership in ECK. It's similar to running a company: you want good salesmen and business executives. If you have a sales representative whose clothes are dirty and whose tie is crooked, then your business will go down in his department. This man is not a good representative of what you stand for; he doesn't reflect your company's image. So I expect more from the ECK leaders. But when someone comes on the path of ECK and he's struggling to get rid of these habits, I usually don't say anything. I know these habits will drop away by themselves within several years.

I know these habits will drop away by themselves within several years.

ECK and Drugs Don't Mix

The objection I do have is to the use of drugs. They not only do physical damage, they also do inner damage. The inner centers are opened to extremely negative influences that come out here in the physical. People who practice drug use are usually of no help to themselves spiritually. The path of ECK is really just for those who are sincere in returning to God.

The drug experience will never bring you God. If someone is serious in their use of drugs and is not trying to drop them, for instance by making a devoted effort through a detoxification program, then I generally suggest that he not step onto the path of ECK.

Spirit, Itself, will not allow something like this within the whole body of ECK. It begins to clean and purify Itself of the dross, and life becomes very hard for the individual who is still under the habit of drugs. It's a kindness when I ask him not to step onto the path. This way he can work things out and drop the drug habit at his own pace. It's not a happy experience for someone who tries to mix drugs with ECK. Spirit won't allow it.

If you have any questions that can be answered or unraveled, I'm willing to take the time. Sometimes this unravels something spiritually, too, which opens up a person to a greater understanding of life.

A Spiritual Exercise Just for You

Q: If a chela asks inwardly what the most appropriate spiritual exercise would be for him, will the Inner Master communicate this to him?

HK: Yes, but the Inner Master will lead you gradually, and you won't necessarily get it on the inner planes. You may be going through an ECK discourse when suddenly you'll find an exercise that seems to strike your imagination; it will seem to pop out at you. Remember to experiment freely with your spiritual exercises in case they are not working. They are guidelines, the basis from which to work. Experiment with them. Use your creative, or imaginative, faculty.

Experiment freely with your spiritual exercises. They are guidelines, the basis from which to work.

The Discipline of Fasting

Q: Are there ways to work out karma without having to go through some of the pain and suffering that normally come as part of life? It seems to come in random ways. I read recently in *The Essene Gospel* that Jesus connected fasting with relieving karma. Is fasting relevant to relieving karmic conditions?

HK: Fasting is one way. It's a discipline. In ECK there are several different kinds of fasts that we use. These fasts are done one day a week for twenty-four hours, usually on a Friday. One is a mental fast, and this can be done in two ways: You can keep your attention on the Inner Master as much as you can, or you can consciously remove every negative thought that comes up. Visualize it being put into the ECK Life Stream where the Light and Sound of God can neutralize it. The mental fast is especially good for those who have health concerns and cannot abstain from food.

The mental fast is especially good for those who have health concerns and cannot abstain from food.

There is also a partial fast where you can eat one meal, or drink fruit juices or eat fruit. Of course, you may choose to do a fast drinking only water, if your health permits. You choose whichever one is right for you at the time, but it changes. Fasting can be beneficial, and it does help.

This doesn't mean you want to go on very long fasts, nor do you want to go on a fast to change another person's state of consciousness. There are people today who will go on a fast in order to try to bring about a change in consciousness about nuclear power and other things. To fast for the purpose of changing another's state of consciousness is a violation of the spiritual law. You pay for trying to move people from their state of being.

Fasting is very good for working out karma. I hesitate to say this because if someone doesn't understand it, he may go on ten-day fasts. He figures if one day is good, ten days is better. Then he starts losing his teeth or developing other imbalances, because he has upset the body's systems. It's better to do any kind of extended fasting under the direction of a medical doctor, to make sure that your health can stand it.

There can be a benefit from it for some, but we are not into asceticism, and most of us do not need such an extreme. Buddha started out living the life of plenty and then went to starvation and fasting until he was nothing more than skin stretched over a framework of bones. But he found that wasn't it, and he finally came to what he called the middle way. When he went the middle path, many of his followers left because they thought you had to starve yourself to become spiritual. In truth, God really doesn't care what you eat or don't eat.

Working in Harmony

Q: If I were to observe some sort of behavior in an ECK leader where I felt I could be of assistance, should I just sit back and wait, or should I approach the person and offer my assistance?

HK: What kind of behavior are you talking about? Something that seems to be holding back the area?

ECKist: Either that or maybe the quality of their leadership skills.

HK: We usually have a chain of command in the leadership, and like anything else, it's not perfect. You know what happens in a marriage when you try to change a spouse because, from your point of view, he could be better. Generally what we see in other people are our own shortcomings.

As leaders, we each have our blind spots; sometimes we don't see what others see. If you feel someone's behavior is standing in the way of other people hearing about the word of ECK, by all means you could mention something. I would. Then leave it at that and put it into the hands of Spirit. Spirit has Its own way of working on a situation. This way, we don't get involved in nagging each other. We can work with each other in the spirit of fellowship and love.

I'd just work quietly to give back in service some of the love that has been poured through me as the Sound and Light.

I'd just let it go and do what I could, working quietly to give back in service some of the love that has been poured through me as the Sound and Light. I'd have to give it out somehow, and if I were not able to work with the leadership, then I'd have to do it quietly myself, even outside the works of ECK. A good deed every day that no one else knows about is a very good way to do it, because this begins to open up the heart center. When we begin to give of ourselves to all life, this is when we find more success with the spiritual exercises.

When we begin to give of ourselves to all life, we find more success with the spiritual exercises.

Make Changes Gradually

Q: On the subject of fasting, you've said that God doesn't care what we eat or don't eat. Yet I've heard many times the concept that vegetarianism leads to spiritual growth. Is that relevant or not?

HK: Eating a vegetarian diet doesn't necessarily make you more spiritual. Some people have found, even in their childhood, that they couldn't eat meat, and for them vegetarianism may be the way to go. But someone who has been a meat eater all his life and suddenly decides to stop eating meat may find it causes problems in his health. In ECK we don't say, If you're not a vegetarian, you're not being spiritual. Some paths decree that their followers be vegetarian, whether or not it's right for them, in the false belief that this leads to spirituality—and it does not.

It's very difficult to make a sudden change of any kind, whether it's in nutrition or in religious teachings. This is why I recommend that someone who is studying the ECK writings, or considering stepping onto the path of ECK, do it gradually. Read the ECK books, study them over a period of months or even years, and make a gradual transition before taking it on. The same with a diet. Life just isn't set up for rapid changes without problems.

Creation

Q: I have a question from my son: Did God really just speak and the world was created?

HK: The children always do that. They get to the heart of a question real fast. As much as we can put it into words—which come from the Mental Plane but are not in the spiritual worlds—I could just simply say, Yes.

ECK and Other Teachings

Q: Are there other organizations and movements in the world which you feel are in accord with ECK?

HK: Some are very close. There are many states of consciousness, and truth is never hidden. If a person will make a search, he'll find that the secret teachings which we speak of in Eckankar are secret only to those who haven't found the source within themselves and how to unlock it. There are teachings that are very close to the path of ECK, and I recognize even those that are far away from the path of ECK. They fill a spiritual need for a particular state of consciousness that is shared by a certain group of people.

Q: Is there anything that you feel distinguishes ECK as being unique from anything else happening on this planet at this time?

What makes the ECK path unique is the ability to have spiritual liberation in this lifetime while still in the physical body.

HK: What makes it almost unique, but not quite, is the teaching of the Sound and Light. There are other paths that teach this up to a certain point only, and then go no further. What makes the ECK path unique is the ability to have spiritual liberation in this lifetime and to gain the kingdom of heaven while still in the physical body. Very few other paths will tell you that you can have this.

We speak of the expansion of consciousness, or Soul Travel, where you gain the ability to go into the heavenly worlds, making a smooth transition from this physical state of consciousness to the spiritual, or the inner. As you do this, you begin to see how people live on the other side; and as you get an understanding of life on the other side, you lose your fear of death. You develop a greater ability to live, understand, and enjoy life while you are here. This is the whole function of the path of ECK: to help develop the greater spiritual man; to work with the whole instead of the parts.

The path of ECK is to help develop the greater spiritual man; to work with the whole instead of the parts.

Most of the other teachings work in the parts. They'll emphasize astral travel, for instance, or speak of the Mental Plane, the Mental bodies, and of the third heaven. Saint Paul spoke of the third heaven, and this corresponds to the Mental Plane.

I can't prove any of this to you in words, but you can do the spiritual exercises and go there to find out for yourself. We can't prove these works to anyone except by giving them the methods. This is another advantage of the path of ECK. You can try the spiritual exercises—over two hundred are listed throughout the written works—and you can begin having your own experience with the Sound and Light of God.

There is some reference in the Bible to the Sound and Light of God, but nowhere that I know of does it give techniques to enable people to have the experiences themselves. Christ said that the things that he did, others shall do and greater; and yet the knowledge of how to do these things was lost by the leaders over the subsequent generations and centuries. The tongues of fire and the sound of a rushing wind that came at Pentecost are two aspects of the Sound and Light that are referred to in the Bible. Saul of Tarsus saw this Light when he was on the road to Damascus. But since the leaders were not able to lead the people to the Sound and Light, they made the secret teachings taboo.

We ought to be able to duplicate these experiences, as Christ mentioned. Yet you find that anyone who admits to having them today is immediately squashed by the orthodox churches. Since the leaders don't know the means and methods whereby an individual may have these experiences in safety, they have to legislate against the practice of it. This was why it was so important to the early Christian church to get rid of Gnosticism.

One can make a real study of the inability of many of today's religious leaders to take their followers into the Light and Sound of God, as their founders did. So now they work mostly with material tools and power—things which have nothing to do with spirituality.

There is much help available through these different paths to God. God created them for the different levels of Soul.

This is not a criticism; there is much help available through these different paths to God. God created them for the different levels of Soul. I don't want to discredit anyone's belief—all of our beliefs are valid, and in a true sense, there is no right or wrong way. The difference is in the states of consciousness we are at.

Balancing the Spiritual and Social Consciousness

Q: Is there emphasis on social consciousness in ECK?

HK: We recognize that the parents must bring up their children to fit into this society. When the ECK writings and teachings came out in the late 1960s, some of the parents misinterpreted what Paul meant when he said ECK is the path of freedom. They let their children run loose and act like a bunch of little monsters.

Children need to learn the laws as well as their duties and responsibilities in society. They can't feel this path of freedom gives them the right to go into a grocery store and steal candy, thinking, *This is my right. Nobody can tell me what to do, because I'm Soul, and I am free.* With that kind of freedom, one can find himself in jail.

The social aspect, in a broader sense, is that when we look primarily for our spiritual unfoldment in life, we ought to be able to enjoy our friends and family in a greater way than before.

Q: Are we our brother's keeper in the sense of being obligated to better the world because we live here?

HK: We don't say Eckankar takes the position that there should be no more hunger in Africa, for instance. As an organization we stay out of the social issues. However, we don't divorce ourselves from life. As we get a greater understanding, we work quietly as individuals. When it comes to having our freedom threatened, such as in a woman's choice of whether or not to have a child, we can speak out as individuals if we choose.

As vehicles for ECK we naturally uplift everything around us. If you want to join a social club or you want to work with a national organization, then by all means do so. Others of you may want to work with political groups to bring about the betterment of society. So do it.

We have to give in some way, but we don't get into political issues by exercising power. We work as individuals, not as the formal organization of ECKists banded together to support some issue and threatening to vote in a bloc against someone because he doesn't suit our way of thinking.

Society is uplifted by our presence, not only because we are silent channels for the ECK, but also because we are active doers in the things that interest us.

As individuals we go out into society, and it is uplifted by our presence, not only because we are silent channels for the ECK, but also because we are active doers in the things that interest us.

Q: Everything in these teachings seems to concern the singular Soul. It's so personal, with no attention to your surroundings. Isn't that being too self-centered?

HK: Before you can help anybody else, you've first got to be able to help yourself. The quickest, most direct method of doing this without bringing more karma into your life, which brings unhappiness, is to raise your own state of consciousness. As one person is lifted, so are all others to some degree. Too many people who want to go out and save the world, you'll notice, are poor. They want to go out and do a lot for other people, but if you really look at them, you find they aren't even able to help themselves and get their own lives in order.

It begins at home, with yourself. If you don't begin here, you open the door to meddling in other people's affairs whenever they, according to your opinion, are not conducting their life correctly. We must start at home; before we can help anybody else, we must first be able to help ourselves.

Exercise

Q: I'm a runner and have done several marathons. When I've completed these long runs, I've noticed an unusual feeling of well-being. As a matter of fact, I've felt like a million dollars. I assume this is more or less due to the endorphin buildup in the body as it exercises. This is a drug, in a sense, and I just wonder if this type of drug would be harmful to spiritual development as are the chemical drugs.

When the Light of God comes in very pure and clear, you want nothing more than to bathe yourself in It.

HK: No. The air actually is the ECK coming in. It causes certain effects, but it's more like the Light of God I spoke of last night: When It comes in very pure and clear, you want nothing more than to bathe yourself in It.

It's better to bathe yourself in the higher aspects of life than in the negative. There's nothing wrong with running if you are healthy, and as long as you do it in balance. You can't run all the time; otherwise, unless you're carrying messages or something like that, you'd be pretty useless to your fellow man. But I don't consider there to be any negative effect from it because of the uplift-ment it brings to many people.

FIRST INITIATION

Q: How do you get your First Initiation?

HK: This initiation comes in the dream state, after you actively step on the path of ECK. It generally comes six months to a year after you begin to study ECK. Some people remember this very clearly—not everybody—but whether you do or not, it comes. Six months is a rough estimate; sometimes it takes longer, other times it comes very fast. The First Initiation takes place completely on the inner. The Second Initiation is given in the physical.

STARTING THE DAY RIGHT

Q: How can we be better channels for the ECK?

HK: You may find it helpful to declare yourself a vehicle for God each morning. Just make a statement such as, I declare myself a vehicle for God. Or you can use the ECK terms: I declare myself a vehicle for the Sugmad (which is God), the ECK (or Spirit), and the Mahanta (which is this high state of consciousness that we look to). Then go about your duties throughout the rest of the day. You don't even have to think about it anymore: You know that every experience that you have that day is for your spiritual unfoldment. If a negative situation comes up with your fellow employees or what have you, there is a way to handle it.

Declaring yourself a vehicle for Spirit and God is a great help in giving you an understanding of the purpose of your everyday life.

You will find that declaring yourself a vehicle for Spirit and God is a great help in giving you an understanding of the purpose of your everyday life.

You'll also find it will help to take those tangles out of the stomach in the morning, when you have to go to work but would rather not.

Making the Transition to ECK

Q: I understand you were studying for the ministry in Christianity at one time. How did you make the transition from Christianity to something like Eckankar instead of another Christian path?

I had searched everywhere, even while a Christian. I had never gotten satisfactory answers about the question of death.

HK: I had searched everywhere, even while a Christian. I had never gotten satisfactory answers about the question of death. Out in the country where we worked, when anybody died—or translated, as we say in ECK—somebody had to dig the grave. This job was usually left to the young farm boys. I would see this big, dark hole, a person in a coffin stuck in it, and dirt thrown on top of it; and I'd say I don't want to be put in that hole, ever. There were other things that bothered me, too, such as salvation being only for those who have heard of Jesus.

Well, this is fine, I thought, but at least two-thirds of the people in the world from the time Jesus was born have never heard of him. The only answer I got from my teachers was either, "We must leave that to God's grace," or "They are damned." I also wondered about all the people before Jesus came who didn't know the prophecies. What about them? What about the Buddhists and Hindus? Did this invalidate their way to God? Their consciousness? In other words, why had God allowed all these different paths? Certainly they, too, had the light of spirituality. These were my personal questions, and I continued to wonder.

Even while technically still a Christian, by the time I got in the service I had stopped going to church. I found it was mostly a social organization that had no way to show me how to find that Light and Sound of God that I'd read about in the Bible.

I wondered how this failure had come about, what had happened to lose the knowledge that must have existed at one time. Then I began a private study that lasted for a number of years through the different aspects of the occult, through different paths such as the Rosicrucians and Edgar Cayce, and through a whole lot of other information. I made a personal study because I wanted to know for myself.

About this time, I came across Eckankar. It rang a bell for me. Everybody comes to ECK in a unique manner. It's not something that can be rationalized or explained or defended.

If you are interested in the works of ECK, I would suggest you look at some of the introductory books that are available. These will give you an understanding of the basics of ECK so that you can get an overview and find out whether or not this is what you have been looking for.

We try to give freedom on this path of ECK in all ways, to all people.

It may or may not be. This is a good way to look, to study, and to get in contact with the Spiritual Exercises of ECK, which you may try in the privacy of your own home, where no one will bother you. We try to give freedom on this path of ECK in all ways, to all people.

Thank you for coming.

Hawaiian Regional Seminar, Honolulu, Hawaii, November 21, 1982

When the compass was invented, and captains first used them on board their ships, their crew members thought it was devil worship because they didn't understand what made the needle turn.

13
Finding a Path to God

An American ECKist went to Hong Kong a couple of months ago to do a musical presentation. When we met there, at the end of his stay, he said that the entire time he was there he felt culture shock. He was more than ready to come home and asked if I'd ever felt any cultural shock of that nature.

I said yes, when I left Wisconsin and moved to Texas for the first time. Texas was about as flat as Wisconsin, but it had no trees that I would call a tree. I wasn't in East Texas, but out in the desert part, in West Texas, where it is flat and sandy with very little vegetation.

We all need something to look up to that's a little higher and beyond ourselves, whether it's in a physical way or in a spiritual way.

The ECKist said the first time he had gone to Wisconsin he experienced culture shock too, because it was so flat. He had come from the mountain areas. I told him when you live in Wisconsin as a native, you spend a lot of time walking in the woods. Anytime you want to see where you are, you look up to the top of the trees to see where the sun is in the sky. This was my mountain. We all need something to look up to that's a little higher and beyond ourselves, whether it's in a physical way or in a spiritual way.

If you take a walk in a city, it's easy to tell the visitors from the people who live there. The visitors are always looking around, rubbernecking. It's very easy for a beggar to spot one, and he won't hesitate to walk right up and ask a tourist for some money. The city dweller, the one who is at home in his town, never looks up. He just plods along looking down at the pavement, because all the sights—the streets and buildings and everything else—have become very commonplace.

Something I do when I get to a city I haven't visited before is to act like a native. I'll look at the ground and watch my feet for about half a block when I see a beggar coming close enough to catch me. They know. Yet if you wear an ordinary jacket instead of a good topcoat and just shuffle along like everybody else, they'll leave you alone.

Of course, there are the ECK Masters who come in disguise. They won't leave you alone no matter where you look. There have been people who had contact with these ECK Masters long before 1965, when Paul Twitchell brought out the teachings of Eckankar. You may be one of those who have had contact with the power of ECK or with an individual who knew and understood a power greater than himself.

States of Consciousness

This life comes but one time, and in ECK we want to live as much of it as possible in full consciousness.

When we are born, we are blessed not only with certain genes but also with a certain state of consciousness. It's rare that a person will go very far beyond the state of consciousness that he gets at birth. It's one thing to be born into a state of consciousness, but it's not good to die there. When you step onto any path, whatever it is, you owe it to yourself to grow. This life comes but one time, and in ECK we want to live as much of it as possible in full consciousness. This is what we are looking for on the path of ECK: full consciousness.

A woman who wrote to me recently said, "When you speak about God-Realization, I have absolutely no idea what you're talking about. But I do know what you mean when you say freedom." She had this enduring flame that was always burning within her, demanding that she have freedom—spiritual freedom.

Unless we have one of the higher states of consciousness, beginning with cosmic consciousness and moving upward, this means nothing to us. When poets and mystics struggle to put their experiences on paper, all we do is read their pretty words. There is no way to explain what it means. The Greeks said, Know thyself. It's not an understanding of a mental kind, such as knowing what kind of clothes you like to wear or what you like to buy in the grocery store. It's something else. And the only way to come to this understanding is through a study of the Light and Sound of God.

There is a saying in business that if you have a product, you emphasize the aspects that are unique. There are different paths that speak of the Light and Sound of God, but they speak of It very indirectly. Very few are able to tell you exactly how to reach this Light and Sound. We can have the intellectual understanding of God, but that's not God, nor is it an understanding of Soul.

There are different paths that speak of the Light and Sound of God, but they speak of It very indirectly. Very few are able to tell you exactly how to reach this Light and Sound.

NEAR-DEATH EXPERIENCES

At the beginning of January, there was a TV program on near-death experiences. It was about people who, at one time or another, were led out of the body—usually through illness, heart attack, or an accident—went into the other worlds, and then came back. Some of the things that happened to them were quite astounding, but one of the greatest shocks was having to come back here to live in the physical world and carry on as usual.

One of the people interviewed was a writer. She

had had an allergic reaction to something that caused her to lose her ability to breathe. A few seconds later she found herself outside the physical body. Someone called the fire department, and they came racing over. While she was out of the body, she could see the people running around trying to administer aid to her physical body lying there. At first she thought to herself, *Oh well, that's me; it's all over.* Actually, Soul doesn't think; It perceives. Finally it hit her: *But that isn't me. I'm me.* And she realized that was merely her body, a physical temple, something which she had been occupying. It was not her True Self.

The principles of ECK teach us and give us confidence about the life hereafter while we are still here in the physical body, so that we can have Self-Realization and God-Realization, as well as move into the kingdom of heaven within this lifetime.

When she looked back, she saw the earth wrapped in a beautiful glowing light. She experienced such peace that it upset her when it was suggested that she had to return to the physical body.

When this woman saw her family and the other people crying and carrying on, she decided she didn't want any part of such grief, so she turned her back on it. Soon she found herself moving rapidly away from earth into space. When she looked back, she saw the earth wrapped in a beautiful glowing light. She experienced such peace that it upset her when it was suggested that she had to return to the physical body.

These people have a hard time readjusting to the physical plane, but the main benefit of their experience is that they no longer have a fear of death. If they don't know the principles of life, they haven't learned that now they must come back and fulfill the destiny for which they came into this world.

Another guest on this program was a school administrator who had left his body and had seen the Light of God. As he got closer and closer to It, the love and joy became indescribable. He said if you were to take the happiest experience you ever had in your whole life and multiply it by a million, you still wouldn't be close.

This is what happens with spiritually awakened people who have these higher states of realization. There aren't that many walking among the human race. When they have it, there is no way they can tell another person what it's like, simply because so often the experience is beyond the Mental Plane. They are working as Soul in the worlds of pure Spirit. Without knowing the way of ECK or the laws of Spirit, they struggle to find the peace and harmony of knowing they are living, right here and now, in a moment that is sacred in eternity because the very ground they walk on is holy.

A Healing in the Dream State

A person saw an ECK Master about four years before she found out about Eckankar. She was going through extremely difficult times in her personal life and had gotten to a point where she even thought about taking her own life. She didn't understand that if life here is difficult, it is simply to offer a way for us to grow. That for every obstacle there is a solution—there is always a way. She didn't know this.

One night in the dream state, an ECK Master came to her. The setting was a beautiful, sandy beach with a clear blue sky.

One night in the dream state, an ECK Master came to her. The setting was a beautiful, sandy beach with a clear blue sky. The man walked along the beach with her to a lighthouse, which for her was the point where the Light and Sound of God came flowing into her. She visited this lighthouse nightly for over a year, until she was again healed emotionally, physically, and mentally.

Then in about 1969, she came in contact with the students of a Sikh master who had left his body. One of these people had come across the book about Paul Twitchell entitled *In My Soul I*

Am Free. When they heard there would be an Eckankar seminar in Las Vegas, several of them went to check out this man Paul Twitchell. Afterward, they said, "Yes, this guy is the one!"

Each of those people went to their own inner master, who wasn't able to serve as a physical master because he had died, or translated, and asked, "Is this the master for me?"

The framework of this question is important. Too often man, in his vanity, feels that if he finds a religious path or a teaching that is good enough for him, it's got to be good enough for everyone else too. No matter which path he follows, there's no religious follower like the zealot, especially one who has just stepped onto a new path. At first, he is enlivened and so full of inspiration that he's an embarrassment to the rest of the church members. They keep away from him until he cools down a little bit and gets some common sense.

Communicating with God

We look for experiences and direct knowledge with the Light and Sound of God because this is communication with the deity: God speaks through the Light and Sound.

This Light of God comes in and purifies us, but the measure that comes to Soul is only as much as we can handle.

When this Light comes on different planes, we see It as different colors. During our spiritual exercises, we may catch glimpses of this Light. Generally at first It will be blue, or sometimes white, yellow, or green. This is the Light of God which comes in and purifies us; but the measure that comes to Soul is only as much as we can handle.

It's best to be careful and not read too many of the ECK books or other books available on the spiritual teachings. Sometimes when we read from two or three paths all at once, our karma speeds up and we wonder why we are having such a hard life. It's very easy to point a finger at the last path we got on and say, This is what's causing all my troubles. The real problem is that we don't have the common sense to back off and not eat our spiritual breakfast, lunch, and dinner all at once. It's all right to eat three meals a day or more, if you can spread them out and not give yourself spiritual indigestion.

The Blue Light may come in different ways. One ECK photographer was processing film in the darkroom. All of a sudden the room was lit by a brilliant blue light.

The Blue Light may come in different ways. One of the ECKists, a photographer who works in a darkroom, told me this story. I could appreciate it because I worked as a cameraman in printing for the last few years. On this day she had a red light on in the darkroom for the film she was working with. As she was processing the film, all of a sudden the room was lit by a brilliant blue light. She said, "Oh, no! Who opened the door?" She was turning around to look when she realized It was the Light of ECK. At that particular moment, as her mind was busy and fully occupied with her work, this Light of God was able to come in. And incidentally, It didn't destroy the film. The Blue Light of ECK doesn't do that.

Thomas Merton, a Catholic mystic, wrote *The Seven Storey Mountain*, which told of his struggle and search to come to some realization and understanding of what God wanted of him. One day, as he was lying with his face in the dust, he said, "God, I know what you want of me. You want me to stop thinking so much about myself." With his face still to the ground and his superior standing right there wondering what was going on, he said, "No, no, you don't want that of me at all. You want me to think more about you." Then he started to laugh out loud. "No," he said, "it isn't even that. You want me to go into the area of consciousness where there is no thought." Thomas Merton had seen the truth that the Greeks spoke of: Know thyself. This is the point where you go beyond the mind. The mind is dropped, and Soul operates by direct perception.

It's something that cannot be explained or defended; all you can do is point someone to the spiritual exercises so they can find truth for themselves.

You will find dozens of creative techniques to experiment with in *The Spiritual Exercises of ECK.* See if these work for you. Let this be the test. It doesn't work for everyone, any more than it's right for everyone to be a Catholic. For some it is right, for others it's not. Some are just there visiting and looking before moving on—maybe next they'll go to the Episcopal Church or become atheists.

One thing Eckankar brings out is that there is a definite difference between the physical body and the Soul body.

Saint Paul said that the body can never reach the Kingdom of God—and it can't. One of the things Eckankar brings out is that there is a definite difference between the physical body and the Soul body.

How Religious Teachings Evolve

Religious teachings can evolve from an original leader who has some understanding and insight into the heavens beyond the Physical Plane and who knows some of the laws of Spirit. He can perhaps travel in the other worlds to the Astral, Causal, Mental, and Etheric Planes—and to the Soul Plane, which is the dividing line between the material and the spiritual worlds. The original leader can travel, and he can see. Then come the disciples who try to carry forth the master's teaching with a little bit less of the Light. But in time these disciples pass on too.

When Jesus said, "Follow me," in a way he was speaking to the primitive state of consciousness of his disciples. And when they said, "Well, we are," they meant, We are walking in the dirty, dusty road with you. Can't you see that? But he didn't mean that. He meant that they should go with him in the spiritual state of consciousness, into the higher planes. They weren't able to do that.

So the original leader takes the message and carries most of the Light, but when he dies, he moves on.

Other people who know mostly the business end of the religion become the leaders. But since they often don't understand about the truth and reality of a person having existence as Soul beyond the physical body, they outlaw such things as Gnosticism—one of the early beliefs in Christianity. And pretty soon the spiritual Light grows dim in that religious teaching.

There is no one religious teaching which is best for all of us. You may be in a particular faith today just because your parents were in it. If you trace back the history of any faith, you will find that it has undergone many changes. I'm familiar with the Lutheran Church; if I were to take it back far enough, I'd see a time when my great-great-grandparents were not Lutherans, because there was no Lutheran Church. Going back even farther, I would see that at one time all the Lutherans had been Catholics, but they had left the church because it failed them. The leaders no longer knew about the spiritual Light and could no longer give direction to their people.

When this happens, the dogma grows stronger, the list of dos and don'ts, shalls and shall nots, grows longer. But as long as a religion performs a useful function for most of the people—and it can be anything, even a social gathering—they may find peace and comfort with their neighbors. This is good—if they are growing.

There is a religion on this earth that will fit the consciousness of just about every individual, except for the atheist and the agnostic. They have their own way, their own ideal, their own mountain, their own treetop.

If you are stepping onto a spiritual path and you actually don't have any experience yourself, what do you do?

Guidance on the Spiritual Journey

If you are stepping onto a spiritual path and you actually don't have any experience yourself, what do you do? You look around and hope to find someone who knows what he is talking about. In ECK I won't promise that your way will be easy, but you will have the assistance of the ECK books where you can learn about the Spiritual Exercises of ECK, and you can try them out for yourself at home. When you try these spiritual exercises—whether it happens in a week, a month, a year, or two years—at some time you ought to begin having experiences with the Light and Sound of God.

Someone will say, "I hear the sound of sparrows during contemplation. What plane am I on?"

Many times we speak of the Sound as the Flute of God. In fact, we have a book by that title that discusses the psychology of Spirit. You may hear the sound of a flute, the twittering of birds, the sound of an orchestra, running water, or the buzzing of bees. Someone will say, "I hear the sound of sparrows during contemplation. What plane am I on?" You may even hear a humming sound, a HU with an *m* at the end of it. It's a variation of HU. Even the word *alleluia* is a corruption of HU. Actually, it's *Allah* and *HU—Allahu*. Gradually it was changed until it became alleluia and then hallelujah. Many people don't understand where these words came from, but they are corruptions of the spiritual works.

You can figure out very quickly how an original idea is changed by playing a children's game called Telephone. One person starts by whispering a message to the next person, until it goes all the way around the room. Along the way each person may hear it a little differently, and by the time it gets back to the originator, the original statement is entirely different. When you ask each of the people what they heard, you'll find some very funny variations.

So finally, the guide has to be you. If you are on a religious path and you feel comfortable and happy there, stay with it. If you are on a path that is not really satisfying but it is better than feeling like you're wandering alone in the dark—and you'd like to test and experiment a little bit—you might try the Spiritual Exercises of ECK.

Before the compass came into use, all the navigation was done by the stars. The sailors, navigator, and captain could tell where they were simply by looking up at the stars. This method had a drawback—if you were in the middle of a storm, you couldn't see the stars. All you could do was hang on for dear life as you were blown off course, and wait out the storm until you could once again see where you were.

Before the compass came into use, the sailors, navigator, and captain could tell where they were simply by looking up at the stars. This method had a drawback.

When the compass came into use, the scientific mind could see right away that it was a useful invention. But the first few captains who tried to take it aboard got a strange reaction from their crews: "Devil worship! Our captain is working with the dark forces!" They didn't know anything about magnetism, one of the lowest forces of the ECK Current, so they couldn't understand what made the needle turn. The captains began to hide the compasses when they took them aboard the ships. They could navigate much better now and tell which way was north, south, east, and west—but they didn't want to be caught with it.

The electrical force is another lower manifestation of the ECK which we've harnessed so that it makes lights shine. It makes microphones work so that I can be heard all the way in the back. We take our lights, heat, and air conditioning for granted—until something happens to deprive us of these conveniences.

In November, we had an ECK seminar in Hawaii. As soon as we left, a hurricane blew in. One of the ECKists and his wife had stayed to vacation in the islands, but for nine days straight there was no sun. It was really disappointing to them because they had come all the way from Connecticut after weeks of very careful planning. It was all ideal except the sun wouldn't shine. They even spent a day out on the beach under the cloudy sky, hoping to get a suntan through the clouds.

One night during the storm, the lights went out—the whole area went completely dark. At that moment they stopped taking electricity for granted. The wind was blowing so strongly that they had to lean forward just to be able to stand. It was so dark that if they went outside the hotel, they couldn't find the door back in. They went through all kinds of interesting moments.

Knowledge Wrongly Used

Electricity was a mystery to man for a long time. He saw that lightning came from the sky, but he didn't know what caused it. All he could do was observe its effects—the burning trees and plains—and try to protect himself and his family by running and hiding from it. This force of electricity that was coming out of the clouds was considered to be a manifestation of the gods, and eventually whole cults were built up around it. Those who claimed to know and understand this light became the priests.

Men who could predict when the eclipse would come could control the people. They'd say, "Unless you give me all your riches, the sun is going to be completely blacked out."

Men who could understand the eclipse were in better shape yet, because if they could predict when the eclipse would come, they could control the people. "You've been bad," they'd say. "The deities are angry with you, and unless you give me all your riches, the sun is going to be completely blacked out." And as it got darker and darker, they knew they had to work fast, so they'd tell everybody, "Hurry up, hurry up! Get your stuff in here!" Soon after that, they could say to the people, "OK, you've done well. The gods are appeased; now we can have the sun back." And the people were so grateful. This is an example of a little bit of knowledge wrongly used.

Truth is simple. It's as simple as going within using the Spiritual Exercises of ECK. I can't take you into the heavenly worlds if you drag your feet and don't want to go. I wouldn't try. Anyone who has any degree of spirituality would never try to pull another into a higher state of consciousness.

Using Discrimination

I talked to a person today who told me that she was a single parent. She has to go out and work while trying to raise her two daughters, and she was having a hard time. Recently one of her friends, a person she respected and who had it a little bit easier, came up to her and said, "You're living your life all wrong. You're too scattered. You're all over the place." The woman said she was totally devastated. It made her wonder if she was a complete failure. I had to explain to her that the people who can harm us the most are sometimes those who are dearest to us, because our hearts are open to them.

We have to use discrimination and be sure the people we are close to really are concerned about us and not just themselves. I said, "This woman was bringing up something about you that isn't true. Your circumstances are entirely different. You're doing very well with what you have to work with. The other woman is frustrated. Her marriage may look happy, but she is bored to tears, and she resents it. That's why she is starting to give you advice."

There is a saying that a person who gives unasked-for advice is actually telling the other person, "You aren't smart enough to know how to run your own life." And what kind of vanity is that? It applies whether we are speaking about another's personal or spiritual life.

The ECK Masters advocate religious freedom for the individual, so that you make the choice and decide for yourself, Is this path right for me?

Standing on Our Own Feet Spiritually

The ECK Masters advocate religious freedom for the individual, so that you make the choice and decide for yourself, Is this path right for me? I can give you the guideposts. I'll tell you that in ECK you will find the Light and Sound of God. And if you don't find It after a reasonable time, then go look elsewhere—it's just not time yet; you're not ready. When you do find It, it's to help you in your daily life so that you can live harmoniously, in cooperation with all life, and not feel you have to look to a God who does everything for you. You'll never achieve self-mastery that way. If I would allow you to rest on my personality, or if any teacher allows you to lean on him, he is doing you a disservice, because you are not learning to stand on your own feet.

We have been spoon-fed with ideas of a God who will heal us no matter what we do wrong. Some people think all they have to do is ask. They feel they can give advice to others that might destroy their lives, and by saying, God, please forgive me, it will all be forgotten. Unfortunately, these people are ignorant of the spiritual law. Saint Paul said, "Whatsoever a man soweth, that shall he also reap," and it means just that.

We can take our place among those who are awake and live a life of responsibility. Once we can live this life of responsibility, we are no longer concerned with guilt.

You can kid yourself. A person can eat wrong until it affects his health and then reason that he can always find a doctor who will take care of him. Or he may ask God for a healing. And if it doesn't work he thinks, *God didn't heal me; therefore, the God of this faith must not be right.* In truth he has incurred a debt to Spirit; he himself must pay it back. No one can help him except himself.

ECK is the path that gives us the understanding of how to live our own lives better, in full consciousness. We can take our place among those who are awake and live a life of responsibility. Once we can live this life of responsibility, we are no longer concerned with guilt. We aren't tied and chained by the guilt imposed by the priestcraft or well-meaning friends or neighbors who are frustrated with their own situation. As we get an understanding, we can have compassion. If someone persists, we simply say, "I don't want your help. Can't you understand?" If they can't, we gradually draw away and find another friend who fits our state of consciousness. No one has the right to make us miserable unless we allow it.

When Abraham Lincoln gave the Gettysburg Address at the dedication of the national cemetery for the soldiers lost in the Civil War, there was also another speaker on the program. This other fellow was Edward Everett, who had been a candidate for vice president of the United States. He was a renowned orator and polished speaker who had been asked a full six weeks before the event if he would give a talk. He was to be the keynote speaker, and it was only as an afterthought that someone said, "You know, maybe we should ask President Lincoln to come too, since this involves a national event."

One commissioner in charge of the event at Gettysburg had doubts. "Do you think President Lincoln will be able to give a talk that is fitting for this occasion?"

One of the commissioners in charge of the event at Gettysburg had his doubts. He said, "Do you think he'll be able to give a talk that is fitting for this occasion?" Lincoln was rough spoken; they thought he didn't have enough polish. In fact, it didn't look like he was going to get reelected the next time. The picture wasn't as rosy as we perceive it today. The man who stood for freedom and against slavery wasn't going to get reelected.

They finally decided to invite him. The other man, Edward Everett, gave the first talk. It lasted for two whole hours, and when he was finished, everyone applauded him.

Lincoln was next. He gave the speech that became known as the Gettysburg Address. He emphasized that the forefathers of our country had set forth to establish liberty—politically and religiously, that the job was but half done, and that we were now in the middle of a fight to regain and maintain this liberation. After his speech, he felt as if he had failed, that his talk was too simple. He said, "I should have said more for the men who gave their lives for freedom." Yet this became one of the keynote speeches of America—an inspiration, a mountain, a treetop for many people to look to spiritually. It's a step.

Yet this became one of the keynote speeches of America—an inspiration, a mountain, a treetop for many people to look to spiritually.

As individuals, within ourselves we will have this civil war between the positive and the negative forces. This happens when Spirit comes in contact with us and our state of consciousness. It will come in and try to break up the mind's solidity, the rigidness that happens as we grow older and become set in our ways. Spirit comes in to break this up so that again we establish the fresh consciousness of a child—except that we become as children, we cannot enter into the kingdom of heaven.

This is what Spirit is trying to do. We have our own civil war going on within us, and it's not bad at all; it is a necessary battle that the ECK Masters help the truth seeker to wage against his own negative nature, to show him the pure positive God Worlds of ECK.

I'd like to thank you for coming. May the blessings be.

Seattle Regional Seminar, Seattle, Washington, January 22, 1983

During World War II, the man's father found himself bathed in a golden light, hovering in a higher state of consciousness above the lifeboat.

14
The Light of God

I went into the children's room yesterday. They were all seated very politely in chairs placed neatly around the room. I was curious, so I asked, "How did you get seated like this? Somebody make you do it?" They said, "No. We just got here somehow."

One young lady told me they wanted to sing a song in the main hall on Sunday. I asked if they would do "Swingin' on a Star." I've always liked it; it has a light, happy approach, and this reflects the spiritual life. It ought to be light and happy, not dark, dreary, somber, and foreboding. One of the children said it was a little high for her range—her voice might break. But they said they would do it, and they came out and performed it for us this morning. It's interesting how the children want to grow and try something new, just as the adults do.

A light, happy approach reflects the spiritual life.

The Blue Star

The star appears in Eckankar. It's the Blue Star that the ECKist very often sees as he does the Spiritual Exercises of ECK. You go into the contemplative state—shut your eyes and look very gently at the point of the Third Eye, the Spiritual Eye. Sing one of the names of God such as HU, as we did just a few minutes ago. Some see the Blue Star and some don't. I can't say everybody will—but this is one of the signs that the Inner Master is coming into your life.

The Light of ECK

I was talking to some friends last night, and one fellow told me about an experience his father had during World War II. He was on a commercial ship coming from England to New York. Because it was wartime, the captain had been zigzagging; but when he got within eighty miles of New York, he decided since they were so close to home they would go in a straight line. Just about that time, a U-boat came along and torpedoed the ship. His father ended up in a lifeboat with a number of other people.

With an incredible sense of peace, contentment, and harmony, his father watched the people down in the boat.

They were on the water for almost two weeks, and it was a very difficult time. One day his father fell asleep, and the next thing he knew, he was hovering above the boat in a higher state of consciousness. He found himself bathed in a golden light that wrapped around him like a cloak. He hadn't ever heard of anything like this before; he didn't know about the Light of ECK. With an incredible sense of peace, contentment, and harmony, he watched the people down in the boat. There was no concern about the fact that he might not make it back to the United States; he just accepted what was happening with full confidence. At that point, he said, he knew what the phrase "God is love" meant.

He had been more than willing to stay in that high state of consciousness and just go into the other worlds, because it was a very happy and warm experience. The lifeboat was very cold, and here he was very warm. But suddenly he heard a firm voice: "Go back." He wanted to argue, but he knew there wasn't any point to it; his destiny here on earth had not yet been fulfilled. And so he returned to his body to become an active person in life who meets obstacles and challenges with creativity.

For forty years he kept this experience to himself until just recently, when he told his son. He had never talked about it to other people because he felt they wouldn't understand. He said others would have laughed at him and thought, Well, the poor guy's gone off the deep end. You can't tell somebody what it is like to experience the Light and Sound of God. It's not possible. He described it to his son as actually bathing in the flowing light that surrounded him as he looked down at the lifeboat and watched his sleeping physical form. In that moment, he had the actual experience of the Light of God.

This is an example of an individual not in Eckankar who has had experience with the Light and Sound. But what does it do to you after you have it? What is the difference between an ECKist who gets it consciously sometime during his unfoldment and a man who gets it uncalled-for, when he doesn't even know such a thing exists? What it did for this individual was to take away the fear of death, the fear of dying; therefore, it took away the fear of living. He was able to go forth in life and do the beneficial things that were needed to fulfill his destiny.

As I was autographing a book, I got to talking with the individual and ended up writing the word spiritual *twice. At that point the question was: Now, how do we get out of this?*

THERE'S ALWAYS A WAY OUT

This morning as I was autographing a book downstairs, I got to talking with the individual and ended up writing the word *spiritual* twice. I started to write, "With spiritual love," and then as we got to talking, I wrote "spiritual" again. At that point the question was: Now, how do we get out of this? So I signed it, "With spiritual love, Spiritually yours"—and pointed out to her that there is always a way out. No matter what happens, no matter what we do, there is always a way out.

It's an interesting thing how language has developed. Latin, in which most of us really don't have any interest, was the language that bound the Christian church together for a number of centuries. We may think there was only one version of Latin that was the common denominator for the Catholic Church throughout all the different countries and cultures, but what is not generally recognized today is that there were corruptions of that language too.

It got to the point where the churchmen, as they traveled from country to country in Europe, could no longer communicate with each other. At one time their language was common, but eventually the French and Italians, for instance, could no longer understand one another. The physical language had become very much like the Tower of Babel.

Our Search for Happiness

Our search for happiness is actually a search for this Golden Age when Soul dwelt in the high worlds of Spirit and the high worlds of God.

There is a natural winding down or dimming of the spiritual light that occurs too. In every event, even within ourselves, within our spiritual evolution, we have actually four stages: the Golden Age; the Silver Age; the Bronze, or Copper, Age; and then we come down to the Iron Age—which is what we are in now.

The Golden Age has a counterpart on the physical plane that took place in ancient times, before recorded history, on other continents.

But the real Golden Age was before Soul came into the lower worlds, and this is what we remember vaguely, unconsciously within ourselves, when we look for happiness here. Our search for happiness is actually the search for God; it is a search for this Golden Age when Soul dwelt in the high worlds of Spirit and the high worlds of God.

Soul's Unfoldment

There was a time, before these lower worlds were created, when Soul resided in the heavens. It's difficult to conceive of such a thing in heaven as a selfish, or ungrowing, Soul; but interestingly enough, It wouldn't serve anyone or anything except Itself. And so God sent Soul down into the lower worlds which had been created specifically for Its experience. The hardships and troubles, even the happiness and joy—the full spectrum of experience that we know through the five senses and beyond—are for Soul's unfoldment, so that one day It may become a Co-worker with God. This is the only purpose of it all.

The hardships and troubles, even the happiness and joy—the full spectrum of experience that we know through the five senses and beyond—are for Soul's unfoldment, so that one day It may become a Co-worker with God.

When a person asks, What is my mission in life? it's very easy to answer: To become a Co-worker with God. But it sounds so simple that often they'll walk away still carrying the question. They are looking for a more startling answer, such as, To become an emperor, perhaps of an Eckankar empire or something. They want to start out humbly—at the top.

Another reaction to that simple answer is, Oh, a Co-worker with God. Gee. It doesn't sound like much fun because they compare it to the days when they sat very rigidly in the pew of a church on Sunday mornings. They'd listen to someone talk for a while and then sing a few hymns—which is fine for many people, but others outgrow it. They suspect being a Co-worker with God means having wings and flittering around out there. This conception of heaven is probably a memory of the Golden Age before Soul was useful, before God said, "You need experience so that you can become a Co-worker." We do not become one with God. We do not merge into God and lose our identity in eternity.

Surrendering to Spirit

Thomas Merton, the Christian mystic, was led to the realization that God wants to take us beyond the area of thought, into the pure spiritual worlds of being. This is what happens in the spiritual worlds—we drop the mind.

When I speak about dropping the mind, I mean regarding spiritual things. It doesn't mean that you no longer want to go to the community college and take a course in computer design because you think Spirit will take care of it. When you go out to look for a job, you are usually asked, "What are your qualifications?" If you try to say, Well, Spirit's going to take care of it, you will soon find that Spirit will take care of it a little better after you get yourself some education and experience.

When I speak about surrender to the Inner Master, to Spirit, or the ECK, I'm talking about spiritual surrender: giving up the problems, cares, anxieties, and worries to the Inner Master and learning how to take care of things out here in our daily life. Then when something comes up, we get the spiritual insight or even the spiritual help to get us through.

The more we scramble, the more stability we find in Spirit and the less we see in material things—even though we may still enjoy them.

More and more we look to Spirit, but more and more we do it ourselves. The more we scramble, the more stability we find in Spirit and the less we see in material things—even though we may still enjoy them. After all, there is nothing wrong with having a nice, heavy coat if you're in a snowstorm.

We don't want to practice austerities; that is not balance. Buddha spoke about this. He had started out his life as a rich young man, protected from seeing poverty or sorrow; and when he went out into the world, he said, Now I must beg and become poor. He tried fasting, and that didn't work out so well. All he got was skinny as a rail. After a while he said there must be some way to live a life that is well balanced. There must be a middle way.

In the spiritual life, we look to find the balance so that when we have this experience of God and see the Light—whether It is the Blue Light or anything else—we are able to carry on. We don't get frantic and say, Will I ever see It again? When the time is right, you will. Others will hear the Sound. These are the two aspects of God which the ECKists, and even those who aren't in Eckankar outwardly, are beginning to learn about and experience in their daily life.

Contact with the Voice of God

I haven't read the autobiography of Carl Jung, the psychologist, but someone mentioned him to me the other day. When he was young, during fits of coughing and pain, Jung saw the Blue Light of ECK. He didn't know what it was, but each time the coughing became so severe that he couldn't take it, this Blue Light would appear. And as he looked at it, his pain would be replaced with contentment and peace.

Any individual who has left his mark in this world in a positive manner has had contact, sometimes consciously, sometimes not, with the Voice of God—either the Sound or the Light.

We find that any individual who has left his mark in this world in a positive manner has had contact, sometimes consciously, sometimes not, with the Voice of God—which may be either the Sound or the Light. Edison, Ford, and others had the ability to move in their state of consciousness to a higher level. They could visit one of the museums which we know very well in Eckankar—the astral museum. There is also a library on the Astral Plane which many of the writers on earth visit in the dream state.

Spiritual Laws and Nutritional Laws

I've got a frog in my throat this morning, and it seems to come after I've eaten a lot of bread. Last night as we were waiting for our food, the service was a little slow. Someone at our table asked for more bread. I know I should have resisted it, but I hadn't eaten since Thursday. I usually work better at a seminar if I don't eat too much. On Friday I had just a little water and kept working, and when it got to Saturday, the schedule was so full that I only had time for about two handfuls of grapes. So by evening, when somebody mentioned there was a Greek restaurant nearby, I thought that sounded good.

We got there at a busy time, and after placing our orders we started eating bread. We waited and waited. In fact, we began to wonder if we'd have to just pay for our bread and leave in order to get back for the evening talk. But you always wait one minute more. So we just sat there eating bread—and really enjoyed it.

I have my laws too, and they are not imposed on me by anyone else. There are nutritional laws and spiritual laws. As we unfold, often we get into another state of consciousness very fast—by that I mean two or three or four years. That is fast considering that many people who come into this lifetime on other paths stay in that state of consciousness for most of their lives. But we don't; we move very fast.

Many people who come into this lifetime on other paths stay in that state of consciousness for most of their lives. But we don't; we move very fast.

Every time you move into another state of consciousness, your nutritional laws may change. Then you start juggling your diet and vitamins. When you finally lose track, you may end up going to a nutritionist. Why? Because you are going through different states of consciousness and your body is responding to the law As above, so below. As you grow in your state of consciousness or as you come nearer to another initiation, things begin to change, and you wonder what's happening. It's simply that your state of consciousness is changing. Even your word, your secret word, may not work anymore, and you must ask to find a new one.

There are many organizations, such as the Masons, that are very good in that they provide a classroom of spiritual education at a certain level where people can learn fundamentals. But there comes a time when we graduate and move on to another step. When this happens, things in our outer life change—including our health—and then we have to catch up. I do too. Sometimes I really have to scramble because I don't have the time to sit down and make a study of what's best nutritionally. As the fads change, you always have a certain food that everybody just knows is the key to eternal youth.

The only key to eternal youth that I can give you is spiritual. The tablets I can give you are not the kind that contain all your minerals, nor are they like the two that have the Ten Commandments written on them. All I can give you are the Spiritual Exercises of ECK. I won't go through a spiritual exercise here—they are found in the ECK books, such as *ECKANKAR—The Key to Secret Worlds*.

The only key to eternal youth that I can give you is spiritual. All I can give you are the Spiritual Exercises of ECK.

THE INNER AND OUTER MASTER

Many years ago I attended a church service where we were all supposed to come up to the front of the room and declare our life for Jesus. But I had gone past that stage. My landlady, as I mentioned in *The Wind of Change*, was determined to save me. She was waiting when I got home that day: "Quick! If you hurry, you can come to church with me tonight." She was a good person, and I really liked her, so when she said, "Come along," I did. Her husband and children really didn't care for church that much, and apparently I looked like I needed salvation as much as anybody.

The minister looked straight at me as we seated ourselves in the front pew. I guess she had passed the word to him: Got a live one coming in! I had come right from the printing department after working a double shift and still had my work clothes on, but they were willing to forgive this of me.

When the minister looked at me, he shouted, "Are you saved?" I thought to myself, More than you can imagine—because I had the Light and Sound.

So when the minister looked at me, he shouted, "Are you saved?" I thought to myself, *More than you can imagine*—because I had the Light and Sound. I didn't need him to tell me anything. But others did, and it was good for them. My landlady said, "Are you going to go up and be saved?" When she started to push me too much, I said quietly, so that only she could hear, "But Jesus isn't coming." This wasn't meant to offend her, but she was in my space. She gave up on me then.

In 1527 the ECK Master Rebazar Tarzs was walking in the Himalaya Mountains, and he heard the Oracle of Tirmer. This is the voice of prophecy that was active many years ago but usually isn't used anymore. Its voice came down from the mountains and said, "Christ is dead." At this particular time, the forces of Charles V, emperor of the Holy Roman Empire, were launching an attack against the pope.

When Rebazar Tarzs heard the statement, "Christ is dead," it meant simply that the power of the Catholic Church of that time was broken; the spiritual light had gone out. In the same period came the Protestant Reformation—in 1517, Martin Luther nailed his ninety-five theses on the door of Palast Church in Wittenberg; in 1529 Henry VIII broke away from the Catholic Church and set up the Church of England; and there were the reforms of Calvin and Zwingli. A great change was occurring.

A church might carry on, but it takes a living master to physically keep things in line out here and to lead people to the Inner Master. You need both the Inner and Outer Master, and a book can't do it.

We read the ECK bible, *The Shariyat-Ki-Sugmad*, and the other ECK books to get information. We use and test this information through the spiritual exercises or the contemplative techniques. We are given the information, but then we are also given the rule of thumb that comes along with it: Is this true? Try it. Test it for yourself. If it works for you, great; and if it doesn't, keep looking for another path that fits you. There is no need to hold on to anyone.

We are given the information but also given the rule of thumb that comes along with it: Is this true? Try it. Test it for yourself.

Survival beyond the Physical Body

I visit different health-food stores, buying a little here, a little there, and pass the time of day with the people I meet there. I don't press ECK on them and usually don't even mention anything about it. But the owner of one of these stores told me this story.

In 1972 he had come across one of the ECK books, *In My Soul I Am Free*, and he decided to try the Easy Way technique, a spiritual exercise that is given in the book.* Sure enough, he found himself in a higher state of consciousness. For protection he had asked that a few ECK Masters be on hand just to make sure he'd be safe, and since he was into karate, he envisioned these guardians as big, bald-headed, strong, and muscular.

Soon he found himself in that state of consciousness where he could view the physical body lying asleep. This brought him a sense of peace and contentment and the knowledge that Soul exists beyond the physical body. But then after a while he started to get a little anxious. Even though he saw these two big guys and knew they were taking care of him, he still got a little nervous, because that's the way we are. We say we'd do anything to have that higher state of consciousness, and then when we get it we say, That's enough for now, thanks.

He put this book away for almost twelve years. As

* See footnote on page 3. —Ed.

we talked, I told him that there are so many people, even on the path of ECK, who would say, "I'd do anything for that experience. If I could have the actual confidence that I would live on after this physical body was dropped in death or translation, I'd be the happiest of people. I would give my whole life for ECK and then, Lord, you could write the ticket."

And you know how that is—promises are easy and cheap. About a year after the experience is over, when life brings us to a higher state of unfoldment and things speed up a bit, some of those same people would say, "I can't take it anymore. This must be the dark night of Soul that Saint John of the Cross was talking about." Things start moving too fast, and they forget how enthusiastic they felt back then. The mind is a funny thing—it forgets. And so we need the opportunity to go back again and again to the source, to the inner temple.

I can tell you stories about people who met the ECK Masters before 1965. You can read about people who had this state of consciousness outside of the physical. But the best thing anyone can do is to show you how to get there yourself—to work with you outwardly, through the ECK books and the ECK discourses, so that you can make the jump to the inner planes and find the understanding and the help that you need to live your daily life.

Your daily life is the spiritual life.

Your daily life is the spiritual life. So often someone will say, "If you will take away this pain and give me a spiritual healing or give me money, I'll be better able to live the spiritual life." They don't realize these are the experiences that will give them spiritual understanding. We learn compassion. This is part of our experience here.

Compassion and Detachment

We are interested in Soul, each one of us. But as we get this understanding, as we become greater in our own unfoldment and move toward the God Consciousness, we also develop many other traits, and compassion is one of them. We have learned, however, to be detached from the problems of other people. We can cry with them when they cry, laugh when they laugh, but the sorrow that comes into our life won't break us. We can get up and face tomorrow because we can see that this was a spiritual experience that was necessary for Soul to gain the spiritual foundation It needs to become a spiritual giant, to become a member of the order of ECK Masters, to become a Co-worker with God.

As you go back home, you carry this Light of God with you.

I would like to thank you for coming. As you go back home, you carry this Light of God with you. It doesn't necessarily shine like a sixty-watt bulb, where you can walk into a room and say, "Hey, I don't need flashlights anymore!" You won't even know your flashlight is on, but other people can tell. When you return from this seminar and they ask if you had a nice weekend, maybe you'll say simply, "Yes, I did." You might not even want to talk about it because they may not be ready to learn about the ECK works or a spiritual seminar or anything of this nature. But they will notice, and they'll be aware.

GIVING OTHERS FREEDOM

You can enjoy the people you work with and live with. Let them have their being. You don't have to push Eckankar on someone, any more than you'd want him to push his religion on you. In the spiritual worlds, the law is Fair is fair; I must give you freedom so you will give me freedom. And yet we know we must stand up to protect what we call the psychic space around us, so we don't allow other people to push their teachings on us.

We don't have to be rude if someone comes up and pushes their religion. We can always just move back very gently and find new friends. As a last measure, we might say, "If your religion is working for you, then let it work for you; but look around and notice that the whole world doesn't share your belief. God has provided hundreds of paths; there is a way for every Soul to find one that fits It so that It is exactly where It belongs." You might suggest that they let people have that freedom.

Practice the love. Practice "God is love." Practice tolerance and compassion.

Practice the love. Practice "God is love." Practice tolerance and compassion. I'd like to thank you in the Light and Sound of God. May the blessings be.

Seattle Regional Seminar, Seattle, Washington, January 23, 1983

Even though there was nobody manning it and no equipment was attached to its wooden frame, people were very carefully stepping through the metal detector.

15
How to Become a Master

Tonight I'd like to touch on how to become a Master. The HU song you were just singing is something I generally like sung before I speak to a group. On one hand, I don't want to impose this sound on those of you who are guests, here for the first time. But on the other hand, I find that it makes things a little bit easier because it uplifts the spiritual consciousness. This is the HU sound that you, yourself, can sing if you want upliftment or help in any way.

How to become a Master means that we take one step more than we have to, one step more than the average man.

How to become a Master actually means something very similar to what merchants mean when they speak of added value. Another way to say it is that we take one step more than we have to, one step more than the average man.

When we go into the dream state, we may be taken to different planes and worlds to have experiences with the beings who live on the planes we will go to when we drop this physical body, either when it's worn out or after we've spent many years here. There comes a time when we realize that anything that begins must end. Spring comes, you go through the life cycle, then comes fall, and the year ends. This is a natural process, and being such, it's interesting that we are so often afraid of it.

We're born, and we come into this life as a child. At that stage, we don't have much say about how we're going to do things; somebody else tells us. Our parents are trying to fit us into the society in which we live. We're little rebels in many cases, and when we start out, our parents call it the terrible twos.

When my daughter went through that stage, I looked at it carefully and said, I'm not going to be captured by this idea of the terrible twos. But you know, there is something to it. Up to this time, you've finally gotten used to being the parent of a little one in a crib. Then, eventually, the little one crawls out of the crib at night to go wandering through the house.

Around the terrible twos, the child really gets into action. There's nothing wrong with the child; it's just that the parents' expectations are being rapidly changed. First it was troublesome to feed the child at two o'clock and at four o'clock in the morning, but you get used to it. Then the child becomes mobile and starts walking around the house. He gets into the kitchen cupboards, tearing dishes down, inspecting them, and dropping some. The parents begin to wonder, What have we done?

Going One Step Beyond

Children have a unique viewpoint which is necessary for those of us who are sincerely looking to go further toward personal mastership.

Children have a unique viewpoint which is necessary for those of us who are sincerely looking to go further toward personal mastership. One time when I had done the Spiritual Exercises of ECK and then gone to bed, I said I wanted to go to the other planes. You would be surprised that so much of the activity that takes place there and what people do is similar to what happens here. There are times we have these glorious experiences with the Light and Sound of Spirit, which are the two pillars, or aspects, of Spirit which we can see and know. Sometimes you have these, but if you are fortunate, you can develop the ability to have consciousness and be aware of what's happening on the inner planes.

This particular time, the Dream Master invited me to a school at a temple, but it wasn't a Temple of Golden Wisdom. Children here on the physical plane, while they're learning math and other things in school, are being taught at the same time on the inner planes; whether it's the Astral, Causal, Mental, or Etheric Plane, they are learning. What we have here is supplementary education for the Physical Plane.

The teacher at this temple school was instructing the students in basic math and said to a little boy, "You have one tomato. Now if you wanted ten tomatoes, how many more would you have to buy?" The little guy didn't even wait. "None," he said. The teacher, of course, was expecting the answer "nine." If you have one and you want ten, you've got to have nine more. Where are you going to buy them? I don't know if the little guy didn't have any money and wasn't thinking the same way a teacher would, or if he was a farmer, but he said, "I'd cut the tomato open, take out the seeds, plant them, and I'd have a lot of tomatoes."

He was using this idea of the merchant of added value, going one step beyond. The teacher was thinking in a tight, closed box of what the expected answer should be according to logic. But the spiritual life, the true spiritual realm, goes beyond mind; it goes beyond logic. It would be impossible for me to explain this because we are listening and we are understanding through the mind. But in the pure spiritual worlds, we're working with perception and consciousness, with seeing, knowing, and being. It's something no one can explain to you. All I or anyone else can do is say there are Spiritual Exercises of ECK in books such as *ECKANKAR—The Key to Secret Worlds*. There are some in *The Spiritual Notebook*, and these may be

The spiritual life goes beyond mind; it goes beyond logic.

used for a few minutes a day. There is also *The Spiritual Exercises of ECK*, which contains over one hundred techniques you can try at your own pace. Look to a Master with whom you are familiar and comfortable. It may be an ECK Master, or it may even be Jesus.

Overcoming the Sheep Consciousness

Early this afternoon I went to the Capitol to look at the Senate chambers. As I was walking up the steps, there was a tour group right ahead of me—a lot of people. It's interesting to observe how easily we become sheep.

In mastership, we develop the ability to get an overview from all sides into all phases of our daily living.

When we are looking for mastership, we have to stop being sheep. It's too easy. A sign tells us to do something—so we do it and never ask why. Is there a reason for this sign, or are we just doing something because the sign says to do it? In mastership, we develop the ability to get an overview from all sides into all phases of our daily living. We look at our situation and our problems from a broad perspective and from this viewpoint make a decision: How are we going to go about solving this problem?

So I walked up the steps. There's a metal detector that people walk through when Senate is in session. Today Senate wasn't in session, and there was no one manning this metal detector. All that stood there was a wooden frame, the way you see it in an airport. Just a wooden frame. There was no attendant, there was no electronic monitor, there was absolutely nothing. You had a choice: you could either walk up to the right side of the steps and go through the metal detector, or you could go to the left, where there was nothing in your way. The sign above the metal detector said something like, Please Walk Through. Even though there was nobody manning it and no equipment attached to its wooden frame, people were very carefully stepping through it. They shook their coats, then braced themselves and popped through. I even saw one woman carefully hand her purse around the wooden frame to her husband on the other side. He took it, then she smiled and walked right through, because the sign told her to.

I even saw one woman carefully hand her purse around the wooden frame to her husband on the other side. He took it, then she smiled and walked right through, because the sign told her to.

This whole crowd of people followed the sheep ahead of them, and they did exactly what the one in front of them did. They had expectations of how things are usually done, but in this case, nobody noticed that the sign didn't mean anything. Children were crowding to go through, one ahead of the other, even though it didn't make any sense. I was going up the stairs, looking back, and I couldn't believe my eyes. A woman happened to be coming down, and I just about ran into her. We got to talking, and I said, "Have you ever seen anything like that?" She stopped and just looked. She had never seen anything like it.

People tried to get around us as we stood there having this nice conversation and watching them do this incredible thing, not using their heads because it never occurred to them that they should. Finally a whole tour group with a guide came through, and we got out of the way. I found this whole experience amazing.

Finding the Living Water

What we are looking for is the living water. It's the same living water that Jesus offered to the woman at Jacob's well. Jesus was walking at the end of a long day, and he was tired. So he sat on the edge of the well while his disciples went into town to get some meat and food. While he's sitting on the well outside the city of Sychar, a woman—a Samaritan—came along and got her water. Jesus said, "Give me something to drink." She didn't quite understand why he said that, because there was a strong prejudice between the Samaritans and the Jewish people—they wouldn't talk with each other—and she said, "Why are you talking to me, a Samaritan?"

He said, "If you'd give me water, I would give you the living water in return." This is the same living water that an ECK Master named Vaita Danu spoke about several centuries earlier to Alexander the Great.

Alexander the Great had come into India intent on conquest. The Macedonians couldn't stand in front of him, nor could any of the other kingdoms. He crossed the Indus River and camped in the lands to the east of it. While he was in camp, the ECK Master, a very aged man, appeared to him. In his hand he held a water bag, and he said, "Alexander, take this and drink." Alexander hesitated for a moment, and one of his officers took a sword and slashed the bag, spilling all of the water to the ground.

If he had taken the water at that moment, his Spiritual Eye would have been opened. He would have gotten this living water of which we speak—the Light and Sound of God. This would have poured into him and slaked his thirst for conquest, which was driving him from country to country.

This is the search for the living water. It is what we are looking for—the eternal truth. We've looked and searched for this truth in many religions throughout many lifetimes.

Vaita Danu said, "You have been tested and found wanting. If you had taken this water, your Spiritual Eye would have been opened and you would have seen the glories of God. As it is, you are destined to die early in life. You shall become a wanderer through life, in birth after birth, to walk the earth until the Living ECK Master again comes to you in some future lifetime and offers you this opportunity." He had told Alexander that his life would soon come to an end, and it did.

This is the search for the living water. It is what we are looking for—the eternal truth. We've looked and searched for this truth in many religions throughout many lifetimes. And when it is offered, we still have to take it. No one can force us to drink the living water.

Contacting the Light and Sound of God

Spiritual enlightenment and illumination come as we have contact with this Light and Sound of God. The ECKist sees the actual Light of God that comes during contemplation. It gives spiritual upliftment and takes away the karma which has been created throughout our past lives and the daily karma from this lifetime.

We can do without the Light, but we can't do without the Sound. It is an actual sound that we hear. It may be that of an orchestra; it may be that of a flute. We have a book named *The Flute of God*.

This is the only way that God can speak to us, through either the Light or the Sound. Whenever we have an experience on the inner and we hear a booming voice, it may be a Master, whether seen or unseen, another being, or an angel of God—but it's not God. The true Voice is what we seek. It gives the wisdom and the truth which surpasses all understanding.

As we begin to get this Light and Sound in our life, it shows in how we conduct our daily affairs. Our daily life is a reflection of what happens inwardly. We may be spiritually successful, but it doesn't necessarily mean we're going to be rich. If we set a goal for a project, we ought to get a grasp of spiritual principles from the experience. These help us succeed in the sense that these experiences take us to the next step in life. What we call success, other people may call failure, because we have a different viewpoint. And because we have this viewpoint, we have happiness and lightness which many other people would dearly love to experience but have never found.

Because we have this viewpoint, we have happiness and lightness which many other people would dearly love to experience but have never found.

Facing the Challenge

One of my neighbors mentioned that he had once joined the sales team of an insurance company. He wanted to be a salesman, but he had a track record of failure. At every company he had previously worked for, he couldn't sell. On his first day of work at this insurance company, the sales manager said to him, "I would like to welcome you and introduce you to all the other men and women. We're in the middle of a sales contest, but I'm not going to put you in it, because we are halfway through it. And anyway, the man who won it the last several times is ahead, and it looks like he's going to win again this time."

This newly hired man, seemingly a born loser, took the challenge. He set up a whole new sales presentation.

But this newly hired man, who was seemingly a born loser, took the challenge. He was willing to take the extra step and face the challenge which he had never been able to face before in his whole life. He told the sales manager he'd like to be part of the contest. The sales manager didn't really want his new employee to become discouraged by getting into a losing race, but he agreed.

The man went home, sat down, and evaluated every job he'd had in the past that related to selling. He wrote down every one of his techniques and reviewed them. It was an important step—he put all his experiences down on paper. Then he went over his notes, saying to himself, I've done this and that, and it didn't work. I'll make some changes here. I'm going to do something entirely different now. And he did it. He set up a whole new sales presentation.

One of the things he came up with was Never begin your sales pitch the second you walk into the client's house. This is one thing he had been doing wrong in his previous jobs, and he had been a failure every time.

This time, he entered the prospective client's home and immediately commented on the home itself. He started talking about the nice pictures on the wall, or complimented the people on what they were wearing. He made them feel comfortable. *Then* he got into the sales part of his visit.

He won the contest. His prize was a suit. It wasn't a great prize—it was a custom-made suit—but he wore it as long as he could. When it was worn out, he hung it up in his closet as a reminder that there is always one more step.

When we have failures, there is a way within our own resources to find success. This is what he did. This is what we can do. The spiritual exercises open up our inner awareness. We get the insight to see what we are doing that we can do better.

The spiritual exercises open up our inner awareness. We get the insight to see what we are doing that we can do better.

Searching for the Next Step

About 1933, James Hilton wrote a book called *Lost Horizon*. This was the story about the sacred city of Shangri-La, a paradise on earth. In 1933, the world was still recovering from World War I. People were very frightened of what the world had gotten itself into. That was to have been the war to end all wars, but in Hilton's story the premise was we're not out of it yet.

In his story, four people who landed in a plane on a high mountain plateau were taken to a lamasery called Shangri-La. It was a paradise in every sense; it was hidden on an enormous mountain that wasn't located on any map. The four people had actually been selected to live there, but they weren't told this.

As time went on, these newcomers were introduced to the lamas and the people who lived there. They found that the purpose of Shangri-La was to preserve the culture of the earth planet in the event of a holocaust. These masters had learned longevity and other secrets. And there was every convenience—even plumbing from Ohio.

When the old lama died, the leadership was offered to Conway, one of the four visitors. Instead of taking the job, he wondered why a person should live so long. Some of these people were several centuries old. They explained that they were studying so that in the event of a catastrophe, they could bring the culture of the human race to light again.

But Conway knew that the true wisdom could never be found on earth. So he left with several other people. They wanted to make him a master of something which was from the impermanent world of time and space, which would never last. He left because he was a true seeker. After that, there were sightings of him, according to this story, in different parts of the world as he kept searching for the next step in his spiritual unfoldment. He had been offered what the others felt was the height of spiritual development; but he looked it over, and instinctively, as Soul, he knew that it was a dead end.

Developing Spiritual Strength

Sudar Singh, the ECK Master, lived until the 1940s before he left the earth plane. Paul Twitchell said he went to Sudar Singh because he wanted to learn about the ECK. He decided to devote his entire life to the teachings of ECK and making them available to anybody who wanted to know about them. As soon as he made this commitment, everything went wrong in his life. He thought he had troubles before—but he hadn't seen anything yet.

Problems try to keep us from the path, but they also serve a useful function. By overcoming the blocks, we develop the spiritual strength necessary to take the first step on any path to truth.

When an individual comes close to the spiritual path or Master, the spiritual currents are stirred up, and the karma that has built up from past centuries begins to work up to the surface in the form of problems. These problems are trying to keep us from the path, but they also serve a useful function. By overcoming the blocks, we develop the spiritual strength necessary to take the first step on any path to truth.

Sudar Singh had another student who said he wanted an answer or a way to achieve all his desires. Sudar Singh was very obliging. He said,

"I'll give you a couple of techniques. Use these, and you will have all your desires."

The man left the ashram and tried them out for a couple of months, and then he came back, very upset. "These don't work!" he said. "You have given me these techniques, and they just don't work. What's wrong with them?"

"It's not the techniques," said Sudar Singh. "It's never any technique. The only answer you can ever find that's true is within you." The man went away puzzled, wondering, What's the point of techniques?

Techniques are helpful to get the Light and Sound, but they are not to be used as an end in themselves.

Committing to an Ideal

In the spiritual life, we always have to take one more step. These incredible odds come against us, but if we have this ideal set before us, which is Self-Realization or God-Realization, and we keep our attention on it and live our life with common sense, doing the best we can without fear of failure, we will make our way to that ideal because we have to. We make a postulate, and it becomes fixed within our being. We say: "I will have Self-Realization; I will have God-Realization. I will come to know my self. I will come to know who I am and what I've been, and I will know where I'm going."

We say: "I will have Self-Realization; I will have God-Realization. I will come to know my self. I will come to know who I am and what I've been, and I will know where I'm going."

An example of people who have been extraordinary in personal success are the co-founders of *Reader's Digest*, DeWitt and Lila Wallace, who started it in 1922. This individual, DeWitt Wallace, had an idea. He could gather stories, put them together, and condense them into a magazine. His first effort, several years after he finished college, was an agricultural publication. He saw some of the excellent articles that the United States Department of Agriculture was putting out for the farmers, but the farmers didn't have time to research all these pamphlets. Wallace gathered many of these into one place. They were published by the firm he worked for, and this was the first step.

Then he decided to put together a little digest for business, but it flopped. Nobody bought it. The one on agriculture was mildly successful; it gave him enough money to travel around the country in his car and promote the publication, but the one on business was a complete failure. He wondered why it hadn't worked.

All of a sudden Wallace's vision widened, and he started looking at a vast readership which encompassed the world.

He sat down with paper and pen and listed all the reasons why it should have worked. He concluded that maybe an agricultural theme worked, but it had a limited readership. What about a general readership? All of a sudden his vision widened, and he started looking at a vast readership which encompassed the world.

After World War I, while he recuperated from wounds in a hospital in France, he read one magazine after another. He put together a number of these articles and condensed them. Then he returned to the United States and went to the Saint Paul branch of the Minneapolis Public Library, where he worked for about half a year putting together the first edition of the *Reader's Digest*. He printed a few hundred copies and took them to publishers all over the country. They looked it over, and nobody liked it. He was a two-time loser. At one point, he even took his idea to publishers and offered to become their employee if they would just let him work on this idea. But no one would take him up on it.

Eventually he met his wife, Lila, and together, with both their talents, they were able to solicit subscriptions. To their surprise, they got some orders. After this, the digest began to grow to what it is today. It's everywhere. I'm not endorsing it, but it is a good example of an ideal that a man carried.

There were many more hardships that he went through, but you go through these, too.

Being an Individual

You don't have enough money, you don't have good health, and you wonder, *What should I do?* There is always a way.

With health, the first step is to go to the source of healing that you are most familiar and comfortable with. If this is a medical doctor, go to a medical doctor and get a checkup. Then go from there. You may decide you want to continue to go to this doctor, or you may decide to go to a medical specialist. You can chart your own path. And there is no one way to eat on the spiritual path. Vegetarianism is no better than meat-eating. God doesn't really care what we eat; not at all.

As we learn how to become the spiritual Master, we have the spirit Paul Twitchell carried—rugged individualism. Paul called it being the Cliff Hanger.

As we learn how to become the spiritual Master, we have the spirit Paul Twitchell carried. This is rugged individualism. Paul called it being the Cliff Hanger: You get the picture of a man hanging on the side of a cliff, looking down to the ground thousands of feet below him. But he's hanging on. The question is, How did he get there? And where is he going? Up or down?

Cliff-hanger was also a term used to describe the old Saturday matinees when some of you were young. They'd have these characters in serials such as Captain Marvel and Mr. Adventure, and later Batman. The idea was to take a story, divide it into equal parts, and then show one part a week. The kids would all run to see the next episode. To make sure the kids would come back the next week, at the end of the show there would be an exciting film clip. Mr. Adventure would be riding in a truck that was going full speed toward a stone wall. All of a sudden you'd see the truck run into the wall with a huge explosion. Then the picture would be cut off, and a caption would appear: "What happens to Mr. Adventure next week? Is this the end of Mr. Adventure?"

The children would sit there and cry, "Oh, no!" And they'd come back next week. For the next episode the filmmakers would insert one more scene: Just before the truck hit the wall, the brave hero, Mr. Adventure, would bail out of the truck and roll in the dirt. When the explosion happened, he was safe because he had jumped out a couple hundred feet away. This was called a cliff-hanger.

The cliff-hanger experience takes you to an apparently foolhardy edge of destruction, in a sense, spiritually. I don't mean out here in the physical; here, we use common sense. But spiritually we are adventurers. We try things that other people would be afraid to do. We look for the Light and Sound when other people are afraid that such a thing might even exist. And when It comes to us, It brings peace, serenity, harmony, and joyfulness beyond words.

When the Light and Sound comes to us, It brings peace, serenity, harmony, and joyfulness beyond words.

Reaching the Spiritual Power

To gain the spiritual power that I'm speaking of, first of all we have to adopt an ideal—God Consciousness, or whatever it is. This is what we are looking for. To do this, you assume, in a sense, that you're always right. If I were to tell this to some people, I know what would happen: they would take it wrong. But if one knows that the first step to getting this divine power working in his life is to assume he's always right, but then he becomes belligerent in his own defense, he is missing the harmony that's necessary.

It actually goes like this: I'm always right, but I never talk about it. It neutralizes the person who would misunderstand this principle and go out there in left field and do something funny. You cannot talk about it. You act as if you are already in the state of God-Realization, and then you carry out your life the best way you can. Another way that you do this is to say, If the Master were here, how would he handle the situation?

ECK, or Spirit, is already working in your life. It's already working every moment. You may then wonder, Why are things hard for me?

The second part of reaching the spiritual power is knowing that ECK, or Spirit, is already working in your life. It's already working every moment. You may then wonder, *Why are things hard for me?* The reason things may be hard is that Spirit wants us to go into the higher states of consciousness, and we are refusing the gift. We want to do things the way we've always done them. And I can assure you: to do that is to stay where you are.

To be on the spiritual path means to follow this Wind of Change, which is Spirit. If you are on a true path to God and you're unfolding in spiritual consciousness, changes are going to come into your life. They can't help but come. Things are going to be different. You may not know what's happening at first, but your friends will see a change in you.

The third point to reach this spiritual power is to chant the name of God. You can chant or sing *God*, or you may sing any one of a number of different names, such as *Spirit*, *ECK*, or *HU*. This is the song we chanted before—the sound of HU.

You can find more about this and how to reach Mastership through the Spiritual Exercises of ECK in the ECK books. You can make your own decisions without anyone coming to you and saying, "This is how it is," and putting pressure on you. You can determine for yourself, at your own pace, at your own time.

I'd like to thank you for coming. As you go out, you are carrying the Light and Sound of Spirit with you. It doesn't mean you're walking around being very solemn or anything like this, but you're going out and enjoying whatever you see, whatever you hear. The young people are going to have the same opportunity tomorrow to live and learn, and to gain the spiritual insight into what it all means.

This is what we are trying to do on the path of ECK: to find out what this life we are living actually means and how the spiritual consciousness can make it better—both now and after we step through the veil into the true worlds of the greater Light and the greater Sound of Spirit.

May the blessings be.

ECKANKAR International Youth Conference,
Washington, DC, Friday, April 1, 1983

The young ECKist's friend tried chanting *HU* and saw the Blue Star of ECK.

16
How to Find God

In the children's room this afternoon, we asked the children if they had any questions. They came up with some interesting ones, such as, When was God born? That was a hard one, so I asked the others if they had an answer. Actually children often already have an understanding which we adults are trying to reach.

The children came up with some interesting questions, such as, When was God born?

Wanting to know when God was born actually fits in with how to find God, the topic I would like to address tonight. How to find God is an interesting pursuit, a worthwhile one as we make our way through the lower worlds, as we prepare for the time that we go to heaven.

A few weeks ago I was talking with an individual about this very topic, how to find God, and he told me what his mother had said about it. As an agnostic who believed that she couldn't know if there was a God, she taught him a prayer she said was the only one he would ever have to know. It is by Joseph Ernest Renan and is called the "Agnostic Prayer." It goes like this: "Oh God, if there is a God, / Save my soul, if I have a soul." It's a prayer that covers all the bases.

Quest for Happiness

This is the quest that we pursue for ourselves. The quest for God is the quest for happiness. We look for happiness in one way or another, and some of them are detours. A drunk who is trying to find happiness through a bottle is actually looking for God, but he doesn't remember that.

The quest for God is the quest for happiness. We look for happiness in one way or another, and some of them are detours.

A Higher Initiate was asked by a Unitarian group if she would give a talk on this very subject, how to find God. She thought it over and decided to do it. She spoke about the ECK principles and what she had done to find the higher states of consciousness that we are looking for: Self-Realization and, ultimately, God-Realization. This means finding out who and what we are and what our mission in life is. When she finished the talk, one of the members of the Unitarian Church said to her, "It is very evident that you have somehow reached a higher state of consciousness, but however did you do it without Jesus?"

And so the question of how to find God must be looked at from another, higher viewpoint. You have to ask, Throughout the two thousand years since Jesus left the earth, how many who have sought the Christ consciousness have ever attained it? Saint Paul did, and he spoke of it when he said that when he is in Christ, he is a new creature. He was speaking of this state of consciousness, and what he meant was When I am in this state of Christ consciousness, then I am a new creature.

When the ECKist gave her talk, the people listened and had the ears to hear that she spoke the truth. But it's not enough to speak truth. It's not enough for a person to say, "I have the truth" unless he can show you the way to find it too.

Someone pointed out a long time ago that as we go up the ladder, we leave the ladder behind so those who come after us may use it too. This is done through writings and through our conversations. We carry this Light of Spirit out into the world in our own way. We don't have to preach, we don't have to collar anyone, we don't have to force anyone to come to our meetings, or anything of this nature. The easiest way to answer someone who wants to find out about ECK is simply to give them a book, such as *The Spiritual Exercises of ECK*. Just tell them: "You can try it and see if it works for you. If it does, you've got gold—eureka! And if not, you haven't lost anything. You've gained information, and it hasn't hurt you."

Blue Star of ECK

A fellow was telling me this story about his nine-year-old daughter, who is a student of Eckankar. She had a friend whose family were Christians. One day the little girl explained to her friend how the Spiritual Exercises of ECK were done and how to sing *HU*, the ancient name for God. Her friend seemed interested to hear more about it, so she said, "I'll just show you how to do it."

When they sat down and began a spiritual exercise, her friend really got into it. After twenty minutes the ECKist decided she had better see what was going on. Her friend finally opened her eyes. The little ECKist said, "What took so long? What did you see?" The other one said, "It was really something! When I shut my eyes and sang *HU*, I saw all these stars. The whole sky was full of stars, and as I watched, they all came together and formed into one huge blue star."

The Blue Star of ECK is a sign of a high state of spiritual consciousness which has come to give you the upliftment and blessing of the moment.

This is the Blue Star of ECK. It is a sign of a high state of spiritual consciousness which has come to give you the upliftment and blessing of the moment. This Blue Star of ECK also may be seen as a blue globe or saucer. You may not see It every day, only periodically, but It is there and It's real. This Blue Light is one of the manifestations of the actual Light of God. God can only be experienced through the Light or the Sound.

The Sound may come as the sound of rushing wind. Its action is a purifying upliftment for Soul.

The Wind of God

The Sound is the more important of the two aspects. It may come as the sound of rushing wind as told in the Pentecost story, where the apostles and others were gathered together and the Holy Spirit came upon them. They saw the cloven tongues like as of fire, and this rushing wind seemed to sweep through and fill the house. Jesus spoke of the Sound when he said, "The wind bloweth where it listeth," and talked of how no one knows where it goes or where it comes from. No one knows because it's not a wind in the usual way we think of wind. It's the spiritual Sound of God coming down and speaking to us through the inner ears. Its action is a purifying upliftment for Soul.

Sometimes it's hard to put these things into words, and I believe any of you who have ever tried to carry the ECK message or tell someone about ECK may agree. In answer to the question, What is ECK? you may find yourself trying desperately to put it into words, and you wonder if you did it well enough. This afternoon I was talking with a speech teacher who said she was afraid to give a talk on ECK. I asked why. She said it was because she wanted to give it as correctly as possible. Since she's a speech teacher, she didn't understand why she was so worried about it.

Any of you who have taken a speech class may think the teacher knows everything and should be able to give a talk easily. Yet, when something is precious to us and we care about it, we're careful not only about the people to whom we give it, but how we give it. We try to give out the message as we know it, in the simplest way possible.

The same little ECKist girl that I mentioned before went to a retirement home with her father to visit an elderly aunt. When they got there, they met the aunt's roommate for the first time. This lady was well on in years and was able to see across to the other side and get glimpses of life on the other planes. Whenever she spoke about it to others, they said, "Poor old Sophie—her mind is going."

The little girl walked into the room, and as soon as the allegedly senile old woman saw her, she said to the young girl, "I know you. I knew you when you were an old lady." The little girl didn't even hesitate. She simply looked at the elderly lady and said, "I knew you when you were a young lady."

The little girl walked into the room, and as soon as the allegedly senile old woman saw her, she said to the young girl, "I know you. I knew you when you were an old lady."

And the aunt said, "Don't mind Sophie. She's getting a little senile." It's easy to discredit both age and youth when they don't fit one's limited knowledge of the spiritual worlds.

Rope of Five Passions

An individual wrote to me and said he wanted to find God but he had realized that the five passions of the mind were holding him back. This lesson came to him in a very peculiar way. While working as a counselor at a camp for the mentally retarded, he was put in charge of a young boy who managed to disappear whenever he turned his back. Every time he looked around, the little guy was gone—and he didn't know what to do.

Finally, in a flash of inspiration, he got a rope and tied it to his own waist. You'd think he'd tie it to the little boy's waist, wouldn't you? But he tied it to his own waist and then gave the end of the rope to the little boy to hold. And it worked. The little guy never ran away again, because the counselor was now his prisoner.

He went home and thought about this, and he said, You know, the negative power has me in the same state.

This rope that's tied around the waist of the negative power has five strands, and these are the passions of the mind: anger, lust, greed, attachment, and vanity.

The ECKist started mulling over the rope of the five passions which holds us in the lower worlds or the lower states of consciousness, the human consciousness. All of a sudden, he asked himself, What am I doing, standing here like a fool, holding on to this rope?

All the ECKist had to do was drop the end of the rope, and he would be free. With this realization, he took a giant step in his spiritual unfoldment.

All he had to do was drop the end of the rope, and he would be free. With this realization, he took a giant step in his spiritual unfoldment. At this point he could begin giving up those things that were holding him back from finding God, from finding the peace, happiness, and joy that we can expect here and now.

What We Are Looking For

We can find heaven on earth. What we are looking for as ECKists is to find heaven no matter what our outer circumstances may be. Then, no matter how negative things seem or how poor we are, we can always find at least a little bit of happiness every day. And it's possible.

Some of you have told me your friends and neighbors notice that even when you are going through hard times, you are not completely destroyed. You may cry, but you come out of it very quickly. They watch and wonder: What secret does this individual have that I would like for myself? This is when they might ask to read an ECK book. It may be another couple of years before they are ready to look a little further and take another step on the path.

This morning, when I was autographing books downstairs in the bookroom, a gentleman came over and said, "Well, I'm kind of new at this." I understood perfectly what he meant. You want to look into something new, but you hesitate because of the fears you are carrying, the fears that have been put upon you. The fear of death, damnation, hell; just name it—every negative thing. But as you get along a little farther in years, you find that you have to make a decision; you are going past the fork in the road. Finally you say, "I've spent so many years on this path. What assurance do I have that any other path is going to work better for me than the one I have?" The energies of life are running low, and you may decide to stay with what you have. It takes courage to take another step, to go a little further.

For those of any age who have stepped on the path, this is the International Youth Conference, where we pay tribute to Soul which has no beginning and no ending. It exists forever, beyond eternity. It was created by God, of course, but outside the arena of time, space, matter, and energy. This being true, it's as paradoxical to say that there was a beginning to Soul as it is to say there was a beginning to God.

Soul exists forever, beyond eternity.

Wheel of Karma

Most of you probably saw the TV miniseries "The Thorn Birds." For those of you who didn't watch it, the story is set in the Australian outback. It begins in 1915 and centers around Father Ralph, a priest who was sent there to serve after he criticized the bishop. He was exiled because they thought this experience would give him a little common sense: maybe in a few years he could be brought back to society. The story follows his life and several generations of the family with whom he becomes involved.

At one point, a fire rages out of control, goes through this family's sheep ranch, and throws everything into turmoil. By then the children of the family are all grown up. One of the sons goes out in the bush to look for his father and finds that the fire has killed him. To signal the other searchers that he has found his father, he takes his rifle and fires three shots in the air. About this time, a wild boar runs out from the underbrush and charges at him. Before he has time to reload his weapon, he too is killed.

His sister, Meggie, realizes that in a very short time she has lost her father, her favorite brother, and most of her home. She cries out, "Why has God done all of this to me?"

Father Ralph tries to console her: "But God brought the rain to put out the fire."

In anguish, she says, "Who brought the fire?"

Father Ralph turned away then because he didn't have an answer. He didn't understand the Law of Karma or the wheel of life. He didn't understand that whatsoever we sow, we reap. If he had, he would have been able to approach Meggie from another viewpoint. If she had understood this principle, this spiritual law, she would never have had to ask the question. It's a fine story, and it will be around in reruns many times.

When looking for the realization of how to find God, we need to have an ideal, whether it is God or an Inner Master or an Outer Master. We have to start with an ideal.

When we are looking for the realization of how to find God, we have to think about what it is we actually want to get. We need to have an ideal, whether it is God or an Inner Master or an Outer Master. We have to start with an ideal.

Hidden Laws of Life

Those in authority very often are more than happy to keep the people in ignorance of the hidden laws that govern life; and in many cases, they don't know these laws themselves. This doesn't apply only to the spiritual laws, such as the one I just mentioned—the Law of Karma, the Law of

Cause and Effect. There are cycles, and there are people who study the patterns to find out, for instance, whether or not we run into a financial crisis every nine years. They have already noticed that when the economy dips, church attendance goes up. It's a very interesting opposition—like sound waves that crisscross.

In one case an insurance man, formerly the board chairman of one of the largest insurance companies in the United States, attended a talk on the subject of cycles. The speaker presented his theory about how he could predict, with a good degree of certainty, what the future would bring. The executive leaned over and said to one of his associates, "If it ever looks as if he's hitting on some truth about these cycles, let's drop the whole thing like a hot potato. Forget it."

Looking ahead, he could see the disastrous consequences to the insurance business if people ever got wind of this foreknowledge of the economy. This insurance man was afraid that if anyone ever got a study of the cycles perfected, people could use this knowledge to decide when it was necessary to buy their insurance and when not. You could say, I'm in a bad cycle so I'd better go down and see my friendly agent and load up on some term insurance. Then when the crisis had passed and you could feel fairly sure that you were OK for probably another year, why pay premiums? The executive saw how this could set a whole chain of events into motion, with the insurance business being the ultimate loser.

You can make a study of the ECK-Vidya, and then, through the dream state and outer study, you begin to get insights into what your future may bring.

Those in power would rather the people did not know some of these laws that govern life—the probabilities of the future. But in ECK we have a book called *The ECK-Vidya, Ancient Science of Prophecy*. You can make a study of it, and then, through the dream state and outer study, you begin to get insights into what your future may bring.

Overcoming the Fear of Death

We get a little knowledge of the spiritual path through the Spiritual Exercises of ECK, some of which are found in the books. *ECKANKAR—The Key to Secret Worlds* has several, and *The Spiritual Notebook* has three more that are also very good. You can try these for yourself. You will gain an insight into the meaning of life and the meaning of death. After all, why do we want to find God? Mostly it's because we're going to have to face this thing called the Angel of Death, and for many it's a time of terror. They wonder how they are going to do it.

With spiritual insight, we are able to have the expansion of consciousness to go into the inner planes, meet the beings who dwell there, have experiences, go back and forth many times in states of consciousness, and actually see where our home will be in the future. At first we may remember seeing this vaguely in a dream, and later we develop the ability to see it in full consciousness. Then when the moment comes, when it's time for us to step across, we find that the veil of death is but a shadow. It's a shadow in the world of light. It's not a barrier, it's not a wall; it has no more meaning or substance than the wisp of a cloud.

When the moment comes for us to step across, we find the veil of death is but a shadow. It has no more meaning or substance than the wisp of a cloud.

An ECK woman told the story about her brother who had been sick for quite some time. Because he lived several thousand miles away, she was not able to be with him physically.

One evening she felt a strong need to contemplate and do a spiritual exercise. At eleven o'clock that night, while doing this spiritual exercise, she was able to see her brother actually stepping across, out of the physical body and into the higher spiritual body. He wasn't an ECKist, though he had known about the ECK teachings.

She saw him standing there shaking his leg, the way you do when you're taking off a pair of pants—

you've got one pant leg free and the other one caught around your shoe, and you shake your foot because you're too lazy to bend over. He was shaking his foot and smiling, and he said, "Hey, that wasn't half as bad as I thought!" And it wasn't. All of his fears meant nothing. He had moved very naturally into a higher world very much like this one, but more beautiful and a lot more enjoyable. When she saw this, she knew that he was happy. In fact, he was laughing! He was in a lot better condition than he had been in that disease-ravaged body. They talked for a while, and then he said, "You know, this is really pretty good." And she watched as he wandered off into his new life.

We can meet our friends and family in this way if it is a blessing for us. I'm not saying that each one of you will see your loved ones go to the other side, but it is possible if you are ready. It is possible if you have developed yourself in a spiritual sense—if you have developed the Soul body through the Spiritual Exercises of ECK. They are very simple, and you do them in your own home, at your own time. You can adapt the spiritual exercises to fit you. You do them as long as they help, as long as you feel confident and happy with them, and you never push yourself into an area that is strange or frightening.

You find the other worlds are natural and full of joy; and when you have the knowledge there is no death, you no longer have the fear of death.

You find that the other worlds are natural and full of joy; and when you have the knowledge that there is no death, you no longer have the fear of death. When you realize you can come back to the body without this fear holding you back, you find your creative imagination begins to blossom. There are no more blocks in your personal life as you set your goals for material success and spiritual unfoldment.

Many times we look for God because we are afraid of death. We know it is inevitable. But when you can overcome this fear, the benefit is that you are now able to go forth and live this life fully and with enjoyment. Once you come into this state of realization, you're going to find that you are happy. There is freedom and joyousness no matter what happens. The sorrows of life may take you down for a little while, but they won't last for the rest of your life. Because you have this assurance, you're going to spring back.

Once you come into this state of realization, you're going to find you are happy. There is freedom and joyousness no matter what happens.

The Wayshower

In some ways, it may sound like an easy matter to find God—you do the Spiritual Exercises of ECK every day, have success, and life is pat. That's it. But there is a subtle little thing that happens as we live here. The negative power has a job: to blind us, lie to us, and tell us happy tales—anything it can do to keep us here, to keep us content with where we are now so that we won't look any further. It throws up all kinds of straw issues that build up into karma, until finally the load becomes so great that we break. And that is when we begin to sincerely look for someone who can show us the path to God.

In Eckankar we look to the Living ECK Master. He, in turn, provides books, and these are the ones we read to take the next step ourselves.

In *Give and Take*, a book about business negotiation, author Chester Karrass tells an interesting story about a woman in Russia who went to see the village wise man.

"We've got a very severe problem in our family," she said. "We live in this little hut with barely enough room for my husband, our two children, and myself. But hard times have forced my in-laws to move in with us."

The sage thought about it for a little while, and then he said, "Well, if the house is very crowded and you're having a difficult time, I can show you how this heavy burden can be taken away so that you can find happiness."

"Great!" she said.

"Do you have a cow?" he asked.

"Yes," she said.

"Take the cow and bring it into the house."

It was a very tiny hut, and she thought this was kind of strange. But he did have a good reputation, so she went home and brought the cow into the house. This proved to be a real nuisance, because every time the cow turned around, the family had to get up off the chairs along one wall, climb over the cow, and go to the other side of the room.

The following week she went back to the sage. "This doesn't make any sense at all," she said. "The cow is a nuisance! We can't even eat, we can't sleep, we can't move, and every time it's quiet, the cow will moo!"

"Do you have any chickens?" he asked.

She was a little hesitant, but she finally said, "Yes, we have some chickens."

"Well, take the chickens into the house with you."

She was just about to tell him what he could do with the cow and the chickens, but then she decided, OK, I've given him only one chance—I'll give him two.

She went back home and brought the chickens inside, and the whole thing turned into one big mess. Every time the cow turned around, the family jumped from their chairs. This frightened the chickens, so they'd fly around in the air and their feathers would fall into the soup. The in-laws were fighting, the husband was screeching, the cow was turning around, the chickens were squawking—and she barely made it to the end of that week.

Every time the cow turned around, the family jumped from their chairs. This frightened the chickens, so they'd fly around in the air and their feathers would fall into the soup.

"I've had it!" she yelled to the wise man. "The in-laws are bad enough, the cow I can barely take, but the chickens—that's too much!"

"All right," he said. "If it would make you happier, take out the chickens."

She went home and took out the chickens. A week later she came back and said, "I am much happier. Things are a lot better with the chickens out of the house. There's no cackling the first thing in the morning, and the children don't have to fish feathers out of the soup."

"I'm happy to hear that," said the sage. "Why not let the cow out of the house too?" She thought that was a wonderful idea. She immediately went home and let the cow out of the house; and she, her husband, the children, and the in-laws lived happily ever after.

You're wondering what kind of spiritual point there could be to this story, right? Well, I'll let you think about it.

You go deep within and come in contact with the Light and Sound of God. It will lead you to your home. This is the Ocean of Love and Mercy, which we know as God.

When you are looking to find God, you think, you plan, you look. First you think, *What is my ideal?* Then you plan what you can do to get there. My suggestion is to read an ECK book. But whatever you want to do—whatever path or personal discipline you choose—is right for you. Then you look. You look at the people who are successful in life to find out what they have done, and you study the lives of the saints and find out what they have done.

You go to books and you study the lives of other people, but more importantly, you go within. You go deep within yourself through the contemplative techniques, and you come in contact with the Light and Sound of God. And when you come in contact with this Voice, It will lead you to your home. This is the Ocean of Love and Mercy, which we know as God. With this I leave you. May the blessings be.

ECKANKAR International Youth Conference, Washington, DC, Saturday, April 2, 1983

"You know, it's unusual to see a man walking around with crutches when he doesn't need them," I said.

17
The Vairagi ECK Masters

I'd like to speak this morning about the Vairagi ECK Masters, their presence, and their significance in our life, which many times is unseen and unknown.

The Vairagi ECK Masters' presence and significance in our life many times is unseen and unknown.

Recently we had a series of Light and Sound workshops which some of you may have attended. The purpose of these workshops was to try to give attendees the opportunity to again have some experience with the Light and Sound of God.

Some of you who joined Eckankar many years ago had vivid experiences when you first stepped upon the path, and in the natural course of events, you forgot about them. You became so used to your own experiences that they lost their meaning, and gradually your memory of them dimmed. With these Light and Sound workshops, the memory was revived and the spiritual experiences again became a living thing as the Light and Sound of God came into the reaches of Soul.

We sent two people to Honolulu recently to conduct one of these spiritual workshops. Before it started, they checked the meeting room to make sure the chairs and tables were in place and that the thermostat control was functioning properly. They were thinking about the ECK Masters as they set up the microphones, feeling the presence very strongly before this important spiritual event. Suddenly they heard a soft, swishing sound behind them. Turning around, they were quite surprised to see the huge movie screen splitting from top to bottom. For no apparent reason, it just ripped right in half. The two workshop leaders started to laugh as they watched it, and all they could say was, "Look at that screen!"

It was like the screen of the mind that has to be split open and pulled apart so that the Light of Soul can come through. The Masters had made sure that the mental powers standing in the way would be split to allow the pure Light and Sound of God to come in so that the workshop would be a success.

Today is Easter. For many of us it has meant something of great significance in the past—a rejuvenation and a revival. The celebration itself came down from pre-Christian times. Its purpose was to symbolize the renewal of life and fertility, which these days is represented by the Easter bunny and Easter eggs. This has become almost as much a part of our tradition as Santa Claus. And it's funny—with this intermixing of the Easter bunny, Easter eggs, and the Resurrection, it's getting hard to separate one from the other. It's interesting how readily we tie things together and make them a part of our deepest beliefs, without ever knowing where they came from.

It's interesting how readily we tie things together and make them a part of our deepest beliefs, without ever knowing where they came from.

The legends about Easter have been woven together from the times of Krishna, Zoroaster, and other saviors of the past. Around 1875 Kersey Graves wrote a book called *The World's Sixteen Crucified Saviors*. It tells of resurrection stories that had been given even before Christianity—stories about Godmen who go through the transition of death, then arise and ascend into heaven.

A book called *Jesus Died in Kashmir* gives an account of the silent years of Jesus. Whether a person believes it or not is a personal matter. In biblical times, right after the reign of King Solomon, Israel was split into two kingdoms. The northern kingdom had ten tribes, the southern kingdom had two; and the kingdoms were headed by Jeroboam and Rehoboam. The two kings got into an argument with each other and started a little war. The northern tribes tried to get help to overrun the southern tribes, but the southern tribes won the battle.

After the northern tribes were taken into captivity by the Assyrians, they disappeared. Ever since then, they have been known as the Ten Lost Tribes of Israel. It is suspected that they were taken somewhere to the East, and even today in Kashmir, Afghanistan, and throughout that whole region, there are a number of cities, towns, castes, and family surnames that are identical to those in the Holy Land.

There are records in monasteries indicating that Jesus traveled through the different lands as a child, as a youth, and even after the crucifixion, which, as this story goes, was not done according to the usual Roman protocol of the times where it was assured that the man would die.

The purpose of the book was to say that Jesus lived beyond the crucifixion and then made the second journey to the east. He took up residence there to finish out his mission to the Ten Lost Tribes. There are physical records with bloodlines and family trees that supposedly go all the way back to when he had a family.

Those of you who are interested can look up the information and study it to your heart's content. Then make up your own mind.

Those of you who are interested can look up the information and study it to your heart's content. Then make up your own mind as to how much of the tradition which we have come to call Christianity was developed from other sources. Perhaps the traditions we know were a convenient way to try to boost spirituality at the time.

The early Christians were very primitive in their state of consciousness. When Jesus told his disciples to follow him, they said, "Well, here we are. Can't you see?" But he was talking about going within; he meant, Come follow me into the high place of God. There were just a very few who understood what he was saying, and yet his disciples were greater in consciousness than most of the people in those times.

The ECK Masters will often speak in parables and stories.

The ECK Masters and many of the other people who bring truth into the world will often speak in parables and stories. Jesus often gave straight parables without weaving in the spiritual meaning. One day after he had given a sermon by the sea, his disciples asked him why he always gave these teachings to the people in parables. He said, "Because it is given unto you to know the mysteries of the kingdom of heaven, but to them it is not given. . . . Therefore speak I to them in parables." He was referring to those who were outside of the circle of his disciples and close associates. So the parables were his teachings for the masses. This is a portion of Christianity that even today is often taken as the key teaching, when Jesus in fact said it was not.

Many masters who are able to go to the inner planes have difficulty expressing what they have experienced. Saint Paul tried to teach this. When he went into the inner worlds, he reported that he had heard "unspeakable words, which it is not lawful for a man to utter." There were things he saw he couldn't put into words. This is true of all masters who are able to go to the inner planes.

The Gnostics and the Orthodox Church

In the early times of Christianity there were at least two groups of thought. One became the orthodox way of thinking, the institutional church which began developing in the first and second centuries. It was in direct opposition to those who were called Gnostics. Paul Twitchell, in *Letters to*

Gail, Volume I, made the statement that he was a Gnostic. He said this because the Gnostics were people who went within for their spiritual authority. The leaders of the orthodox, institutional church didn't have the ability to go in their state of consciousness to those heavens within, and so they had to rely on an artificially constructed apostolic tradition. And so the two came into opposition with each other.

The curious thing is, the early orthodox church put a great deal of emphasis upon the truth. So after Jesus died, what happened then? Who would be able to carry on the teachings? Someone who had known him in the physical body. The succession that occurred was through people like Peter, who had known Jesus while he was alive. In later centuries they would say that Peter started the church, that Peter was the first one who saw Jesus after his resurrection. But this was not the case. It was Mary Magdalene.

I am going into this a little bit on Easter because there is an interweaving of how the ECK Masters work and how some of these traditions have become a watered-down, corrupted offshoot.

The apostle Paul was an interesting man. It was he who developed Christianity, the very basis of what is known today, from the teachings of Christ. He took Judaic thought and blended it with Christianity, thereby making it palatable to the Romans. The Roman soldiers weren't going to allow a bunch of people coming in with strange, foreign ideas.

Paul had the ability to go to the inner planes and say that when he is in Christ, he is a new creature. He meant in the Christ consciousness.

Yet the leaders felt there was something wrong with naming Paul as the head of the church. The problem was that he had the ability to go to the inner planes and say that when he is in Christ, he is a new creature. He meant in the Christ consciousness. None of the others had this ability. Paul's authority was Christ on the inner planes, both in his experience on the road to Damascus and later. His tradition was based on the inner man, and this was something the church could not accept. It was Paul who really developed the teachings that became the Christianity we know today. It was not Peter at all.

The Gnostics were coming out with writings that said they talked with Jesus. This brought forth a whole field of thought which was based on inner experience. The Gnostics believed a high form of spiritual revelation came from the man who took his master's words and expressed them through his own creative imagination. The orthodox, institutional church felt the other way—that the highest person was he who could repeat the ancient scriptures word for word, sometimes without knowing what meaning the original sentence intended to give the seeker. It was very interesting how this whole thing occurred.

Once we get within, we go outward into the worlds of God.

Paul Twitchell was a Gnostic. And in the sense of being inner-directed, having the ability to go within, so am I. And then once we get there, we go outward into the worlds of God.

Contemplation versus Meditation

There's a great distinction between meditation and contemplation. Traditional meditation teaches one to go inwardly and sit quietly. It is the heavy spiritual technique of the East, whereas contemplation is the very light one of Eckankar. Meditation has people going inwardly, sitting there trying to still the mind. In so doing, they become passive and quiet. They fall into inertia, a trap of the negative power, and their whole life can become one of dissolution and poverty. India is an example of a country that has gone to meditation en masse—and look at the poverty there.

Contemplation is an active way. We sit down for twenty minutes, chant a sacred name of God such as HU, and look for the Light and Sound of God. As It comes through, it is not meant to be just one experience for your whole lifetime; but It comes in many different ways, at many different times, in many different intensities.

The Light and Sound uplift and purify Soul, bringing the joy and happiness that can never be known by a person who believes and trusts only in the outer teachings. This is why the ECK Masters say you can never put total reliance upon any outer teaching. The ECK writings are only to lead you within. There is much good information and understanding in all the books, including *The Shariyat-Ki-Sugmad*, but these are only a physical translation of the full book which is found on each one of the different planes in the heavenly worlds.

HOW THE ECK MASTERS HELP

The ECK Masters work with us quietly. They come at a time when we need a lesson, when we need insight or inspiration or a little push to help us to the next stage of our spiritual life.

The ECK Masters work with us quietly. Often they will meet us on the street and we won't recognize them. They come at a time when we need a lesson, when we need insight or inspiration or a little push to help us to the next stage of our spiritual life. In the physical plane, this may even reflect in our job and where we live.

One time while I was still living in Wisconsin, I had become very restless. My job no longer offered opportunities for personal growth, and the place where I lived had also become very confining. All I had to do was say it's time to get it together, then gather all my energy, make a decision to move, and find another job. But I couldn't break out of the inertia and take the step.

One winter night, I put on my coat and went out for a walk, just to get my thoughts together. A few snowflakes had started to fall; later it would turn into a snowstorm. I walked for a number of blocks and came to a little shopping center. It was closed due to the lateness of the hour, but two bars on opposite sides of the street were still open. As I got nearer to the bar on my side of the street, I saw a man lounging on the steps, just leaning against the building. He had two crutches under his arms, and in the light from the doorway I could see that they were brand-new. He looked sturdy enough that I could tell he didn't need them for walking.

I was hoping he would strike up a conversation as I walked past, and he did. "Got a light?" he asked.

Just to pass a little time, I was hoping he would strike up a conversation as I walked past, and he did. "Got a light?" he asked. "I don't smoke," I said and figured, *Well, there goes our conversation.* But I made an effort to keep it going. "You know, it's unusual to see a man walking around with crutches when he doesn't need them," I said.

He gave me the most intense stare then, and without saying one word, he picked up his crutches, walked across the street, and went into the other bar. If he had said anything to me, the whole experience would have passed by without another thought on my part, because actually it had come to its completion.

In making up posters, advertising agencies use a certain technique. Maybe you could call it the shoe-that-didn't-drop technique. You're downstairs when you hear the clunk as someone upstairs removes one shoe. You wait and wait for the sound of the other shoe falling, and you can't sleep all night, wondering why the guy won't drop it.

Advertising agencies stir up the same kind of anxiety with posters. They seem well balanced and look very good to the untrained eye, but somehow they incorporate an element that makes you feel the message is incomplete. And what you want to do then is find out what's missing. Quite conveniently there happens to be an order blank attached so that you can send for the missing part—and very subtly they have accomplished what they set out to do.

It was the same with this man. If he had given me an answer to why he was walking around with crutches, the experience would have seemed complete, and I would never have bothered to wonder about it again.

When I got back to my room, I sat and thought about this perfectly healthy man holding on to two crutches that he no longer needed. Why keep carrying them around? Why not just leave them behind?

"Wait a minute!" I said. "*I'm* carrying two crutches, too—one is my job, and the other is the place I live." I needed them at a certain point in my life to get back on my feet after going through difficult times, but lately I had been wanting to get rid of them. So why not just do it? Out loud I said, "OK, I got the picture!"

Was this man one of the ECK Masters who walk quietly in the background and never tell you who they are? It's hard to say. You are going to meet them, but you won't know it, because they will never tell you.

Anyone who steps on the path of ECK to become an ECK Master in hopes of recognition and acclaim is usually disappointed. The ECK Masters work quietly in the background. The Living ECK Master must work in the forefront, but when his job is finished, he turns over the duties to a successor who is most qualified by his specific talents to take the message of ECK into the world for the next leg of the journey. And from then on, the former Living ECK Master works quietly in the background.

We are learning to work with intuition, which actually is Spirit speaking to us and giving us the gentle guidance to make our life better.

LEARNING TO WORK WITH SPIRIT

We are learning as we go, even though we have the Light and Sound, even though we are tuned in. We are learning to work with intuition, which actually is Spirit speaking to us and giving us the gentle guidance to make our life better. Spirit is always with us, always guiding, always protecting, always attempting to bring joy and make our life better, but that doesn't mean that we are always aware and listening.

Spirit is always with us, always guiding, always protecting, always attempting to bring joy and make our life better, but that doesn't mean that we are always aware and listening.

A few years ago when I was selected to go to Europe and speak at an ECK seminar, I boarded a jumbo jet leaving from New York. In the minutes before takeoff, the entire plane was filled—except for the two seats on either side of mine at the front of the cabin. And as it got closer to departure time, my hopes rose higher and higher that I would have all three seats to myself for the all-night flight. This meant I could sleep, arrive rested, and beat jet lag. My luck continued to hold even after the doors were secured and the plane took off.

Just as I was starting to get comfortable and relaxed, a flight attendant came over and said, "There's a very elderly lady way in the back, and she wonders if she could come up here and sit by your window." I wasn't exactly thrilled at this change in my plans, but filled with the goodwill of ECK, I said, "Of course."

It seemed like no more than a few seconds had passed when this little old woman came bounding up the aisle as fast as an Easter bunny. She didn't even give me time to get out of the seat—just squeezed right by me and plunked herself down next to the window.

I was in the center seat, about to move over to the aisle, when she said, "My husband is still in the back of the plane. His legs are bad, and he has to sit on the aisle so he can stretch out and keep them straight."

Now remember, I am an ECKist; I'm supposed to be tuned in and know what the score is—but I was more like a child in the wilderness.

She pounced for the kill: "Would it be all right if my husband came up here and took the aisle seat? This way we could talk a little."

And what am I supposed to say?

As soon as the plane leveled off, she went hopping over me again as quick as could be, and in record time she and the husband with the bum legs returned to torment me even more. She jumped in by the window, he took the seat on the aisle, and there I sat between them. At this point he became filled with conversation, leaning across me to talk to his wife, all the time giving me these hard stares that said, What kind of a turkey separates a man from his wife?

They weren't finished with me yet. The woman could tell how uncomfortable this was making me, so she said to her husband, "This young man has kindly offered to go and take your seat at the back of the plane." I couldn't believe I was hearing these words. But the next time the flight attendant came by, the woman said, "This young man has volunteered to go to the back of the plane so that my husband and I can sit together and talk." In a daze, I gathered my things and followed the attendant to the very last seat in the plane, right next to the lavatory, in the smoking section.

"I think she took me," I said to myself as I sat back there, realizing how fast those two worked. She and her husband had gone through this little routine many times before. And so I learned something and became much wiser.

We walk this path to God, and we do the best we can. Along the way we get help both from the Inner Master and the ECK Masters who walk among us.

The same kind of thing has happened on many flights since then—father and little son or other combinations—and others traveling with me immediately jump up and relinquish their seats. As I sit there observing this, I say to myself, "Their generosity will be blessed many times over—but I'm not moving!"

So we walk this path to God, and we do the best we can. Along the way we get help both from the Inner Master and the ECK Masters who walk among us. They may come in disguise, they may be well-dressed, they may appear to be businessmen; but they will be speaking the words of Spirit which are needed by us at that particular moment.

The Detached State

Detached means seeing the play of life—crying when we must, laughing when we can—but at all times looking at life from the viewpoint of Soul, knowing that even this shall pass away.

These ECK Masters of the Vairagi are able to do this because they have attained the detached state. Detached means seeing the play of life—crying when we must, laughing when we can—but at all times looking at life from the viewpoint of Soul, knowing that even this shall pass away.

A poem with this title was written by a man named Theodore Tilton. It tells the story of a wise king, a seeker who was looking for the spiritual truths. But he already had the state of detachment which we look for on the path to God as we make our way toward personal mastership.

This king had all the wealth of his position, including the finest jewels from across the oceans. But while others were swayed by such riches, he was not. He often looked at the signet ring he wore on his hand, which bore the seal of his kingly office. On it he had inscribed the words "Even this shall pass away." This reminded him to keep a detached viewpoint so that he could enjoy the moment without being caught up in the pain of loss or blinded by the illusion of power or wealth. It kept him in balance and allowed him a clear, levelheaded view of life.

Even as he gazed at his lovely bride, the most beautiful young woman in the kingdom, he was seeing with the eyes of Soul. He said, "Mortal flesh must come to clay—even this shall pass away."

He enjoyed the moment, and he enjoyed his life, because he was able to have the overview that we are seeking for ourselves.

Time passed, and the king went off to war. During the battle a lance went through his shield, wounding him badly. His men carried him to his tent, and while he was healing, the pain was almost beyond his endurance. But as he slowly healed over the weeks that followed, he often said, "Even this shall pass away." It gave him perspective. It gave him the spiritual viewpoint.

One day he went into the square where a statue had been erected in his honor. In disguise he walked among the people, and humbly he said, "What is fame? . . . Even this shall pass away."

The king grew to be a very old man, and now, faced with the specter of dying, he wondered what awaited him on the other side. As he lay on his deathbed, his heart calm and confident, a beam of sunlight appeared through the curtains and struck his ring. He looked down at it and saw the words, "Even this shall pass away."

He knew now that there was life beyond, that physical life was but a step in the existence of Soul as It gains the maturity to become a Co-worker with God.

Through the spiritual exercises, we gain the detached state of the Vairagi ECK Masters.

We go within, and we find the Light and Sound of God. Through the spiritual exercises, we then gain the detached state of the Vairagi ECK Masters. We gain illumination and enlightenment—the true enlightenment which is beyond the emotional and the mental planes, beyond cosmic consciousness and beyond the ECKshar. When this happens—when we have reached the highest consciousness that is known on this physical plane—then we have joined this order of the ECK Masters.

Know that the Light and Sound are always with you. On your journey homeward there will be safety and joy; and as you come home, spiritual unfoldment. May the blessings be.

ECKANKAR International Youth Conference, Washington, DC, Sunday, April 3, 1983

Her way of giving Ray and me more time to talk was to set the clock back one hour to 9:30 p.m.

18
The Creative Power of Soul

The topic this morning is the creative power of Soul. At each seminar I try to give stories, techniques, or something that you can take home with you: some little thing that's helpful so that you can say it was worth it to attend the seminar.

Backstage someone just handed me this greeting card. It's the kind that Soul would give.

Backstage someone just handed me this greeting card. It's the kind that Soul would give. On the front it says, "All-purpose generic greeting card." And then at the bottom, very carefully, it lists the size: five inches by seven inches. Generics make sure of every detail. The message that comes with the card is: "Whatever"—which is generic, of course. And there's a nice little note handwritten inside: "Living the basic fundamentals of ECK daily allows me to be a basic, nongeneric, all-purpose initiate of the Light and Sound; and all I ask is to be of greater service to Spirit."

Getting Confident in Spirit

Yesterday someone told me about a conversation that took place among four young ladies, just about ready to become teenagers, who were riding up in the elevator. Though still in their swimsuits, with big towels wrapped around them, they said, "We're going upstairs to see the Master."

Some of the people in the elevator were ECKists, some not. Even the ECKists couldn't help wondering what made these girls sound so sure. A man attending an insurance convention at the hotel couldn't figure out what they were talking about. He said, "Master? What do you mean by 'Master'?"

They said, "Do you know anything about ECK?"

"No," he said.

"Then you wouldn't understand."

As the elevator moved upward, they talked among themselves: "Do you suppose it's really right to go see the Master in our bathing suits and towels?"

The doors opened on one of the upper floors, and sure enough, there I was—just standing in the hallway. Without even batting an eye, they said, "Hi, we came to see you." I said, "Yes, I know."

Many of the young people are getting confident in Spirit and in their inner experiences of Light and Sound, which are the two aspects of God that uplift and bring the maturity of Soul we are looking for. They become so confident, in fact, that they have to learn to be careful at school in what they say about ECK to their friends. It's how you live it that counts. Let other people have their freedom.

It's how you live it that counts. Let other people have their freedom.

At school my daughter is quiet about her involvement with ECK because she has learned it's wise to keep it to herself. The few times she tried to talk about it, her friends gave her funny looks.

She's going to graduate from the fourth grade on Wednesday, and for the last two weeks of school they got to use a computer. The computer represents a whole new era in education. Computers sometimes drive me wild—the buttons won't go, the thing locks up on you, and even when you shake it, it either won't spill out the words you've put in there or it manages to lose them. But the youth are learning how to work with them very naturally. They're growing up with them, and it's a very interesting part of their education.

Her class was given an assignment to put together some kind of pictograph on the computer. She decided to write *ECK*. She made a great big *E* out of little *e*'s, a *C* made up of little *c*'s, and a *K* made of little *k*'s. She hasn't gotten it printed out yet, but she said, "I know what my friends are going to say when it prints out. They'll ask, 'What's ECK?' and I'll just say, 'It's Spirit. Don't you know that, man?' "

The children aren't apologetic about ECK, because it's a part of their life. We adults have come into ECK through the back door—by way of other religions. Often one tries to compare ECK with what he knew before: Does it fit this path? Is it as good? Does it show us the Time Track as quickly? Do we remember dreams as well? What about knowing the future? All these funny little things go on in the mind.

Encourage children to get their own answer. Just say, "Go back in the dream state tonight and see if you can find out what it means, and let's talk about it tomorrow morning."

The ECK children have the Light and Sound, and if an inner experience comes—such as from a past life—they absorb it. They'll speak with their parents about it and ask, "What does it mean?" You can try to give them an answer, or better yet, you can encourage them to get their own. Just say, "Go back in the dream state tonight and see if you can find out what it means, and let's talk about it tomorrow morning. Let's see if you understand it better."

FINDING OUR OWN ANSWERS

A real Master or a real authority tries not to put himself in the position of giving all the answers to one who is seeking truth. He wants the individual to find his own answers. Some people routinely come to an ECK Master for a solution to their problems.

A real Master wants the individual to find his own answers.

One individual, for example, was trying to decide if he should buy some property in another country. He wanted to buy a farm, and this involved a whole change of life for him.

He said, "I can buy it in one of two countries, and I'm more of a native in one country than the other. Which should I buy?"

I said, "Well, make a very good study of the whole situation. Sit down and make a list of all the positive aspects and all the negative aspects. Lay them out side by side, and investigate it thoroughly."

I was trying to get him to look at it objectively himself, so that he could better determine what was involved in making such a big move. It was a major transition from his present clerical occupation to farming. He wanted to grow things, but it can be a hard life. You've got to have money to start with as well as some knowledge about the crops. Will they grow? If they don't, do you have enough money to live on until next year?

Soon after our talk, he wrote me a letter: "I've made up the lists and studied all the information. Now what should I do?"

I didn't give him the answer that he wanted. I wrote back to him with this message: "What happens when you have to make a decision about which kind of fertilizer to buy? Suppose I'm not there or your letter gets lost in the mail for two or three months. What are you going to do with your farm then? So make up your own mind. What do you want to do? What are you going to do? Where have your talents brought you up until today? This is your starting point."

FOCUSING OUR ATTENTION

Working with the creative power of Soul means learning how to focus your attention. Often I hear, "I can't make my mind still long enough to do the spiritual exercises." It's something you have to work with, because if you're going to be good in anything, you have to put some effort into it—whether you are studying to be a doctor or whatever else.

The power of Soul is ignited by the chanting of your word.

The path of ECK doesn't eliminate the five passions of the mind; we learn how to control them. How? By focused attention, the power of Soul, which is ignited by the chanting of your word. By chanting your word, you instantly have the power to raise yourself in consciousness to the point where you are able to step back from any situation so that it doesn't overwhelm you. Then you can look at it objectively and unemotionally and figure out what's happening. Ask yourself, Is it in my best interest? or Is someone using his creative imagination to trap me within the dimensions of his time and space?

BECOMING THE AWAKENED SOUL

We're looking to become the conscious, awakened Soul. This means being completely free of outer influences by anyone else. Then when you walk into a grocery store, you won't be so swayed by all the silent fingers tugging at you from the shelves, wrapped in pretty colored boxes that say, "Buy me! Buy me! If you do, you'll be healthier, wealthier, and wiser!"

I went into a fast-food restaurant two nights ago with my family. You know the kind—three minutes after you walk in, you're sitting at a table, eating your meal out of a box.

Working in those fast-food restaurants offers a good opportunity for young people to take that first step toward becoming self-sufficient. It's hard to work there, and usually the best thing that can be said for it is that they learn very quickly there must be a better way to make a living. But in the meantime, it gives them something to show on a résumé, so that when they apply for another job, they have a better chance to be chosen over someone who has no experience at all.

These restaurants are almost like corrals for the customers to be herded through. Before we even got all the way in the door, the young man behind the counter was saying, "May I take your order?" I tried to ignore him, because if you walk in with your wife and daughter, it's not an easy thing to immediately come up with one order. It takes a little negotiating to finally get it together so the person at the counter can make sense out of it and ring it up on the cash register. He doesn't understand that you're doing him a favor by stalling.

The young man's fingers were reaching out, and I could feel that he was just itching to ask us again for our order. I continued to try to ignore his message, even turning away from him and standing back about ten feet from the counter.

As we left the restaurant, I tried to smooth things over. Paul Twitchell did the same thing one time for a woman who had snuck into an Initiates meeting.

He finally couldn't hold himself back anymore. "What do you want to order?"

"Hold it!" I said. "Will you give me a chance to make up my mind?" He didn't mean to get in my space, but he was all over it. This took away some of the goodwill and happiness from him and from me, and we both wished it hadn't happened. As we left, I made a point to say a few nice words to him about the good job he was doing and tried to smooth things over.

Paul Twitchell did the same thing one time for a woman who had snuck into an Initiates meeting. Paul had said it was to be a meeting for Second Initiates and above, and she wasn't an initiate at the time. She came in and began to ask many, many questions. I couldn't make heads or tails out of them. I was very nervous. You see, I wasn't a Second Initiate either, but I hadn't snuck in! I had explained at the desk that my initiation was scheduled for the next day, and I received permission to attend.

When this woman began to ask all these funny questions about psychic and occult things, I said to myself, "Is this ECK? What is going on? Did I come on the wrong path?"

All of a sudden Paul looked at her and said, very sharply, "You don't belong here." I wondered if maybe he meant me too.

This is an example of imagination running wild. Yes, I belonged there, but even though I had permission to come in, I couldn't help thinking, *Oh no, what's going to happen to me now?*

When the meeting was over, Paul apologized to her. He said, "I shouldn't have been quite so harsh about this," and he smoothed it over very nicely.

Setting Goals for Ourselves

A principle of Soul is to be timely. If you're going to set a framework in this world, if you're going to set a goal, also set a deadline to accomplish it. What are you going to do, and when will you finish it? No matter what it is, set yourself a goal and a deadline, because this is how you begin working with the creative imagination.

A principle of Soul is to be timely. Set yourself a goal and a deadline, because this is how you begin working with the creative imagination.

You start by saying, I'm going to do something. Make it small enough at first so that you can actually accomplish it. You don't want to be like the gardener who keeps planting seeds in a garden that never bears fruits or vegetables. Pretty soon, if you keep putting seeds in the ground without getting results, you become discouraged.

Set your goals so that you can reach them. If you are planning to reach into the higher states of consciousness for Self-Realization and God-Realization, you're going to have to set goals for yourself. And where do you practice setting goals? In your daily life out here.

If something in your life is making you unhappy, whether it's the amount of money you earn or a person you work with, set new goals—for yourself, not the other person. Do this in the name of Spirit while chanting your word and acting as if your goals were already attained. This is using creative imagination; you live the wish fulfilled.

Understanding Protection

Letters to Gail, Volume I, gives you some of these techniques. You might look at them and say, "Isn't this psychic?" On the other hand, look at your body: "Isn't it physical?" We have psychic bodies; they're part of us. We have the five passions of the mind as well as the five virtues. As long as we are in this world, they are going to be with us.

Never allow any thought to come in that can harm you in any way, because you are Soul. You are eternal—and nothing can hurt Soul.

How to defend yourself when someone sends you a psychic attack is described in the book. Whatever you do, never allow any thought to come in that can harm you in any way, because you are Soul. You are eternal—and nothing can hurt Soul.

If you fix this strongly in your consciousness, you build the outer protection so that nothing can come through. You have to know and understand that this is one purpose of the word that you use. You create a spiritual foundation where you become so strong that no matter what comes up, you instantly remember to chant your word. By doing so, you open yourself to the full help of Spirit that is already around you and available to you. What it does is open the floodgates of your understanding.

This is why we speak of the circles of initiation. If you are an initiate of the Second Circle, it opens you to the circle of awareness which corresponds to the degree of help you are able to accept from Spirit. When you get to the Third and Fourth, correspondingly you reach a greater circle of awareness of the help you can accept from Spirit, which is already there. This is what is meant when the Master says, "I am always with you."

Your word helps you to open up and accept the protection that is your heritage.

Your word helps you to open up and accept the protection that is your heritage. This includes information needed to improve your health and guidance in finding the best doctor, dentist, or nutritionist you can. That's how we do it here in the physical world.

That's what I do too. In the year before I got this job, I really didn't have time to study health matters, and I didn't exercise. Eventually I found that I had to catch up on my nutrition and exercises, because this physical body has to be a good vehicle. We keep it in the best shape we can.

There are times you're strong and times you're weak. When you're weak, you figure out how to get your strength back up, how to work with what you have, and how to get the most mileage out of yourself.

Using the Creative Imagination

I would like to tell you about someone who uses the creative imagination in an interesting way. This is the wife of Ray, the Good-Rumor Man, whom I mention in *The Wind of Change*. Ray's wife is not a student of Eckankar, but she has her method of living the ECK life in a very natural way. She never worries because, she says, "Ray does most of it for us—and he does it quite well."

It used to upset her when her checking-account balance fell below fifteen dollars—but not enough to stop writing checks. Eventually she figured out a way to overcome her worry: She simply stopped subtracting when she reached the fifteen-dollar level.

The first time she received a notice from the bank, she showed it to her husband. "Ray, what does *NSF* mean?"

"Oh, no!" he said. "That means, 'not sufficient funds.'"

"Oh," she said.

But she had stopped concerning herself with whether or not they had enough money to cover the checks which she continued to write. A few days later, when another notice came from the bank, she went to Ray and asked again for an explanation of those enigmatic initials, *NSF*. "You told me the other day, but I forgot. What did you say *NSF* meant?"

"Oh, no!" he said.

Ray wondered how he could keep their marriage together and his wife, who refused to live by other people's rules, out of jail. Finally he figured out a way to sneak more money into the bank account without letting her know.

So she writes checks as needed and stops subtracting when the balance drops below fifteen dollars. He deposits money in the account on the sly. And with each one using their creative imagination, they have managed to keep peace in their marriage.

With each one using their creative imagination, Ray and his wife have managed to keep peace in their marriage.

Of course, this won't work in an ECK family, because if you're writing checks that bounce, your spouse is going to say, "I heard that talk, so don't pull it on me."

We pay our own way. We don't try to get something for nothing. We find out that it doesn't work anyway and that we're going to have to pay for it. But within that family unit, they figured out a way to balance this out.

Ray's wife also has her own way of dealing with time. It doesn't bother her at all. She never looks at her watch the way I do; she simply rearranges time to fit herself. She is working as Soul. She creates her own world; nobody does it for her.

I visited with them about a month ago. Ray and I sat and talked for quite awhile that evening, and when it got to be 10:15 p.m., I thought it was about time to go. I said, "You have to get up for work in the morning, so I'm going to leave at ten thirty. I don't want to take up your whole night."

"No big thing," he said.

His wife walked in just then and overheard us. "Don't worry about it," she said. "Ray stays up until at least midnight every night." She's very open with life. She volunteers freely of Ray's time.

After she left the room, Ray said, "Listen, if she thinks you're planning to leave at ten thirty, she'll just walk in here and turn back the clock."

"You're kidding," I said.

"No, I'm not. I know her."

At 10:30 p.m., Ray and I stood up and started to say good night. She walked back in and said, "Why are you leaving?"

"Because it's ten thirty," I said.

"No problem." She walked over to the grandfather clock, opened the door, changed the time to 9:30 p.m., and slammed the door shut. "There," she said. "Now you have more time." And she left the room.

Ray and I sat back down.

"Don't you feel a lot more comfortable now?" he said. "And have you noticed that the pressures of time don't weigh on you so much?"

I said, "You know, it's really true. I feel much more relaxed than I did—and much more relaxed than I will an hour from now."

After his wife left the room, Ray said, "Listen, if she thinks you're planning to leave at ten thirty, she'll just walk in here and turn back the clock." "You're kidding," I said.

That was one of the creative techniques she used in her daily life; she refused to allow a small thing like time to rule her world.

We are learning how to survive as Soul, and the key is always the Spiritual Exercises of ECK and the word that you use every day. Experiment with your spiritual exercises. Develop the ability of randomity, which Rebazar Tarzs has spoken of. Experiment. If something works, go with it; stay with it until you become tired of it. Then try something new.

Invent your own spiritual exercises. You can create your own because you are Soul, and in Soul you are free.

Look through the basic exercises given in the ECK books. Use these as supplementary exercises if you find you want to try something fresh. Or use the ones you find in the ECK discourses. Whatever works for you, use it. Invent your own spiritual exercises. You can create your own because you are Soul, and in Soul you are free.

ECKANKAR Creative Arts Festival, St. Louis, Missouri, June 12, 1983

You can't even steal a little thing like a baseball without somebody looking over your shoulder.

19
My God Is Bigger . . .

Sudar Singh, the ECK Master, had a problem learning how to speak about the message he got when he went to his inner worlds. It sounds as if it should be an easy thing. But I know those of you who have tried to talk to others when they ask about ECK have found it's not always so easy. When another person asks about ECK, he's inviting you into his home, into his state of consciousness.

When another person asks about ECK, he's inviting you into his home, into his state of consciousness.

This afternoon I met a little boy outside the hall. We took a walk together. Along the way he stepped on a rock. "That one got me!" he said. He gave me his whole family history during our little stroll, and then he said, "See the tent back there? That's where I sleep."

Just to see what he'd say, I asked if it would be OK if I stayed overnight. He looked the tent over, trying to decide if he should invite me to stay. At first he said, "I think it's too small." Then he thought about it for a while longer. "Well, maybe there's room."

What Are We Looking For?

A big question is, What are we looking for when we say we are looking for God? You can take a hundred

You can take a hundred people, all members of the same church, and you will have a hundred different understandings of what God is. This is because each one is Soul, and Soul is a unique being, a spark of God.

people who all consider themselves members of the same church, and you will have a hundred different understandings of what God is. This is because each one of those people is Soul, and Soul is a unique being, a spark of God.

When I was studying the Christian faith, on the one hand I'd say to myself, "God is good"; but when I got sick, I'd say, "Dear God, please make me well." It's a funny paradox. If I had stopped to think a moment, I might have realized that if all things come from God, and God brought this illness to me, then maybe I should just accept it instead of questioning God's judgment by asking for it to be taken away.

Sometimes I would rationalize it: When I'm well, it's God; when I'm sick, it's the devil. But sometimes we become ill simply because we eat too much of the wrong kinds of food. Our system gets out of balance and we get colds, flus, or stomach upsets, and then we want a miracle. We're sick one second and well the next, and as soon as we're feeling better, we go back and eat some more of the food that caused our illness.

I was joking with a person who was traveling with me recently. Both of us had gotten airsick on the plane—not much, just enough to feel unsettled. Even though the smoking section is in the back of the plane, the smoke is constantly blowing and being recirculated, and you get to inhale it again and again. Pretty soon you may not feel so well.

By the time we landed neither of us was feeling very well. I had read somewhere that gingerroot was good for settling the stomach and had been thinking of experimenting to see if it really worked. "I read in one of the business magazines that gingerroot is supposed to be good for motion sickness," I said to my companion. "Would you like to try it?" He took some, and so did I. But at the same time we went for a walk outside to get some fresh air.

Soon we both felt better. The question now was, What made us feel better? Was it the walk, or the gingerroot? Or neither?

This is the interesting thing about asking God to heal us. When a healing occurs, it sometimes comes about in such a natural way that we just take it for granted. For instance, a friend may come to us and recommend a doctor. Spirit uses every form, and we may never recognize that this doctor was the instrument for the divine healing that we requested.

Wanting to Know the Future

Besides wanting to be healed, another fascination people have is wanting to know the future. This is often based on fear. Entire industries are built around this fear of the future. Insurance is one example. You've got to have it for your health, your car, and everything else. There is nothing wrong with insurance, except when it's based on fear. Of course, if the state law requires it, I take out car insurance. But people want to know the future so that if trouble is coming, they can sidestep it. This stems from the fear of death or, worse yet, fear of a lingering illness that can only end in death.

Before any major event in an American Indian's life, he was apt to fast. Then he would go into the woods and wait for a revelation from the being we know today as the Inner Master.

The American Indians used a technique called a vision quest. Before any major event in an Indian's life, he was apt to go on a total fast for three to four days. Then he would go into the woods and wait for a revelation from the being we know today as the Inner Master. He would go within, to the heart, where he would contemplate, reflect, and look for a vision or some sign that would give him an insight into the future. This was his way of going within and talking with God to find out how he should direct his life.

The oracle at Delphi in Greece was another attempt by the people to learn what the future held. The oracle itself was underground. There was a woman through whom it was believed Apollo spoke. When a person came to see the oracle, he would have to stand outside for a couple of weeks or even a couple of months, until one day the high priestess would come and say, "The oracle will see you." The person would descend to the underground room where the woman, speaking with a man's deep voice, would give a prophecy.

A man with a very bad stammer walked in to see the oracle at Delphi, hoping to find a cure.

In one case, a man with a very bad stammer walked in, hoping to find a cure. Before he could even say a word, the oracle spoke out in a loud, booming voice: "You have come for a voice!"

He waited, expecting to hear the solution to his problem. The oracle continued: "Go to Libya, conquer the land, and raise abundant flocks." At first he protested. All he wanted was to be able to speak well without stammering. But after considering the answer, he decided to go.

In Libya, he and his men got into battle with the soldiers there and won the fight. When it was all over, the man realized that he had lost his stammer. And with that conquest, he now had the land and material goods to lead a better life.

In a way, he had been asking Divine Spirit to heal his voice. He was directed through the oracle to a way that would earn him this healing. When he objected, it was because he did not understand that Spirit actually was arranging for his well-being in a much broader sense: Not only would his speech impediment be cured, but he would also gain those things which were good for his spiritual unfoldment in this life.

Unfolding Spiritually

This spiritual unfoldment continues even with our children. I've got a little model airplane, the hand-launched kind. My brothers and I used to spend a lot of time, when we were young, making gliders and flying them in our field. My older brother was very good at making model airplanes. He threw around words like *dihedral*, *conical camber*, *ailerons*, *elevons*, and all these fantastic-sounding things. Since he was older, I studied and learned from him.

We would make up a prototype of a glider. Then we'd put a notch on the plane, cut an old inner tube into long strips, and use it like a slingshot to launch the plane into the air. These things would go high. We created our own designs with little delta wings, and if the plane didn't fly quite right, we would take it back to the drawing board and redesign it until it was perfected.

When we were young, flying model airplanes was important to us because it made us look up to something. When we flew the plane, it was like we had launched a bird.

Flying the model airplanes was important to us because it made us look up to something. When we flew the plane, it was like we had launched a bird. It was a secret yearning that you had inside as a child, but you couldn't put your finger on it. It found expression when you could fly a kite or send a model airplane soaring.

So even though we live in the city, I got my daughter a little hand-launched plane. I cut a notch in it and got some big rubber bands. We take it out to the school yard once or twice a week, and whenever we fly the plane, I make a point to run after it. That's my way of getting exercise.

One day we were flying the plane at one end of this field, and at the other end were some people playing baseball. They were hitting fly balls, and pretty soon the guys who were shagging the balls decided to run in and rest. The others continued to hit them, and in a short time there were baseballs all around the outfield. In the meantime, I launched my plane. It took off with a *zing* and flew quite a distance, landing near a baseball that had gone farther than all the others.

Along comes this little guy about nine years old. He runs over to the ball and calls back to his friend who hadn't yet spotted it, "Hey, look, here's a baseball." He's trying to act as if it just happens to be there for no reason, ignoring all the other baseballs lying about ten feet away.

I stood right behind him, kind of watching to see what he would do. With a quick glance to the left and right, he bent over, picked up the ball, and very carefully eased it into his pocket. He didn't realize that the players way off in the distance were noticing that he had taken one of their baseballs. I said to him, "That ball belongs to those fellows over there; I bet they'd be really happy if you carried it in for them." The little guy was startled; he didn't know anyone was behind him.

His friend ran up then, and I heard this little voice say, "Hi, Harold." I looked around and saw that it was an ECKist. The other little guy, with a sheepish grin on his face, quickly pulled the ball out of his pocket and threw it on the grass.

Although the ECKist had been way off in the distance when his buddy lifted the baseball, he came over in time to make an interesting observation: You can't even steal a little thing like a baseball without somebody looking over your shoulder. The one who happened to help you to learn this lesson about the Law of Karma is also the individual who works with you on the inner.

There is a saying that the closer a person comes to God, the more refined he becomes in character. This is true.

We teach our children to respect the rights and property of other people. There is a saying that the closer a person comes to God, the more refined he becomes in character. This is true.

Understanding Boredom

My daughter knows better than to ever tell me she's bored. I've told her, "There is always something to do, or life wouldn't have placed you where you are, so don't tell me you're bored. It means you haven't looked inside deeply enough to figure out what to do with yourself right now."

One day she forgot. She was just lounging on the couch when she said, "Dad, I'm bored"—and for some reason she fell right off the couch. From down on the floor, she looked up at me and said, "Dad, I'm not bored anymore."

The saying as given in the Bible is, "For as he thinketh in his heart, so is he." Thoughts are things, and it's important to keep our thoughts of a spiritual nature, where we put our attention on living a life which is a clear step toward growth. In whatever we do, are we growing? Are we learning? Are we enjoying this lifetime while we have our strength and our health?

In whatever we do, are we growing? Are we learning? Are we enjoying this lifetime while we have our strength and our health?

The idea is, we become what we think. We live our lives according to our spiritual understanding of life, and before we find the path of ECK or another religious path that fits us, we are like fish out of water. We're like the ugly duckling; we don't fit.

The Law of Cause and Effect

Someone wrote to me from a farm in Africa. He said a hen laid a bunch of eggs that were fertilized by a funny-looking rooster whose head and neck were bald. Every time the rooster would come in the yard, the family would all laugh at it.

It was all pretty funny until the eggs hatched. One of the chicks came out looking exactly like the rooster—bald head, bald neck. Because the little thing was so ugly and small, the other chicks picked on it and finally even broke its leg. To protect it, the family had to bring it into the house.

The person who wrote the letter said, "You know, it's interesting how we laughed at this rooster that was bald-headed and bald-necked, and now all of a sudden we find that one just like him has taken up residence in our home!"

The person from a farm in Africa said, "We laughed at this rooster that was bald-headed and bald-necked, and now all of a sudden we find one just like him has taken up residence in our home!"

Thoughts of any nature are going to come home to roost. This is called the Law of Karma, or the Law of Cause and Effect. The ECKists are quite familiar with it.

It reminds me of a friend of mine who likes to go camping. To him this means staying in a tent and roughing it, but to his wife, it means going to a motel with a color TV and a pool.

One day after a disagreement on whether or not to go camping, he took his son and stormed out of the house. She was just as happy to stay home—she's a very easygoing sort. He jumped in the car with his son, and they drove off into the country, about two miles outside the city.

Children at a certain age have a peculiar knack for doing strange things that you can never put any rhyme or reason to. For some reason, his son started playing with the car keys. He tossed them in the air for a while, and then he threw them into the tall grass. Something else must have caught his attention, and he just forgot all about them. Later he simply could not remember what he'd done with those keys.

After their overnight outing, my friend came back to the car, and he couldn't get in. He was out in a remote area, and finally he had no choice but to call his wife. "Listen," he said, "we're going to be late. We've spent the last hour scratching around in the grass looking for the keys."

She started laughing. "You know you had it coming," she said. "That's what you get. That's your payment." She isn't an ECKist, but she understands the laws of life. She didn't call it karma because she didn't know it in those terms, but she knew about the Law of Cause and Effect. His anger had come back to him quickly; now he very patiently had to look for the keys.

The key to the self-mastery we are looking for is self-discipline. If something comes up, we don't fly into a blind rage, because Soul is in control of our emotions and of our mind.

The key to the self-mastery we are looking for is self-discipline. If something comes up, we don't fly into a blind rage, because Soul is in control of our emotions and of our mind.

I've been working with my daughter, trying to teach her things about science and the Law of Cause and Effect. I bought her a little science kit that is supposed to demonstrate this law. The kit contained a boxlike cut-out made of very light, thin plastic. You were to make a catapult on top of it and pin wheels on the bottom to make a wagon.

I said to my daughter, "What you need is not pins, but a straight rod going all the way through. That little box they gave you is too light. If you stick a pin in it and try to use that for an axle, you'll only have three wheels touching; one's going to be tilted up."

Children being the way they are, she wouldn't believe me. She worked and worked and somehow got the whole thing together, but it was barely holding. I tried to tell her it was a foolhardy thing to do and that she was wasting her time, but she went right on to the next step. The whole principle was that when a marble shot out of the catapult, this lightweight plastic box, now a wagon on wheels, would take off in the other direction.

She put the marble in the sling and cut the restraining string. The marble went shooting off, the wagon didn't budge, and she yelled, "It worked!"

I said, "I'm afraid you don't get the point of this. It wasn't the marble you were supposed to be watching, but the wagon. It was supposed to move in the opposite direction of the marble."

"Oh," she said. "I guess it didn't work then, did it?" She's very patient in learning the laws of life.

Spiritual Understanding

As we start out in our own searchings, we may pray to God for this or that. As we go farther, we learn much prayer is asking God to change what God has already allowed. Maybe God allowed this for our own learning. And then our prayers change from "God, take away this illness" to "God, let me understand why this has been given to me." In other words, we begin asking for spiritual understanding.

As we go farther, our prayers change from "God, take away this illness" to "God, let me understand why this has been given to me."

At first, we look for a Master to teach us about spiritual unfoldment, to help us find truth, to show us how to find the Light and Sound of God. Then when we find the Master, we expect him to do everything for us.

You're probably familiar with the characters in the Beetle Bailey cartoons—the sergeant and Beetle. In one cartoon the sergeant has his left hand clutched around Beetle's throat and his right hand clenched into a fist, drawn back and ready to let Beetle have it. Beetle is just standing there, his mouth in a curvy line, pretty much resigned to it. The sergeant says, "Beetle, you've been my greatest disappointment."

In the center frame, the sergeant continues his talk. He still has Beetle by the neck with his left hand, his right fist is still drawn back, but he hasn't yet punched him. He says, "Why can't I make you change? Why can't I make you grow?"

Beetle, of course, isn't ready to take on any of the responsibility himself. In the third frame, he throws it all back to the sergeant: "Well, maybe you just don't have a green thumb."

You know, there's a spiritual principle in practically everything. It's in Beetle Bailey cartoons, it's everywhere. People ask for help from a spiritual master, whether it's Jesus, Buddha, Krishna, or any of the modern-day saviors, expecting that master to do everything for them.

The Motivation to Find God

The Living ECK Master will give you certain disciplines and say, If you want to see the Light of God, you do this. We want to see the spiritual Light, and the Master gives the directions, but sometimes we're just too lazy to follow them.

He'll tell us to try certain disciplines: Do the Spiritual Exercises of ECK, spend time contemplating upon something that is sacred and beautiful to you, and you will also hear the Sound of God. Those of you who are in ECK and have the experiences of the inner planes know the Voice of God can be heard as the music of the spheres. This comes when you're sitting quietly in contemplation. Some of you hear It as a flute, a symphony, the twittering of birds, or the buzzing of bees. Sometimes It sounds like the roar of a train going by.

Of those who want to walk the spiritual path, I would ask this question: What motivation do you have that is strong enough for you to look for God in every waking moment of your day?

But when the Master has given you techniques to go about finding the way to God—to get this pure essence of God coming into you for your spiritual unfoldment, to give you healing, to give you an insight into your future—some people are too lazy after the first couple of tries to give it any more effort. Then they try to throw the blame back to the Master and say, as Beetle Bailey did, "Well, maybe you don't have a green thumb."

They are saying the Master doesn't have a green thumb, when it's the spiritual student who doesn't have the self-discipline.

Of those who want to walk the spiritual path, I would ask this question: What motivation do you have that is strong enough for you to look for God in every waking moment of your day? Sometimes it's loneliness.

A Christian missionary, who was also a mystic, traveled to the island of Mindanao in the Philippines to work with the natives. His mission was to bring his religion to the natives, but he soon found that they had their own religion and their own ways.

He was unhappy there, a stranger in a strange land, and lonesome because his wife couldn't be with him. After some time, it occurred to him that if he could learn about the people and what was important to them, maybe he would have more success in being happy himself. His idea was If I can't be joyful and happy in my own life, what right do I have to come here as a Christian missionary and try to change people from their path?

So he began a life of study and observation where he tried to walk moment by moment in the presence of God. He realized it wasn't possible to do it all the time, because if you put your attention on God to the point where you forget your duties to yourself and family, you become worthless to those around you. God didn't put us here to be fed and catered to by others, but to get the rich experiences that Soul needs to one day become a Co-worker with God. This is the mission of Soul. This is our mission.

The ECKist thought about it and said, "I don't know about you, but the times I was happiest were when I was giving."

MY GOD IS BIGGER . . .

One of the ECKists told me this afternoon about a very interesting person he had met. His new friend was a Christian. They liked each other and felt an instant rapport. The Christian man was the kind who liked to stir people up and make them think. As they talked he said something to this effect: Give me two instances when you were absolutely the happiest in your life.

The ECKist thought about it, and then he said, "I don't know about you, but the times I was happiest were when I was giving."

The other fellow said, "You know, I like you. I don't know where you get your ideas, but I agree with the way you're thinking, except for one thing: My God is bigger than yours."

The other fellow said, "I agree with the way you're thinking, except for one thing: My God is bigger than yours." The ECKist started laughing so hard.

The ECKist started laughing so hard that the other man was quite astonished. "You mean you aren't upset that I said my God is bigger than your God?"

"Not at all," said the ECKist.

"Why not?" he asked.

"Your God is bigger," said the ECKist, "because your needs are greater."

On other paths, you were taught to give reverence through prayer to the divine being that you knew and worshipped. You prayed to God, and it worked for a long time, but prayer often puts one in the position of a helpless petitioner. The real purpose of this life is to learn the spiritual laws so that we become masters in our own right.

Beyond Prayer

Beyond prayer is what we know in ECK as contemplation. One contemplative technique is to read something inspirational—a biblical verse or a passage from the ECK writings—then shut your eyes and look inwardly, very gently, at the form of an ECK Master, Jesus, or any figure you feel is a spiritual traveler. Ask to be shown the truth. You can ask for love, wisdom, and understanding, but something greater than these three things, which are only attributes of God, is to ask for the realization of God.

Through contemplation one comes to an understanding of the mental and emotional bodies. There are also other ways to approach life. Another step is to make a study of who and what you are and make an effort to learn the spiritual laws, such as the Law of Cause and Effect. The third step whereby one can learn about the pure spiritual truths is through service. Service means giving in some way. If you expect to grow spiritually, you have to give of yourself. There is no other way you can unfold spiritually and rise into the high heavens of God.

If you have never used a spiritual exercise before, and you would like to compare it to prayer, then pray in the evening before you go to bed, and try a spiritual exercise later. You can look to Jesus or anyone else while singing *HU*, this love song to God. Try it for yourself, and see if there is a difference between how prayer works for you and how a spiritual exercise works for you.

No longer bound by the hand of destiny, we then become spiritually free to mark our own course for this lifetime and into the worlds beyond.

What we want to do is contact the Voice of God, which is the Holy Spirit. This Voice of God can be known through the Light and Sound that uplifts us so we can reach into the high states of spiritual consciousness. No longer bound by the hand of destiny, we then become spiritually free to mark our own course for this lifetime and into the worlds beyond.

Beavers Bend Campout, Broken Bow, Oklahoma, July 9, 1983

Her first parachute jump was almost her last, but an out-of-the-body adventure saved her life.

20
A Brief History of ECK

I'd like to go into the history of ECK just briefly for those of you who are new. Paul Twitchell brought the teachings of ECK out again in 1965, but they come from a source that predates modern history. In fact, the teachings of ECK predate even the Aryan civilization, which began shortly after Atlantis went into the ocean.

Rama's Mission

The Living ECK Master at that time was a man named Rama, who came from the dark forests of Germany and traveled to Tibet. On his way there, he left the message of ECK—the teaching of the Sound and Light of God and how to reach the kingdom of heaven in this lifetime—with the primitive people of northern Europe.

On his way to Tibet, the Living ECK Master at that time, Rama, left the message of ECK with the primitive people of northern Europe.

Even today, there is a faint remembrance of HU, the secret name of God that he left with the people. This word can be chanted or sung quietly to yourself when you are in trouble or when you need consolation in time of grief. It gives strength, it gives health, it opens you as a channel for the greater healing of Divine Spirit.

When Rama spoke of HU, he was referring to the divine Light and Sound. The Sound of God, the Audible Life Stream, is the purifying element which uplifts Soul, so that one day It may return home to God, Its creator.

Eventually all that remained of Rama's teachings was a dim memory of the Light, and the brightest light they were aware of was the sun. This is why historians today claim the Druids worshipped the sun god HU.

The word *HU* was later used among the Druids, but they eventually lost the information about its true meaning. All that remained of Rama's teachings was a dim memory of the Light, and the brightest light they were aware of was the sun. This is why historians today claim the Druids worshipped the sun god HU.

Rama brought the message of God, the Divine Being of which we can have realization. When it comes, it's called God-Realization, where we know the meaning and purpose of life and how to live it. We learn the laws of Spirit. We learn how to avert illness instead of being at the mercy of destiny and feeling that somehow life has dealt us a bad hand.

Rama then went on to Tibet, there to be taken out of the body to the Temple of Golden Wisdom in the spiritual city of Agam Des, where sections of the sacred writings of ECK are stored. From there he carried the message of ECK to Khara Khota, which was the capital city of the ancient empire of Uighur. But the priestcraft were more interested in maintaining their control over the spiritual welfare of man, so it wasn't long before he was driven out of that country, which today lies buried beneath the sands of the Gobi Desert.

Rama went back to Tibet, where he founded the Katsupari Monastery. Then he traveled down through Persia, which today is Iran, and there he established what was later to become the Magi Order. Once again he left the seeds of ECK among his followers, some of whom were the ancestors of Zoroaster. Eventually there were even offshoots of the Magi. The Magi later traveled westward at the beckoning of the star which announced the birth of Jesus, who came from another line of masters. Christ lived at a time when Zadok, the Living ECK Master, was active in Palestine. They met, but their missions were different.

Rama continued his journey and went to India. Here he left the teachings, again in seed form, from which evolved the Hindu religion and its many offshoots.

Soul's Journey Home

The original teachers came to bring the inspiration and motivation for Soul to seek Its way back to God. As their teachings were passed from father to son and to grandson, the message became more and more diluted. The teachings got twisted, corrupted, and lost. But there is no reason to ridicule the people of any faith, for God has provided a way—a religion, a faith, a belief—so that every Soul that is seeking a path back to the original Source can find the one that suits It.

You are Soul. You are a unique, individual being because all your experiences—both the sordid and the happy—make you completely different from any other being in this or any other period of time.

This brief history is the foundation of what we know today as Eckankar. It is a teaching which allows others to follow their own path to God, recognizing that each of us is at our own level of spiritual understanding—and rightfully so. Earth, after all, is a training school for the spiritual children, such as we are, in their quest for spiritual maturity.

We retain our individuality throughout eternity.

The mission of Soul, very simply, is to become a Co-worker with God. Never to become one with God, but to be a Co-worker. We retain our individuality throughout eternity.

KNOWING THE FUTURE AND PAST

There was a time when I wished to know the future, as I know many of you do. Part of the teachings of ECK relate to the ancient science of prophecy—the ECK-Vidya—and this is called the God-knowledge. It is merely an aspect of the full teachings of Eckankar. Many who follow the path take up the study for themselves, not only to learn and understand the future, but to gain a deep insight into their feelings.

If needed, we can look into the past, sometimes in the dream state, so that we can see the experiences that made us what we are today. Furthermore, we can see what kind of experiences lie down the road for us tomorrow, and then we have a choice of whether or not to take the path that leads to a problem situation. But not many of us will do that. If we see something coming ahead that isn't very pleasant, we tend to walk around it.

A step beyond prophecy is the spiritual element of the works of ECK, and that is the ability to live in the moment.

A step beyond prophecy is the spiritual element of the works of ECK, and that is the ability to live in the moment.

SPIRITUAL PRINCIPLES IN *THE MYSTERIOUS STRANGER*

Mark Twain, the American humorist, wrote a story that took him twelve years and three versions to complete. The shortened version is entitled *The Mysterious Stranger*, but in its full and final form it is called *No. 44, The Mysterious Stranger*. The story is set in medieval Austria, about forty-five years after Gutenberg invented the printing press.

In those days of the Inquisition, anything with the printed word was considered the work of the devil. It undermined the work of the church, which at that time was very interested in keeping the people in ignorance. They were kept too busy trying to stay alive to have any time to learn. It is known that whoever has knowledge can find his way out of the lower worlds and into the heavens in this lifetime; so education was not intended for the laborer or the farmer, and certainly not for women. It was reserved for the monks.

The purpose of Satan and the entire earthly existence is to hold us here, not just by the evil things, but through the pleasures and the good times. Soul goes to sleep in the carnival atmosphere of life where It wishes nothing more than just to go on enjoying the wild, blinding pleasures without realizing that one day this is all going to become tiresome.

So if it becomes tiresome, what then? At this point I would offer Eckankar as a next step, though it may not be the way for everyone. If the path you are now following is no longer holding your attention or your interest, you owe it to yourself to find another one. It should be one where you can grow and learn what you must know so you can take the next step. One of the principles or laws of ECK is that there is always one more step. There is always one more heaven.

Mark Twain's main character was actually a being from another level of consciousness.

Mark Twain's main character was a printer who actually was a being from another level of consciousness. He came from the pure worlds beyond the mental regions, which in the Bible are known as the third heaven. Saint Paul spoke of a man he knew some fourteen years earlier who had been caught up to the third heaven. This corresponds to what we know as the Mental Plane.

This being came down in the guise of a printer's apprentice, about sixteen or seventeen years of age. He came to a huge castle where a master printer was allowed to use a small space, and in this castle they were protected from the superstitions of the townspeople.

The young printer's full name was Number 44, New Series 864,962—but for short he asked to be called 44. He had marvelous abilities and could perform all kinds of tricks. At one point he befriended another apprentice whose name was August. Another character in the story was the priest who acted as the chief swordsman of the Inquisition in the town.

Forty-Four went at any task set before him with love and anticipation, while August spent his time trying to convert his friend. Forty-Four said he would rather not be converted. August asked him why not.

"I should be too lonesome," he said.

August said, "Lonesome? How?"

Forty-Four said that then he'd be the only Christian.

Mark Twain had a caustic view of religion. He looked very carefully at the Christians who lived one kind of life on Sunday morning and an entirely different one for the rest of the week. And this is why he had 44 indicate that if he became a Christian, he would be the only real one—a very lonely being.

Forty-Four taught August a secret word to develop the ability to become invisible. It was very similar to the use of the secret word in Eckankar, which we use not to become invisible, but to tap into Spirit. This is a word that can enable a person to Soul Travel by going out of the physical body in the Soul body.

Forty-Four said that where he came from, he could know the future. August thought this would be a wonderful gift to have.

Forty-Four mentioned a peculiar thing. He said, "The place where I come from . . . " And August wanted to say, Where is that? but every time he tried, he was tongue-tied. Forty-Four had certain powers, and he didn't want anyone to know that he came from a region of Light. He said that where he came from, he could know the future. He could know everything that would happen in the moments to come, he had insight into the present time, and he knew the past.

August thought this would be a wonderful gift to have. Forty-Four responded in terms of a production process. He said that the only relief he gets from knowing the future is when he comes to earth. Because of the peculiar construction of earth, he can shut off the prophecy works and not be bothered by the future.

Forty-Four would walk around disguised as the magician to whom he had been giving a lot of credit for the miracles he himself was doing. At one particular point the townspeople and the priest came after him to burn him at the stake. As the torch-carrying crowd filled the streets in front of the castle, he exclaimed to August how wonderful it was: At that moment he didn't know what the future held! But he wasn't worried—he knew the art of invisibility and many other things.

The point is that these principles of Spirit are imbedded in the literature and in our culture. Truth is never hidden. It's always available for the Soul who wants to take the next step.

How Spirit Heals

Another area of interest is miraculous healing. It is not always understood that Spirit heals through the common channels of medicine, such as the doctor or dentist. And if it is our money situation that needs healing, it may come by way of an accountant—a CPA or something of this nature.

These creative techniques release the spiritual power that brings whatever is of benefit for our spiritual unfoldment.

Use the Spiritual Exercises of ECK such as the singing of HU every day. These creative techniques release the spiritual power that brings whatever is of benefit for our spiritual unfoldment.

This is not to say that Spirit and the secret word or the holy names of God are to be used for material gain, because they are not. But we use the spiritual words which are given in the ECK writings for the upliftment of consciousness. And as you grow in spirituality, your whole life must improve.

Those of you who have used prayer for many years and are satisfied with it—by all means, continue. But those of you who have felt that somehow there must be a better way to address the divine power may now wish to try a spiritual exercise. The Easy Way technique shows you how to work with a master with whom you are familiar. It can be Christ, it can be Buddha, or it can be one of the ECK Masters—a familiar figure that you trust and love.

Love is an important element here, because when you pray or when you do the spiritual exercises, first of all it must be for the greater good. Too often one prays for his neighbor to have hard times so that he himself can prosper. Or he breaks the laws of Spirit by asking God to take a burden away, forgetting that God has allowed the burden so that the person could learn the laws of Spirit.

The Voice of God

For many the Audible Life Stream, the Voice of God, sounds like the buzzing of bees. Sometimes It is like an electrical motor whirring at a very high frequency.

There is something called the Audible Life Stream, and this is the Voice of God. It is a current, like a wave, that comes from the heart of God and flows out into all the worlds. Soul must catch this wave and learn how to ride this Voice of God and how to work with It. The only way we can know the Voice of God is through the Light and Sound.

If in your contemplation you hear a deep, booming voice, it may be a Master who is speaking as an instrument or agent for God, but this isn't the supreme God which can only be known as the Light and Sound.

The Sound can be heard in numerous ways, such as the single note of a flute. For many It sounds like the buzzing of bees. Sometimes It is like an electrical motor whirring at a very high frequency; other times It can sound like an orchestra or like thunder. The way you hear It depends upon where you are in your state of consciousness as you chant your word.

We can be taken from the physical state of consciousness to the Soul Plane; or it may be to the Mental Plane or to the Causal Plane, where we have memory of our past lives. The Master often works in the dream state because it is easier to get through. Fears can inhibit and prevent one from exercising the freedom and power and wisdom which are the birthright of Soul. In the dream state, the Inner Master can begin working with you to familiarize and make you comfortable with what comes on the other side.

The purpose of learning the ways of ECK is to overcome the fear of death, and this is done by learning that Soul lives forever. It has no beginning and no ending. One of the great laws of God is that Soul exists because of God's love for It.

Soul Consciousness

A woman told me last week about her adventure with her first parachute jump a number of years ago. Her first jump, in fact, was almost her last.

She jumped out of the aircraft with the parachute strapped on, arching her back for the fall, as she had been taught. But she arched her back too much, and this curvature created a vacuum so that the air pressure was running over the front of her. Because of this, when she pulled the rip cord, the parachute wouldn't open. She didn't have the presence of mind to pull the cord of her reserve chute. In a panic, she screamed as loud as she could, "God, help me!"

All of a sudden she found herself at a point above the falling physical body, with the perception of Soul.

All of a sudden she found herself in the Soul body, at a point above the falling physical body. With the perception of Soul, which is infinite and instantaneous, she could see what caused the problem. That's all it took. She immediately returned to her body and straightened her back, and with the vacuum gone the parachute opened.

She was really shaking when she got to the ground, because when you get into something adventuresome like that, you want to have a second chance. For a moment she wasn't so sure she was going to get it.

This was her first experience with consciousness out of the physical body. From then on, she began looking to see how she could again have this experience of being in the greater awareness, to live and work in the Soul body so that she could gain mastery over her life.

We become greater, we become stronger. Our vision is deeper, and we have a greater understanding of where we are, where we belong, and of the need to one day begin the journey back to the heart of God.

When we work from the Soul consciousness, we can shape our own destiny. No longer are we the slaves of our passions. I'm not saying that you are not going to have sickness; I won't say the further you go on the path, the easier it gets. If others could see the burdens you carry as you go further, they would say, If this is spirituality, forget it.

But we become greater, we become stronger. Our vision is deeper, and we have a greater understanding of where we are, where we belong, and of the need to one day begin the journey back to the heart of God.

Those of you who would like to learn more can try the Spiritual Exercises of ECK to see if indeed they do fit you. You owe it to yourself to find the path to God that is right for you.

Johannesburg Afternoon with ECK,
Johannesburg, South Africa, July 16, 1983

Read *The Shariyat-Ki-Sugmad* and see if you can find a word there to chant.

21
Steps to Self-Mastery

The path of ECK is primarily for spiritual growth. But as we gain in our spiritual unfoldment, we also begin to reach out into the community and start doing the things which make our own life easier and better. And we carry other people with us.

Going Step-by-Step

Some express the attitude "I've been in other groups. Since I am already so knowledgeable, why do I have to start in Eckankar with the First and Second Initiations?"

The spiritual exercises—chanting the name of God—are really important. If you expect to make any progress whatsoever, this has to be done. People say to me, "I'm having such a hard time with the spiritual exercises—they don't work for me." If I were to ask them, "Are you doing the spiritual exercises regularly?" they would simply answer, "Yes." What does that mean? Once a month? Once a year? They will find a lot of help in doing them every day for twenty minutes.

A lot of times we hear someone express the attitude "I've been in the Rosicrucians and a number of other groups. Since I am already so knowledgeable—practically a crown prince of God—why do I have to start in Eckankar with the First and Second Initiations?"

One's opinion of himself is generally much better than anyone else's. He has a false value of what his true experience really is, and he is unwilling to go step-by-step.

Allowing Others Freedom

Earlier today someone was talking about a local Christian man who joined a Satsang class so he could pretend to study with ECKists while actually trying to convert them. I don't know how the class managed to put up with him for a full year. One day he decided to travel to America to attend one of the major seminars, where he hoped to convert the Living ECK Master. But he never got farther than London. His wife got sick, and he had to come back home. It must have really frustrated him.

He never realized that Spirit was behind the whole thing, allowing other people to have the freedom to follow their own path without interference.

One of the good things you will find in ECK is a community of beings who can recognize some of the subtle things that happen.

One of the good things you will find in ECK is a community of beings who can recognize some of the subtle things that happen. If you try to tell it to your neighbors, they'll think you're a little bit funny—that there is something wrong with you. You try to tell an orthodox mind how Spirit works, and they won't believe you. If you say too much, they back away; and if you persist, they put you in a hospital. Every effort is made to discredit the person who doesn't fit into the orthodox way of thinking so he can't stir up trouble and get people thinking for themselves.

Practicing the Friday Fast

Someone asked about the purpose of the Friday fast. The benefits of the Friday fast include self-discipline, giving the body a break by not eating so much, and being in contact with chelas throughout the world since we are all doing it at the same time. It's similar to when you become an initiate of the Second Circle and have an inner communication with other Second Initiates. Some of you are aware of it; others aren't.

The Friday fast is a time designated to put a little attention on the spiritual disciplines. When we are locked in the human consciousness down here on earth and we have the problems of the five passions that hold us down and keep us miserable and unhappy, we find that the spiritual exercises and the Friday fasts begin to pull us up, little by little.

We find that the spiritual exercises and the Friday fasts begin to pull us up, little by little.

Occasionally someone asks that a lot of karma be taken off all at once. I usually recommend against it. I've had it taken away fast myself, and it makes a mess. It creates a vacuum in our lives, and then the rest of the karma falls into the hole where the ECK has suddenly taken a huge chunk out. This is why the ECK Masters often work through the dream state. This allows you to work off some there, work off some here, and it's done in a gradual way so life doesn't cave in on you.

If you are having a hard time in your family or at work and you want to get ahead of the game, you can do a Friday fast. There are different ways you can do the fast. There's the mental fast, the partial fast, and the water fast. Any one of these is as good as the other; it depends upon which one is right for you. You may want to do one kind this week and another next week. It depends upon your work schedule or your doctor's orders. You may have a certain condition, such as low blood sugar, where you have to eat regular meals in order to be able to do your job. This is one of the realities of living down here.

I have found that, when times were especially hard, it helped to do a fast on Tuesday also. Sometimes I would do more than one kind of fast at the same time; keeping the attention on the Mahanta, you can do this. I would do the mental fast at the same time as a partial fast. Then I would sometimes do a water fast on Friday.

There are several ways to do the mental fast. One way is to take all negative thoughts out of your mind. If anything negative comes up, just get rid of it. The other is fixing your attention so fully upon the Inner Master that a negative thought can't crowd in.

At one time somebody was trying to fire me at work; I didn't have money saved and didn't know what to do. So when times were really bad, I would do a juice fast on Tuesday. That used to balance the week out. This was not intended to control anyone else; I merely wanted to purify myself spiritually so that I could get through the situation. But sometimes all kinds of unusual things would start to happen in the lives of those who thought they were attacking me. They began to have so many problems that they didn't have time for me.

The Friday fast helps us develop the ability to handle our problems with much more facility. It's an excellent way to take a step toward our own mastership.

The partial fast is another way to do the Friday fast. This means eating only fruit or drinking fruit juice or having just one meal that day. There is a lot of latitude—you find what suits you best. What it does is to start moving you out of the karmic environment in which you find yourself today. Spiritual unfoldment begins where you are today. So the Friday fast is a way to help us pull ourselves, degree by degree, out of our karma. It also helps us develop the ability to handle our problems with much more facility. It's an excellent way to take a step toward our own mastership.

Avoiding Gossip

As ECK leaders, one thing is essential: If you hear gossip, stop it and stop it fast. Get to the heart of it. If one person says something about another that has to do with spreading the message of ECK—not their personal life, but spreading the message of ECK—then get to the bottom of it. If someone is reported to be disrupting a Satsang class, first go to the Arahata and see if it can be resolved there. If it can't be resolved there, then work with the local Higher Initiates.

Handle gossip right away, and don't get caught in the trap. It leads downward. It feels good to gossip, but all of a sudden you find yourself on the short end. Your spiritual experience is stopped, and nothing works. Then, without knowing why it happened, you come asking for help. I can't do anything but stand back and let you realize for yourself what is causing your problem. It's an important point. If you hear a person talking about someone else, don't listen to it.

I would recommend that you, as ECK leaders, keep your personal lives private. Myself, I don't care how you conduct your personal lives—it makes no difference to me—but I do care when it's brought out hand-in-hand with the ECK message. When you bring your problems from home to the Satsang class, you involve the other ECKists. Marital or love relationships are the favorites. When people bring their problems in, this affects and upsets all the rest of the people. And it has nothing at all to do with giving service to the Sugmad, which is what we are learning to do in enjoyable ways.

Giving service to the Sugmad is what we are learning to do in enjoyable ways.

If you have any questions or comments, just raise your hand.

Creative Fasting

Q: Let's say on a Friday I'm expected to attend a business luncheon that is necessary to clinch a deal. The ten other people attending know nothing about

ECK, but as an ECKist I want to fast. Do I just bluntly tell them, "Excuse me, I'm fasting," and then let my business career fall where it may?

HK: Do any of you have comments about what you would do, or what you already do, if something like this comes up on a Friday? How do you handle it?

ECKist: You could compromise and just have a light meal.

HK: This, of course, is the partial fast. On that particular day you could do a partial fast by having just that one meal. Any other comments or ideas?

ECKist: How about just fasting on Saturday?

HK: You can, but Friday is a better day. You'll find it more powerful. Much more beneficial. You can do the mental fast on Friday, and then just watch—you'll be surprised. It takes a little while, but if Spirit wants you to be fasting in a different way, It is going to make it work out on Friday. So trust Spirit too. Do what you can among the fasts that you have to work with, and when the time comes, you will be able to do the fast that you feel you would like to do.

ECKist: When it's possible, I reschedule the meeting for some other day. If it's not possible, and depending on who the people are, I may not eat, but I won't tell them why. I'll just say, "I don't eat on Fridays."

Use any of the fasts that feel good and work out right for you.

HK: There's a good suggestion. Be discreet about it. Make it a very straightforward statement. It takes a little bit to work up to abstaining from food all day, and some of you won't be able to because of your health or your work. But if you can and you want to, by all means do it. Use any of the fasts that feel good and work out right for you.

ECKist: Another suggestion is just to tell the people, "I don't feel much like eating today, but I'll join you and have something to drink."

HK: That's another good idea. He's using the creative faculty. This is the treasure of Soul—how better can you say it?—where you are working with your own mastership.

The fast has thrown you into a problem situation, and the first thing that might come to mind is, Why am I bothering with this? Then pretty soon you say, But on the other hand, I have experiences with the Light and Sound and the Inner Master; and if this is part of how I get them, so be it.

You are learning how to work around situations, and that's very good.

Q: What do you do when your boss tells you to stop fasting and eat?

HK: If it means getting fired, I'd eat.

Letting Others Give

The ECK Masters let people give.

The ECK Masters let people give. There is the story about Jesus letting the woman anoint his feet with fragrant ointment. The whole scenario probably happened a little bit differently than the way it is known in biblical history today. There were likely a lot of other little details that were taken out by writers throughout the centuries. For instance, we don't know how life changed for the woman who was able to anoint the feet of Jesus, yet that probably is the most important part of the story.

To get a point across about what is sometimes given to people so that they can open themselves up to Spirit, I'll tell this story about Paul Twitchell. Paul allowed people to have their space. We have all these ideas of what an ECK Master is and what he is not. Some of the things he does may seem shocking, but the purpose is to cause a reaction in the chela in some way that will help him to come to grips with himself. Then he can take a real hard look and decide, How important is my concern about what society thinks when compared with truth?

Very often we are locked into misery, pain, and loneliness because of what our neighbors will say. We're afraid to step out for ECK, for Spirit, and live our own life because of what people may say. That's the social consciousness. But in one way or another, the ECK Masters will draw the individual out. Sometimes they may even embarrass the chela. I don't usually try to do that, at least not on purpose, so rest easy.

One time Paul was staying at a hotel for an ECK seminar. Being a writer and a newspaperman, he learned by reading the works of other people, not only for enjoyment, but to see how they put writings together. There was, of course, an evolutionary period in his literary style too. As you read his different ECK works, you can see how Paul was developing spiritually. This is one of the principles of ECK: There is always one more step. And this includes the ECK Masters.

Paul was relaxing, reading a mystery novel, when the phone rang. The caller was a woman who said she would like to come up and anoint his feet.

He was relaxing, reading a mystery novel, when the phone rang. The caller was a woman who said she would like to come up and anoint his feet. This sounds almost bizarre these days, but for her it was not. The Inner Master had told her that for her this would be a great gift of love, so she asked Paul if it would be all right.

"Well, yes," he said.

"When would be a good time?" she asked.

"Now would be a good time," he said.

"I'll be right up."

He hung up and went back to reading his mystery novel. Soon the woman arrived at the door, her arms loaded with all her oils and perfumes and towels. Paul had never had his feet anointed before. So she said, "Can I anoint your feet now?" He said, "Yes, go right ahead." He sat back down, stuck his feet out, and went on reading his mystery.

It takes a lot of faith in ECK to go ahead and do something like this. It was a gift of love to Spirit, because as the Mahanta, the Living ECK Master, Paul was the vehicle for the divine ECK, and sometimes divine Spirit has you do things that might make others worry about what the neighbors will say.

An ECK Master isn't bothered by that, and when you gain your own mastership, you won't be either. This doesn't mean you are going to flaunt things in the face of your neighbors so that you end up with a modern-day inquisition on your heels. You use common sense. You try to get through this life as smoothly as you can.

She finished anointing his feet, very carefully dried off his toes, and then she said, "Thank you very much, Paul."

"You're welcome," he said. She went out the door carrying her towels and the ointment, and he kept right on reading his mystery.

Someone who heard about it later was quite shocked. The ECK Masters will work in whatever way is necessary to unlock the doors of Soul, to get you to see that there are no sacred cows on the spiritual path.

The ECK Masters will work in whatever way is necessary to unlock the doors of Soul, to get you to see that there are no sacred cows on the spiritual path.

Learning Spiritual Survival

We're all scrambling. It's called spiritual survival. And we learn that to survive, we do whatever is necessary to make something work, especially when we see it is part and parcel of our spiritual self, the Soul body.

I'll give you an example. You're doing the spiritual exercises, using the word you were given at the Second Initiation. Lo and behold, two weeks pass, and the word doesn't work anymore. Here you are out in a remote area of South Africa, probably at least a couple hundred miles away from the nearest ECK Initiator, and you wonder, *What should I do now? I got a word, but it doesn't work anymore.* Sometimes your word will last throughout all the different initiations, from the Second on up; other times it will last for two initiations, and then you need a new one. So what do you do?

Finding a New Word

You begin working to find another word. Read *The Shariyat-Ki-Sugmad*, and if you find a word there—perhaps *Anami* or another name which refers to the God realm or the Sugmad—chant it; try it that night. See how it works.

As you go further, more and more responsibility will be given to you for working with the spiritual exercises and finding a word.

Try a different word and experiment with it, because as you go further, more and more responsibility will be given to you for working with the spiritual exercises and finding a word. The responsibility rests with you. You have to figure out how to do it, and there is a way.

If your word has stopped working and you need another word to carry you through the rest of your Second, Third, or Fourth Initiation, whichever you happen to be in, first go into contemplation. Blank the mind, and see which words come to the forefront of your mental screen.

Let's say the initiation you are in requires a one-syllable word. See if one of the words or thoughts or impressions that just happen to come to you can be reduced to whatever number of syllables your word had when you were given the initiation for the particular circle you are in. See if you can do this. When you find a word, then use it, try it out, and see if it works. If it doesn't, wait about a week or two and try another word, because you are the one who is going to have to find it. If it still doesn't work, you can become more earnest with your Friday fasts. That's what I did.

As far as I'm concerned, if once a month you have a Light-and-Sound experience, see the Inner Master, or have an inner experience that you know is spiritual, that's fine. You actually are having many more. I want you to remember at least one a month to keep your confidence up. But better still is being aware of Spirit's help in your daily life.

I want you to remember at least one inner experience a month to keep your confidence up. But better still is being aware of Spirit's help in your daily life.

SAYING YES TO SPIRIT

Somebody was needed to coordinate the arrangements for this seminar. I can just imagine how this person felt when she was asked to coordinate this event and figure out how to communicate with the staff back in the United States in an economical way.

What were your first feelings when you found out that you were so lucky as to be the one to help out?

ECKist: My very first thought was, Will I be able to do it? Then I said, All right, if I was asked, then I should have the capability to do it.

HK: A really good start is to say yes; that was step one. Then came the time for step two, and she just had to sit down and think: Now what? Find the location for the seminar. She tried to visualize the end goal. How many people would be sitting in the room? She took that step, and once she visualized it, she went ahead and tried to find it.

Well, the physical world being what it is, there wasn't a reasonably priced room available for two hundred people. Everything kept falling through. So as the time came near, she had to make a commitment, which she did for this hall. And she did all this step-by-step.

This is an ECK principle: When you see a big job in front of you, you break it down to its smallest, logical first step, whatever it is. You set just a little goal to start with, and then you set a deadline for yourself. You work from there. This is the grand scheme.

SOLVING PROBLEMS

Some of the ancient Greek philosophers used to think from the whole. They would consider the overview. Western man usually thinks in terms of the parts. Most people think only in fragments; and because they do, they can't step back and take a look at the whole situation, so a problem defeats them before they've taken even one step.

It is also good to be open to help from others. If you don't know the answer, start calling around to other ECKists and get help. You don't have to know everything as a leader in ECK, any of you; gratefully, the Sugmad has arranged for somebody to be there who's just waiting to help. You find them by the expansion of consciousness.

Your awareness expands to accept and recognize the help that the ECK has already put at hand.

At the initiation of the Second Circle, your awareness expands to include a certain level of help that is already there. And again at the Third, your awareness expands to accept and recognize the help that the ECK has already put at hand. This is what is meant by living moment to moment—a solution is at hand for every problem; all we have to do is find it. It may not be the final solution, but it is a first step. But you have to have enough confidence in yourself to take the first step, whether it's with ECK or any other area of life. You've got to learn how to say, Yes, I can. And once you learn this, the world is yours.

UNDERSTANDING MOTIVATION

On the spiritual path we say, Don't ask questions; but that refers to a certain kind of question that asks, Where do I stand now in my spiritual unfoldment? In relation to what? In relation to yourself? Then the question disappears in itself. It's not important where you stand spiritually. That is the kind of question that you don't really need to ask. All you need to do is say, How can I find a way to have experience with the Light and Sound of God? How can I meet the Master in the dream state? How can I Soul Travel? These are things that take motivation.

Someone mentioned they didn't know how to find people with motivation or how to motivate them. And really, you can't. You find people who are motivated at any particular moment. Some are motivated for awhile, and then they go into a rest period—the rest points in eternity. There is a natural cycle that we run: activity, rest, activity, rest. An ECKist learns how to walk the middle path where he can make the activity and rest work for him, so that he becomes a conscious Co-worker with God twenty-four hours a day.

There is a natural cycle we run: activity, rest, activity, rest. An ECKist learns how to walk the middle path and so become a conscious Co-worker with God twenty-four hours a day.

APPROACHING LIFE WITH COURAGE

Q: With regard to spiritual gluttony, is it not a good idea to do the spiritual exercises for twenty minutes, three times a day, if one feels that is the way to get the Light and Sound?

HK: You can do it, as long as you're careful not to become introverted. A person can become introverted; even an ECK Center can become introverted. All of a sudden the meetings are just for us. We've forgotten to go out there. And the real joy of living is in being courageous enough, for instance, to go out on the street and figure out how to find a new job if you've lost yours. It may mean throwing out a lot of old ideas about how much you should be paid and what you should do. It takes a lot of courage.

Too often when we start on the spiritual path we carry the feeling, as I did, that this life is one grand mistake. The only thing I wanted to do was Soul Travel so I could get out of the unpleasantness of my surroundings. I was stationed in Japan then, and all I wanted was to go back to the farm. It's all very nice, but you can't live life by running from it, and that's what I was trying to do. Living life fully takes a sense of adventure, but we grow into it gradually, at a pace we can handle.

Living life fully takes a sense of adventure, but we grow into it gradually, at a pace we can handle.

Anybody have a good story to tell?

ECKist: When I was introduced to Eckankar some four years ago, I had the problem of convincing my family that I was doing the right thing. I was pressured to go to a psychiatrist to be examined. It occurred to me that this was one indirect and subtle way to spread the message of ECK, because obviously the psychiatrist had never heard of Eckankar. So in order to provide a fair chance for us to discuss ECK on the right level, I took a couple of ECK books along to the meeting.

My wife was delighted that I was willing to at least consider the possibility that I was doing something erroneous. I had agreed to abide by the results of the psychiatric evaluation.

In the first meeting, I said to him, "Doctor, my problem is not a problem really. It's a matter of coming to grips with life as I see it. And to help you understand why I am what I am, you can read through these books."

He took the books with equanimity and paged through them as if to say he already knew about all these crackpot ideas. I could almost hear him thinking, *I've gone through medical school, I've heard all the conceivable notions of man, and this guy is just another crank—probably has aces up his sleeve.*

When I got home, my wife said, "How do you feel now that you've seen this headshrinker?"—as she referred to him. I said, "Well, he can't seem to make heads or tails out of it. I don't know if the words are beyond his ken or whether he's got the appropriate vocabulary or if he requires an Oriental dictionary, or what. I even gave him the *ECKANKAR Dictionary** just to help us communicate."

This went on for several weeks. I allowed myself to be subjected to three different psychiatrists, because I knew I was right. I just knew. But my family felt it was up to them to confirm it. After the third psychiatrist could find no problem, my family decided there was nothing they could do except leave me alone.

I feel if you are inspired with an inner knowingness that what you are doing is right, you just carry on and do it. As Paul Twitchell has mentioned, it's only the bold and adventuresome that succeed.

This man's family stood against him when he wanted to walk the path of ECK.

HK: This man's family stood against him when he wanted to walk the path of ECK. As part of their condition of whether or not to leave him alone, he agreed to subject himself to a psychiatric evaluation. He also had to accept the psychiatrist's decision. His family thought, *He's a lunatic, and the psychiatrist is going to convince him to drop this ECK business.* But he subjected himself to three psychiatrists, going far beyond his original agreement to abide by one psychiatrist's verdict, and none of them were able to say he was crazy.

It takes a lot of courage to even put yourself

* Expanded and republished as *A Cosmic Sea of Words: The ECKANKAR Lexicon.* —Ed.

through something like that. You have to be very strong. If you know within yourself that you are right, then you have to follow it out if you want to live with yourself. It's the life of ECK; a very courageous approach to life. He was willing to do whatever it took and to take whatever went with it.

Being on Time

We've got just a couple of minutes more. In reference to that, another really pertinent point is starting and ending on time. You will find that much of your success as leaders depends on setting a starting time for a meeting and then starting at that time, even if everyone isn't there. When it's time to quit, quit at the time that you have agreed upon. If you go a few minutes longer, that's fine; but you don't want a one-hour class to run two hours.

We can set the agenda to fit within the schedule, allowing time for discussion, and then stick to it. Setting goals and making deadlines will carry you a long way in the material and the spiritual aspects of your life.

As you go further, you find the ECK actually weaves the material life and the spiritual together so smoothly that there is no difference. It is all the spiritual life.

Living the Spiritual Life

ECKist: I just wanted to say that the other disciplines that I've studied seem to bring about a separation between the spiritual life and the material life. The ECK path somehow seems to continuously integrate the spiritual with the material.

HK: When you first get on the path, you see a distinction between the material life and the spiritual. But as you go further, you find the ECK actually weaves the two together so smoothly that there is no difference. It is all the spiritual life.

If you try to make a distinction and say this

is material and that is spiritual, it's saying in essence that this physical life has no meaning in your spiritual unfoldment. It has all the meaning in the world, because we work off our karma as we meet other people. It doesn't generally happen with inanimate objects—unless you kick your car that just got a flat tire, and you work off that karma by getting a sore toe. It has nothing to do with what the car thought; it's because of what you did. There is this blending in life, and that's a very good insight.

Your experiences carry out into the world, and they help bring upliftment for the whole of mankind.

Next weekend we're going to be at the European Seminar in the Netherlands. In my travels I sometimes get stories and ideas as I listen to you. Your experiences carry out into the world, and they help bring upliftment for the whole of mankind.

Thank you.

Leadership Meeting, Johannesburg, South Africa, July 16, 1983

These are the three steps that can help the individual enter into the states of Self-Realization and God-Realization.

22
The Three Steps of Knowing

People are fascinated by the future. The oracle of Delphi held a peculiar fascination for the Greeks. They would come and wait for as long as two months, until finally one day the high priestess would say, "The oracle will see you now." They would humbly stand before the oracle, while the voice of Apollo came thundering through the high priestess with a prophecy.

How Spirit Works

I recently told the story of a man who went to see the oracle to get rid of his stammering problem. The oracle told him to go to Libya, conquer the land, and raise flocks of different animals. This upset him very much because the oracle, even as the ECK, will hardly ever give us exactly what we ask for. It will come about in a better way. If we are open and understand the ways of Divine Spirit and the laws of life, It will give us far more than we expected.

The ECK will hardly ever give us exactly what we ask for. It will come about in a better way.

Spirit, working through the oracle of those times, heard the man's request, but the answer offered to him required a little bit of faith on his part and the willingness to take his own step toward reaching the goal. The man did follow the will of the oracle. In Libya he and his men got into battle with the Libyan soldiers. When he won the fight, he suddenly realized he had regained full control of his voice. The stammering was gone. And since he had conquered the enemy, the land was now open for him to raise his flocks and to prosper.

Spirit won't do it for us. If you ask for a healing, It may cause a friend to tell you about a good doctor. But if you are not aware of how Spirit works, you may discount the help that you receive and give credit to the doctor, without ever understanding that the doctor is another means, another instrument of divine Spirit, to bring healing into this world.

An elderly man once came up to me after a seminar talk. Very quietly, so no one else could hear him, he said, "While I was in there, all of a sudden my hearing was restored. Thank you for the healing." Rather than go into a long story with him about thanking me, I just said, "You're welcome."

Those of you with experience in being an open vehicle for Spirit have seen healings occur around you. Often the person wasn't aware that the healing came because you were an open vehicle. You didn't direct rays, you didn't lay hands on him, you didn't crack his back like a chiropractor—although that is a good method of healing too. You were an open vehicle for Spirit, and Spirit then did the healing. This is what we are looking for as Soul.

The mission of Soul is to become a Co-worker with God, to taste of the Light and Sound, the effervescent food of God.

The mission of Soul is to become a Co-worker with God, to taste of the Light and Sound, the effervescent food of God. The Voice of God can only be heard as Sound and seen as Light. This is the Audible Life Stream. This is what the Bible called the Word. John wrote: "In the beginning was the Word. . . . And the Word was made flesh, and dwelt among us."

The ECK-Vidya

The prophecy of the ECK-Vidya works in small, subtle ways. The original art of the ECK-Vidya is the highest method of reading the Soul records of this life and past lives for an understanding of who and what you are today. This ability to study yourself, either through a direct reading of the Soul records or through the dream state, where you can see pictures of past lives and gain insight into your life today, is all an aspect of Eckankar. It is but one small piece, one small phase. As much as we like to know the future, there does come a time when knowing the future becomes dull.

Until one knows how to read it and see it, he may say, "Oh, Lord, the greatest gift of all would be to see the future, so that I could make my life happy and prosperous. And being happy and prosperous, I would give many gifts back to you." You know how that goes: Please make me rich, Lord, so I can give it back to you. With a little thought, the petitioner would realize that if God wanted to be rich, He could simply bypass the middleman and get it all. And it's a fact that when the money is run through man, not much goes back—despite his generous promises. Instead, it's "God, give me more yet because the tax man taketh a bite." And when more comes, it's strange how even less is given back.

A friend locked himself out of his car one night. As I stood there watching him try to get back in his car, all of a sudden the ECK-Vidya, the ancient science of prophecy, opened up.

I'm not saying this means everyone or that we're down on the rich and boosting the poor, because this is not the case. Spirituality does not depend on the thickness of your wallet or the size of your bank account.

The ECK-Vidya works in its own way. A number of years ago when I was working at a certain company, a friend of mine locked himself out of his car one night. As I stood there watching him try to get back in his car, all of a sudden the ECK-Vidya, the ancient science of prophecy, opened up. This is an ability I call the Golden-tongued Wisdom. I watched him, and suddenly I understood that I was about to be fired from this company; I was being locked out of my job.

I watched him, and suddenly understood I was about to be fired; I was being locked out of my job.

Soon a man drove up and gave my friend a wire coat hanger to use. In a very short time he was able to get into the car. When I saw him open the lock with this wire, the way to handle my situation became clear to me: I would make a phone call to my boss; and as I talked with him about something else, the conversation would open up in a direction that would help him to again recognize the contributions I had made to the company. And this is how it was resolved. This is one way that the ECK-Vidya works, and it hardly ever works the same way twice in a row.

The reading of tea leaves is a corruption of the ECK-Vidya. It is similar to how a monkey would react if he observed an ECK Master reading the ECK-Vidya. The monkey would try to recreate the outward actions that seemed to bring about the results.

A monkey watching the above incident, for example, would conclude that there are certain steps you have to take in order to see the future. First of all, he would figure out how to lock the car door. Then he would run around looking for a wire and fiddle with it until he could finally open the door. From then on, it would become a tradition that the monkey would pass down to his son and his grandson, and in time, even those facts would become distorted. Eventually it would have to be a certain model car. You would have to use a certain grade of coat-hanger wire and spend a certain amount of time trying to get in.

This illustrates how the corruptions of the original practices and teachings of the ECK Masters come about. The basic teaching is split again and again, and the result is the many different denominations and sects in Hinduism, Buddhism, and Christianity. Yet each person in each religion, in every corner of any particular denomination, can find exactly the message of Light as it applies to him. It fits him, but it won't fit his neighbor. Soul is a unique being. It is different from Its neighbor because of Its different experiences in this life and in all past lives, not only on the physical plane but in the planes or heavens where It exists before coming to this world.

Much of this information is given in the ECK books. *ECKANKAR—The Key to Secret Worlds* is a good book for those of you who are new to ECK. If you have tried prayer and would now like to try a spiritual exercise, begin with chanting *HU*, an ancient name for God. Let your heart fill with love and trust for a spiritual master, and this can be Jesus, Buddha, Krishna, or it can be one of the ECK Masters. Shut your eyes and go into contemplation in a very light, gentle way. You may find results in a day, a week, a month, and for some it may take a year. You can try it and find out for yourself what the difference is between prayer and the spiritual exercises.

How Do You Find God?

How do you find God? What makes you yearn for God?

How do you find God? What makes you yearn for God? It's an indefinable something; and I can only say that often it helps if you have pain, suffering, and loneliness. When life drives you against the wall and you have nowhere else to go, you finally give up trust and confidence in yourself and in your material possessions. And when you can give up attachment and reliance upon anything in the outer world, only then do you have a chance to see the door open for the inner truth of God. Only then can you find the way to spiritual freedom.

The way to spiritual freedom is always through the Spiritual Exercises of ECK. You may have tried prayer, as I did for years. Eventually you will outgrow certain kinds of prayer, such as asking God to change the will of another person to suit your own. As you go further on the spiritual path, you understand that using prayer to change another person's mind is black magic.

The way to spiritual freedom is always through the Spiritual Exercises of ECK. You may have tried prayer, as I did for years.

Many people in the orthodox faiths feel it is their right and their privilege to pray for another person to come into their particular religion in order to be saved from hell. It's the vanity of man, the same vanity which once had man believing that the earth was the center of the universe. Galileo tried to tell the church that by his observations he had found something far different, and he was subjected to the Inquisition. I understand just in the last year a special dispensation was allowed so that the stigma of the Inquisition was lifted from him by the church.

A Life of Trust in Spirit

An ECKist told me about an incident which struck me as somewhat amusing. He worked with a Christian man who ran an airline salvage business. It was his job to fly into Mexico when an American plane crashed there. He would try to get it airborne and back to the United States. By Mexican law, any plane that stays down in their country for a certain length of time automatically becomes government property. The only way to avoid this seizure is to send in an expert pilot and mechanic to see if they can get the thing flying long enough to take it back across the border and land it just on the other side of the Rio Grande, which is the dividing line between Mexico and the United States.

This individual, in his own way, had learned how to work with Spirit, which we know as the divine

ECK. He said he would just look at the plane, replace a few parts, and without even having to start the engine he could tell whether the plane would fly or not. His life depended upon his decision every time, and he was always right. If he determined that the plane was beyond repair, he would remove all the expensive radio and navigation equipment, load it in his plane, and leave the rest of the worthless hulk behind.

This man and the ECKist had developed a mutual respect for each other. One day he said to the ECKist, "I don't know where you get your ideas"—they had never discussed Eckankar—"but as much as I like you, there's one thing I have to tell you: My God is bigger than your God."

The ECKist responded by laughing. The other man couldn't figure out why he didn't get angry. "Aren't you going to defend your God? Doesn't it upset you that I said my God is bigger than your God?" The ECKist was able to stop laughing long enough to say, simply, "Your God is bigger because your needs are greater."

You do what you can to make your life right, and when you have done 100 percent of everything you can do, then Spirit steps in to help with the miracle.

He was able to concede the point because he had learned to live a life of trust in Spirit. This means you do what you can to make your life right, and when you have done 100 percent of everything you can do, then Spirit steps in to help with the miracle. The apostle Paul said: "I have learned, in whatsoever state I am, therewith to be content."

While traveling recently in Greece, I found a peculiar thing. The people are happy and joyful because, from what I could see, most of their heaven is right here on earth. They have food, they have drink, they have family, and it's everything a person could want. They are totally happy right where they are, so why look for a heaven after this lifetime?

It's curious that in the cultures where a religion is failing its members, the mourning and grief at the passing of a loved one are the greatest. In the cultures where they understand the laws of Spirit, the Wind of Change, there is very little of the deep, heavy grief that might otherwise last for so many weeks or months.

We can cry when our loved ones leave, because we've gotten used to each other—but we can pull ourselves out of the grief much faster. It's all right to cry; it's a natural reaction, and we don't have to suppress our feelings, but we do learn how to control them. When we have cried enough, we can put it aside and say, Life goes on. It always has, and it always will. And finally you can just say, Life is. ECK or Spirit is. Life exists beyond eternity.

The Three Steps of Knowing

Someone told me that as he tried to bring the message of ECK to people, he would tell them that this is the path to spiritual liberation—wisdom, power, and freedom. Then he would say, "To reach the high state of God and the attributes which come from it, we go through the stages of Self-Realization and God-Realization." But, he said, the words are so big that they don't mean anything to people. They have no idea what it means when you say Self-Realization and God-Realization.

What can be said to people about seeking the state of all-knowing? The first step is contemplation. This is where we learn to bring the mind and the emotions under control.

The question is, What can be said to people about seeking the state of all-knowing? What can lead them a step at a time so they can unfold spiritually, to then enter into the states of Self-Realization and God-Realization?

There are three steps. The first one is *contemplation*, or the Spiritual Exercises of ECK. This is where we learn to bring the mind and the emotions under control. This is absolutely essential if one is to learn how to live in the detached state of consciousness like the great ECK Masters. Detached does not mean unemotional; it means that no matter what we have in life, we will not be crushed if it is taken from us. It means we have the attitude of total trust in life to give us what is for our own spiritual benefit.

The second step is *study*. We study our own makeup or spiritual constitution and the spiritual laws of life. We make an actual study of what it takes to live in this world with happiness and joy instead of being the victim of destiny.

Service means that every move, every thought, everything we do gets the best advantage. We look to excel in every way.

The last step is *service*. Service means that every move, every thought, everything we do gets the best advantage. No matter what thought we have or what action we take, it results in the most productive deed we can do as Soul learning to become a Co-worker with God. I have often referred to this service as the Law of Economy. It means that in every way we look for the best. We look to excel in every way. If we are going to paint a picture, it will be the best we can do today. Yet tomorrow we will be able to do it better. If we write a book today, it's going to be great; but the book we write tomorrow will be even better. We use the Law of Economy: Only as many words as we need, and that's all.

So we have the spiritual exercises, we have study, and then we have service, or the Law of Economy.

If you are new to ECK, I can only recommend that you try the spiritual exercises. Practice them. Try a spiritual exercise at night when you go to bed. For those of you who are in ECK, I would recommend that you continue with the spiritual exercises every day. This is the key to spiritual unfoldment.

As an ECKist you will also find it of great benefit to daily declare yourself a vehicle for the Sugmad, which is God; for the ECK, which is Spirit; and for the Mahanta, the high state of consciousness which is the potential that you have as Soul. Do this every morning.

Those who are willing and adventurous and would like to learn in the dream state will find that either an ECK Master or one of the other masters will come to you. An ECK seminar is a good time to pay attention to the dream state, to see who comes and shows you about the mysteries, about the music of God—the flute, the thunder, the orchestra—the purifying sounds. And to see which of the Masters comes to show you the Light—the blinding white light, the yellow light, the blue light, or even the green light.

The Light and Sound are the purifying elements of Soul, and each of you may reach them.

The Light and Sound are the purifying elements of Soul, and each of you may reach them.

ECKANKAR European Seminar, The Hague, Netherlands, July 23, 1983

About the Author

Award-winning author, teacher, and spiritual guide Sri Harold Klemp helps seekers reach their full potential. He is the Mahanta, the Living ECK Master and spiritual leader of Eckankar, the Path of Spiritual Freedom. He is the latest in a long line of spiritual Adepts who have served throughout history in every culture of the world.

Sri Harold teaches creative spiritual practices that enable anyone to achieve life mastery and gain inner peace and contentment. His messages are relevant to today's spiritual needs and resonate with every generation. *Kirkus Reviews* comments, "The powerful optimism of these teachings should resonate with all readers, even those unacquainted with ECK."

Sri Harold's body of work includes more than one hundred books, which have been translated into eighteen languages and won multiple awards. The miraculous, true-life stories he shares lift the veil between heaven and earth.

In his groundbreaking memoir, *Autobiography of a Modern Prophet*, he reveals secrets to spiritual success gleaned from his personal journey into the heart of God. Find your own path to true happiness, wisdom, and love in Sri Harold Klemp's inspired writings.

Next Steps in Spiritual Exploration

- **Browse our website: www.Eckankar.org.**
  Watch videos; get free books, answers to FAQs, and more info.
- **Attend an Eckankar event** in your area.
  Visit "Eckankar around the World" on our website.
- **Explore advanced spiritual study** with the Eckankar discourses that come with membership.
- **Read additional books** about the ECK teachings.
- **See "Contact Eckankar" page 358**.

Advanced Spiritual Living

Go higher, further, deeper with your spiritual exploration!

ECK membership brings many unique benefits and a focus on the ECK discourses. These are dynamic spiritual courses you study at home, one per month.

The first year of study brings *The Easy Way Discourses* by Harold Klemp, with uplifting spiritual exercises, audio excerpts from his seminar talks, and activities to personalize your spiritual journey. Classes are available in many areas.

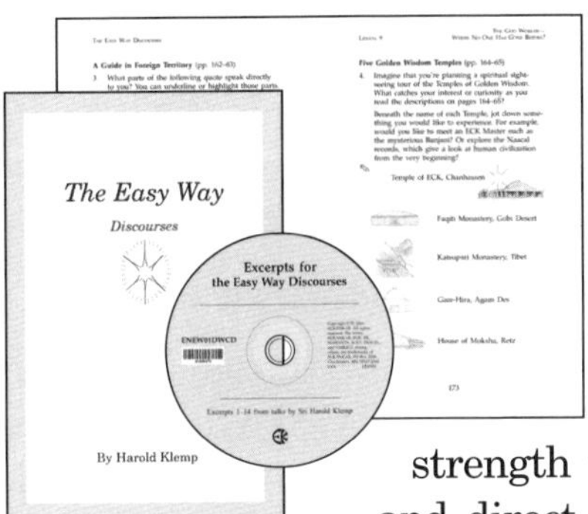

Each year you choose to continue with ECK membership can bring new levels of divine freedom, inner strength to meet the challenges of life, and direct experience with the love and power of God.

Here's a sampling of titles from *The Easy Way Discourses*:

- In Soul You Are Free
- Reincarnation—Why You Came to Earth Again
- The Master Principle
- The God Worlds—Where No One Has Gone Before?

BOOKS

You may find these books by Harold Klemp to be of special interest. They are available at bookstores, from online booksellers, or directly from Eckankar.

Past Lives, Dreams, and Soul Travel

These stories and exercises help you find your true purpose, discover greater love than you've ever known, and learn that spiritual freedom is within reach.

The Spiritual Exercises of ECK

This book is a staircase with 131 steps leading to the doorway to spiritual freedom, self-mastery, wisdom, and love. A comprehensive volume of spiritual exercises for every need.

Autobiography of a Modern Prophet

This riveting story of Harold Klemp's climb up the Mountain of God will help you discover the keys to your own spiritual greatness.

Those Wonderful ECK Masters

Would you like to have *personal* experiences with spiritual masters that people all over the world—since the beginning of time—have looked to for guidance, protection, and divine love? This book includes real-life stories and spiritual exercises to meet eleven ECK Masters.

The Spiritual Laws of Life

Learn how to keep in tune with your true spiritual nature. Spiritual laws reveal the behind-the-scenes forces at work in your daily life.

ECK Essentials

Your keys to spiritual living. These ECK essentials from the Master nourish, guide, uplift, heal, reveal and strengthen the desire and resolve of Soul to reach Its sacred goals. Open your heart to the Master, and you will hear inner, secret whispers of truth.

CONTACT ECKANKAR

For more information about ECK or ECK books, or to enroll in ECK membership you may:

- Visit www.ECKBooks.org
- Enroll online at "Membership" at www.Eckankar.org (click on "Online Membership Application"), or
- Call Eckankar (952) 380-2222 to apply, or
- Write to:
  ECKANKAR, Dept. BK150
  PO Box 2000
  Chanhassen, MN 55317-2000 USA

Glossary

Words set in SMALL CAPS are defined elsewhere in this glossary.

Arahata An experienced and qualified teacher of ECKANKAR classes.

Blue Light How the MAHANTA often appears in the inner worlds to the CHELA or seeker.

chela A spiritual student, often a member of ECKANKAR.

ECK The Life Force, Holy Spirit, or Audible Life Current which sustains all life.

Eckankar *EHK-ahn-kahr* The Path of Spiritual Freedom. Also known as the Ancient Science of SOUL TRAVEL. A truly spiritual way of life for the individual in modern times. The teachings provide a framework for anyone to explore their own spiritual experiences. Established by PAUL TWITCHELL, the modern-day founder, in 1965. The word means Coworker with God.

ECK Masters Spiritual Masters who can assist and protect people in their spiritual studies and travels. The ECK Masters are from a long line of God-Realized SOULS who know the responsibility that goes with spiritual freedom.

God-Realization The state of God Consciousness. Complete and conscious awareness of God.

Gopal Das The guardian of the SHARIYAT-KI-SUGMAD at the Temple of Askleposis on the Astral PLANE. He was the MAHANTA, the LIVING ECK MASTER in Egypt, about 3000 BC.

HU *HYOO* The most ancient, secret name for God. It can be sung as a love song to God aloud or silently to oneself to align with God's love.

initiation Earned by a member of ECKANKAR through spiritual unfoldment and service to God. The initiation is a private ceremony in which the individual is linked to the Sound and Light of God.

Kal Niranjan The Kal; the negative power, also known as Satan or the devil.

Karma, Law of The Law of Cause and Effect, action and reaction, justice, retribution, and reward, which applies to the lower or psychic worlds: the Physical, Astral, Causal, Mental, and Etheric PLANES.

Klemp, Harold The present MAHANTA, the LIVING ECK MASTER. SRI Harold Klemp became the Mahanta, the Living ECK Master in 1981. His spiritual name is WAH Z.

Living ECK Master The spiritual leader of ECKANKAR. He leads SOUL back to God. He teaches in the physical world as the Outer Master, in the dream state as the Dream Master, and in the spiritual worlds as the Inner Master. SRI HAROLD KLEMP became the MAHANTA, the Living ECK Master in 1981.

Mahanta An expression of the Spirit of God that is always with you. Sometimes seen as a BLUE LIGHT or Blue Star or in the form of the Mahanta, the LIVING ECK MASTER. The highest state of God Consciousness on earth, only embodied in the Living ECK Master. He is the Living Word.

planes Levels of existence, such as the Physical, Astral, Causal, Mental, Etheric, and SOUL Planes.

Rebazar Tarzs A Tibetan ECK MASTER known as the Torchbearer of ECKANKAR in the lower worlds.

Satsang A class in which students of ECK discuss a monthly lesson from ECKANKAR.

Self-Realization SOUL recognition. The entering of Soul into the Soul PLANE and there beholding Itself as pure Spirit. A state of seeing, knowing, and being.

Shariyat-Ki-Sugmad The sacred scriptures of ECKANKAR. The scriptures are comprised of twelve volumes in the spiritual worlds. The first two were transcribed from the inner PLANES by PAUL TWITCHELL, modern-day founder of Eckankar.

Soul The True Self, an individual, eternal spark of God. The inner, most sacred part of each person. Soul can see, know, and perceive all things. It is the creative center of Its own world.

Soul Travel The expansion of consciousness. The ability of SOUL to transcend the physical body and travel into the spiritual worlds of God. Soul Travel is taught only by the LIVING ECK MASTER. It helps people unfold spiritually and can provide proof of the existence of God and life after death.

Sound and Light of ECK The Holy Spirit. The two aspects through which God appears in the lower worlds. People can experience them by looking and listening within themselves and through SOUL TRAVEL.

Spiritual Exercises of ECK Daily practices for direct, personal experience with the Sound Current. Creative techniques using contemplation and the singing of sacred words to bring the higher awareness of SOUL into daily life.

Sri A title of spiritual respect, similar to reverend or pastor, used for those who have attained the Kingdom of God. In ECKANKAR, it is reserved for the MAHANTA, the LIVING ECK MASTER.

Sugmad *SOOG-mahd* A sacred name for God. It is the source of all life, neither male nor female, the Ocean of Love and Mercy.

Temples of Golden Wisdom Golden Wisdom Temples found on the various PLANES—from the Physical to the Anami Lok; CHELAS of ECKANKAR are taken to these temples in the SOUL body to be educated in the divine knowledge; sections of the SHARIYAT-KI-SUGMAD, the sacred teachings of ECK, are kept at these temples.

Twitchell, Paul An American ECK MASTER who brought the modern teachings of ECKANKAR to the world through his writings and lectures. His spiritual name is Peddar Zaskq.

vairag The spiritual virtue of detachment.

Wah Z *WAH zee* The spiritual name of SRI HAROLD KLEMP. It means the secret doctrine. It is his name in the spiritual worlds.

For more explanations of ECKANKAR terms, see *A Cosmic Sea of Words: The ECKANKAR Lexicon*, by Harold Klemp.

Index